MAFATU'S
HAWAII DIVE LOG

LIFE WITH MY
WATER FAMILY

BY BRYAN D. ENOS

ISBN: 1449985459
ISBN-13: 9781449985455
LCCN: 2009914004

For a glimpse of heaven on earth,

dive under the waves, look into the sea.

For Aila,

so that she will know her father's life in the ocean.
Aila has been my strongest supporter and most
demanding first draft editor.

ACKNOWLEDGEMENTS

So many people have helped to make this book a reality. Thanks to my wife Sandy who served as a tireless reader of so many rough drafts and my dive buddies who were invaluable and did so much to clarify my thoughts.

My sincerest thanks to a most skilled editor and educator Shannon Trial. Mahalo Shannon! Many thanks to Joey Cruz, Graphic Designer and Consultant, whose assistance was critical in bringing the maps and charts to life.

For all my family and friends, the dive buddies in Hawaii Kai and the Texas Gulf Coast that read the early drafts and offered constructive advice, Mahalo Nui Loa!

PRIVACY

The events described in "Mafatu's Hawaii Dive Log" are based on true to life occurrences and real characters. Some of the names and incidents have been altered to protect the privacy of the individuals involved.

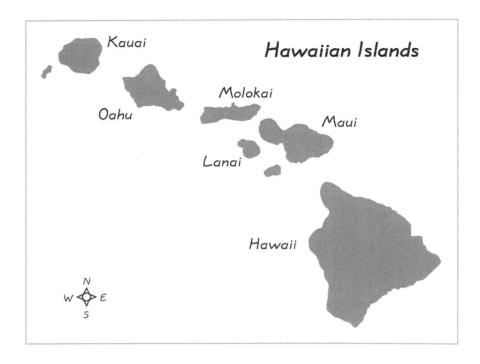

Kauai

Hawaiian Islands

Molokai

Oahu

Maui

Lanai

Hawaii

N
W ◆ E
S

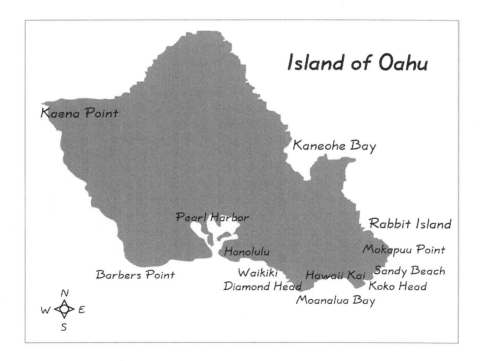

Island of Oahu

Kaena Point

Kaneohe Bay

Pearl Harbor

Rabbit Island

Honolulu

Makapuu Point

Barbers Point

Waikiki

Hawaii Kai

Sandy Beach

Diamond Head

Koko Head

Moanalua Bay

N
W ◆ E
S

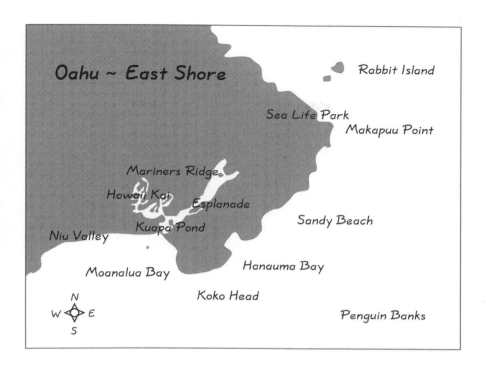

Oahu ~ East Shore

Rabbit Island

Sea Life Park

Makapuu Point

Mariners Ridge

Hawaii Kai   Esplanade

Sandy Beach

Niu Valley   Kuapa Pond

Moanalua Bay

Hanauma Bay

Koko Head

N
W   E
S

Penguin Banks

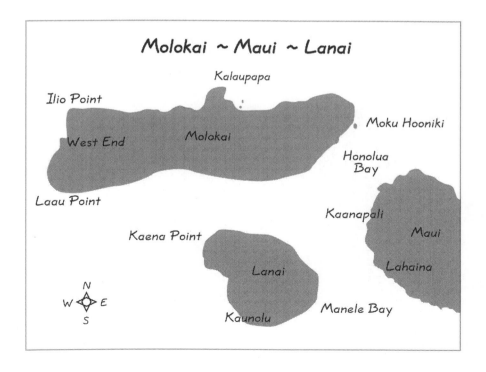

Molokai ~ Maui ~ Lanai

Kalaupapa

Ilio Point

Moku Hooniki

West End   Molokai

Honolua
Bay

Laau Point

Kaanapali

Maui

Kaena Point

Lahaina

Lanai

N
W   E
S

Manele Bay

Kaunolu

Fish Chart

ULUA
Giant Trevally
29 to 191 lbs.

OMILU
Blue Fin Trevally
10 to 28 lbs.

UKU
Gray Snapper
4 to 39 lbs.

UHU
Parrot Fish
2 to 18 lbs.

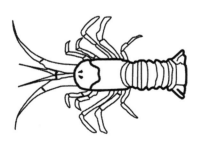

BUGS, SPINIES
Hawaiian Spiny Lobster
2 to 6 lbs.

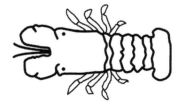

SLIPPAS
Hawaiian Slipper Lobster
2 to 4 lbs.

TABLE OF CONTENTS

CHAPTER ONE

MALOELAP CHARGE

Will it end for me here, so far from home? Will fear and shame overpower me in this pristine lagoon? In a chance, life-changing moment these questions roared through my mind. I knew that this horror might become the twisted mark of my life's end.

Only a few minutes ago I remarked to myself, "What a glorious dive!" My spirit was at such peace. I floated gently, resting on my hands and knees at the sugar-sand bottom that stretched into endlessness. The visibility was awesome, 150 feet or more. I paused to gawk at the ocean's natural beauty. This dive surpassed all of my dreams of what it would be like to spearfish in the perfect lagoon of a deserted Marshall Island atoll. My teak long-gun floated slightly upward as I pulled the leader line in to retrieve the discharged spring-steel shaft lying empty of its intended fish. The backup three-prong pole spear lay beside me resting in the sand. There was no need to rush this experience; it was too enriching to miss any one of these elaborate sensory impressions. I was oblivious to the raw terror that prepared to engulf me with the flicker of a distant shadow.

Our Hawaiian dive group had been invited aboard Chief Juula's yacht for a week of atoll hopping and spearfishing in the Marshalls. Our local contact, the senior member of a royal clan, worked out the details with our trip organizer, Hughsan (Hugh Fraser.) Hugh's contact was a longtime business associate and close friend of his. It was by the good grace of these connections that we'd be traveling with the chief as he visited the islanders. As part of the pre-arranged deal, we would pay for the diesel fuel and tag along as guests. Juula was very accommodating, allowing us to take all the time we needed to dive the atolls while he entertained local officials aboard his vessel. It was the perfect deal for us all.

The chief's yacht was a modern-day replica of the classic American World War II Patrol Torpedo boat that had prowled the South Pacific during the mid-1940's in America's fight with Japan. His vessel was custom-designed and built in Japan to the chief's specifications for inter-atoll service. In an interesting twist of fate, an American military vessel designed in America to defeat the Japanese was now being built in Japan for an American protectorate in the Pacific. The recently-delivered ship was used as the floating home for Juula's official and unofficial trips throughout the Islands.

When our group arrived at the dock early that morning, the chief stood amidst his four-man crew on the aft deck of the yacht. There was no mistaking him; he was the leader. There was something noticeably different about him and his relationship between these native men. I had never seen a ruler or any other royal person before, but knew when I saw him, he must be the royal.

The group of natives seemed more like a gathering of friends rather than a ruler surrounded by his subjects. Dressed in casual dark slacks and a fresh laundered red and blue Hawaiian shirt, Juula stood out, but it was his worn black flip flops that gave him a flair of character. The ship's captain, mechanic, and two young deckhands were attired in casual garb appropriate to their duties. The Marshallese men were having a relaxed conversation in their native tongue when we arrived.

Juula was physically different from the others. Statuesque, he stood a half foot taller with a strong, confident posture. His striking physique, rich wavy black hair, light brown eyes, broad nose, and powerful facial features set him apart as unique. He was quite imposing with his bulk; the crewmen were smaller and lighter boned than their liege.

I could see the chief's authority in the way he interacted with his crew. The captain and his men spoke in a reserved, respectful manner, and the melody of their speech and body language flowed in a comfortable but courteous tone. It was impossible for us to know what they spoke about, as they kept their dialogue private from their guests.

Their behavior was not unusual, but I was curious about their conversation. We came from the modern age of a big city, not the tribal times of a distant atoll shrouded in an age of chieftains and kingdoms. Perhaps the new world didn't come to these islands so deep in the Pacific Ocean. As I thought about this, I cautioned myself that I was only a guest. It would be wiser to keep any personal opinions to myself. This was not the United States but a sovereign territory of an independent nation. Juula's word would be law.

The last of our divers boarded and made his way to the aft deck for introductions. I was very excited and couldn't wait to get underway, as I was about to embark on my dream dive trip through the Marshalls with the chief on his royal yacht. Our conversation with the natives was brief. Juula, while very pleasant, was a quiet man. On the other hand, his hired captain seemed more hospitable and quite talkative.

It wasn't long before the skipper made it clear that he wanted to shove off as soon as possible. I figured his plan was to reach our destination before dark. We hurriedly loaded our dive gear in the aft deck compartments and stowed our personal items in the guest cabins below. My buddy Craig and I, being the youngest divers, drew the floor space in the main salon as our sleeping quarters. It was to be a source of humor as we slept side by side on the cramped cabin floor.

Absent of any farewells, we departed. The captain shouted no orders, instead giving hand signals and head movements to direct his crew. It was a polished operation. In a matter of minutes we left the dock, turned the bow around, and pointed the long, sleek hull to the lagoon pass. The ship's engines sprinted to life and the yacht's forward squat fell off as the hull planed at higher speeds, skipping atop the bay's surface ripple and chop.

Our divers settled in with the drone of the diesel motors and the soft rocking of the ship. It would be a day's trip to the outer atolls. We spent our day onboard exploring the ship, preparing our gear, and relaxing. We knew before this day was done, we'd be at our first stop, Maloelap Lagoon.

The divers were a pretty rugged group of experienced reef hunters. As spirited and independent as they were, it was amazing how well everyone got along. Most of the divers' relationships spanned many years, even through the occasional ups and downs of disagreements and heated arguments. At the core, these relationships had the common bond of the ocean and the need to be under the sea hunting.

A steady stream of divers drifted in and out of our group, but this crew was pretty close to the inner circle. Depending on the weather, family duties, and social obligations, there were a dozen or two divers in our loose-knit horde of weekend warriors. Like any living organism, our dive group continued to refresh itself with new blood. On weekends or holidays there would be at least one full boat of divers, and sometimes two scouting the reefs for game. Almost always, Hughsan's boat *It's Time* led the charge.

There was no official structure to the dive troop. No patches, t-shirts, meetings, newsletters, dues or any other semblance of formal order. Hughsan served as chairman and communications director of dive central. He took the lead and organized the roster for our dive trips.

Originally from Long Island, New York, Hughsan was an enthusiastic Irishman in his mid-fifties. Some thirty years before, he made his way from the East Coast to Hawaii representing a national insurance company. It was during this tenure as a manager for the company that he traveled the Pacific basin for business. He took time to dive many of the islands and atolls that he regularly visited. Hughsan, by no election or personal choosing, served as organizer of our extraordinary collection of ultra aggressive, prima donna divers. He knew each of us well, our dive habits, personal quirks, and strengths and weaknesses. In spite of it all, he held this band of wayward divers together. A sensei, teacher, and dive guru, he was the unofficial dive master of the drift-diving fish killers from Hawaii Kai.

Also on this trip was Hughsan's constant companion and dive buddy, "V" (Vivian Fraser.) The dive boys call her V but often referred to her as "Mother Fraser." Hugh's wife, the bag lady of fish and game, tended to her husband and onboard crew of overgrown boys with great care. A onetime Hawaii model, her long blond hair, attractive features, and warm, caring personality made her our beautiful unofficial den mother.

"Gordon" (Gordon Damon) took the position of our senior

diver and old-time marine environmentalist. He and Hughsan went way back. In the early days, I heard that Gordon was quite the underwater sheller. Now, he worked hard to keep us legal with the fish and game regulations. A lanky Englishman with thinning white hair, his ancestry traced back to the missionary days of Hawaii. Well-educated and socially cultured, Gordon was also a successful real estate entrepreneur.

Without question, "Craw" or "Crawman" (Craig Craw,) was the most technically competent diver we had on the team. A mid-framed, all-around waterman in his early forties, he could do anything in the water with skill and grace. Although an adventurer of many talents, diving and spearfishing were his passions. He usually took the lead on all equipment, logistics, and diving tactics for our trips. Craig was fearless, yet always safety-conscious. He and his wife Susie were also a great dive couple like Hugh and V, but unfortunately she could not make this trip.

I was the youngest diver of the group and the newest to diving remote locations. As a lifelong ocean enthusiast, I'd been in love with diving, snorkeling, spearfishing, and surfing all of my life. Although in my mid-forties, I still considered myself a youthful and passionate spearfisherman.

Many of our other dive buddies in Hawaii who could not make the trip knew they were missing out on the trip of a lifetime, but work schedules and family obligations dictated that they pass on this adventure. Being the good dive buddies that we were, none of us would make them feel any worse, except when we returned home with all the glorious fish stories.

It was a long day at sea, but late in the afternoon a long thread of land appeared in the distance, two points off the bow. It was Maloelap, a cluster of seventy-five islands floating together in blue paradise. The combined landmass of these atolls was only four square miles, but this fragile ring of land enclosed a fertile lagoon of over four hundred square miles. It was one of the finest Edens of marine life on the planet. The atoll's lagoon is encircled by tiny slivers of protective reef walls, silted up sandbanks, and palm tree vegetation growing wildly on every spot of exposed land.

None of us had been in the water all day, so we were dying to get wet. Our excitement grew as we closed in on the island. We hoped that we'd get a dive in before dark and shoot a few fish for dinner as well.

Crawman and I stood at the starboard side of the aft deck watching Maloelap unfold before us. It was astonishing! A perfect picture of God's watery magic rushed at us. Salty, moist wind blew against our faces as our hair flew wildly in the stiff headwind. We leaned forward, buffeted by the wind and entranced by the beauty of it all.

As we neared the shallow pass that pierced through the islands protecting the inner lagoon, azure waters lightened and turned to various hues of green. Sharp brush strokes of vivid blue turned to emerald green then to lighter wisps of green and white. We motored forth, the sea sped by and light patches of sand darted at us from below. The green fluid soon gave way to white sand and larger patches of brown and dark colored seaweed that covered the reef. It was a marvel.

We slowed down through the ocean pass and beheld a vast expanse of marine treasure laying behind the thin curtain of tropical palm vegetation that enclosed the lagoon. An ever-expanding natural beauty unfurled before us. Every imaginative vision of deserted, sand-swept islands lovingly protecting a pristine lagoon was fulfilled for me. I was in awe.

Then, in the middle of this miracle, the rusting steel bones of an old freighter came into view. An ancient death peered out through the tranquil lagoon waters. Of another time and place, it didn't fit in with my vision of a heavenly ocean garden. There ahead lay a sunken World War II Japanese freighter. The yacht slowed and kept a modest distance from the wreck. The Captain overshot the ship and dropped a secure anchor just 100 yards off the freighter's port bow.

Craig looked at me with a childish glimmer in his eye. He's got mischief on his mind, I realized. "Craw, What are you thinking?"

"Brynos, let's check it out. This calls for a dive."

I nodded in agreement. We walked aft and made arrangements with the skipper to put the skiff in and ferry us back and forth to the wreck. After consulting with the other divers, we agreed that Craw and I would snorkel the wreck to see if there was enough game to support a full assault by the group. It would only be a quick reconnaissance run. We suited up and climbed into the dingy manned by one of the deckhands. In less than a minute we were circling the freighter's aft deck. Craig signaled the motorman to cut the engine, and we rolled over the side in unison.

In on a backward flip, I immediately regained a surface position, cleared the snorkel, opened my eyes, and waited for my bubbles to clear. Then, just below me in the most perfect water, an endless silvery wall of fish appeared. It was good eating fish, omilu (blue fin trevally.) As far as my eyes could see, there it was, an enormous school of game fish, just waiting for me to take as many as I wanted. The fish were just begging to be speared. They were like locusts, milling about with absolutely no fear of us. It would be a shoot fest! As quickly as we dropped in the water, we were back out and in the dingy on our way to the ship for the dive gear and guns. The excitement was overwhelming.

The anticipation back onboard ran high as we organized into two dive teams. The young warriors would make the first assault, while the senior crew of Hughsan, V and Gordon would follow close behind.

It wasn't that the most bloodthirsty hunters rushed into the water first to slay the fish and bring the meat back to the clan. It was just that the older guys didn't get all wound up; they had seen it and done it all before. They knew they'd be diving in the same ocean with the same fish. Perhaps getting the first shots wasn't such an advantage compared to their years of shooting experience. After all, the senior shooters almost always brought back as much game as the younger guys but did it with less haste and drama.

Craw and I chatted as we prepared. My adrenaline was flowing. The vision of shooting all those beautiful omilu kept me very excited and aware of the moment. Our preparations were fast completed, and soon we lowered ourselves into the dingy. I did one last mental check: mask, fins, snorkel, gloves, regulator, fish stringer, guns, and power head. Yes, all was in order.

The freighter lay resting ahead, the dead warrior and centerpiece of a funeral display. There may have been an ember of life in her, but by all appearances, death and decomposition was the ship's fate. I wondered what she'd look like underwater. Would it be more of the same rusting steel? Would this death ship give birth to a whole new marine habitat? And what of the merchant men who left their loved ones never to return from these swallowing seas? I reminded myself to be reverent and hunt this ship with respect for the lives that passed here.

Craw and I were crammed together on the floor of the dingy only partially suited. Our asses and elbows were all over each other in a most awkward mess of gear and bodies. We carried the dive tanks in our laps rigged with backpacks and regulators at the ready. Our mask and fins were in one hand, a long-gun and pole spear in the other. Staying upright was difficult, but in no time we were in position 50 feet off the stern of the freighter. I slipped into my vest and tank, pulled my fins on, and made one final adjustment to my facemask. Like a drill team, we went off the side together. The precision of our unified entry was as much a matter of not giving the other diver an early shooting advantage as balancing our small inflatable launch.

Each shooter proceeded to fan out to his prearranged stalking area. However, as was usually the case, as soon as fish showed up, plans were abandoned. So, as we started to fin our way from the entry point, omilu swam in, long-guns were drawn, game chased, shots fired, and in less than forty-five seconds fish blood gushed through the water.

The school of fish was mature, with most of them running in the fourteen to eighteen inch range. Omilu don't resemble a common fish profile like trout or salmon. Instead, they look rather flat, with a much taller body and a forereaching blunt head. Looking at its classic big lips, piercing eyes, and stubby head, it's easy to visualize the omilu's great skill at charging smaller fish. The real beauty of omilu is its inspiring rich colors visible in a profile view. A soft white underbelly turns to a glow of light green, flowing into a darker green at the top of its back. Brilliant spots work their way throughout the body, except for the thick gill plates at the head of the fish. Imagine hundreds of these omilu running wild, splashing vibrant colors everywhere.

Omilu teemed in all directions. It was hard for me to choose just one. I jerked my gun from one beautiful target to another as the fish swam in a frenzy. Finally I pulled the trigger on the very next one in haste. "Slam," my steel shaft went into the fish forward of the belly, too low from the spine and too far away from the gill plate for a good kill. With a short struggle the omilu ripped itself free of my black nylon leader line. What a lousy shot. There'd be another, I consoled myself. I could see Craw working on his second fish. He already had one beauty threaded on his stringer.

The fish soon thinned out with all the activity. I swam to the ship's tail to begin my hunt of the starboard hull. Our dive plan would place me hunting the starboard side and Craw the ship's deck. Then if we had time we would circle back and catch the port side of the ship.

I swam alone to the steel transport which sat nearly upright in 45 feet of water. Finning slightly above the mid-water level, I had a panoramic view of the intersection of the ship's side with the sand bottom. That was the sweet spot for fish activity. With this mid-water strategy I could shoot a fish that swam to me here or shoot the occasional free-swimming fish above, or drop down to the bread-and-butter killing zone below. I swam closer to the ship and stretched my gloved hand out to place it on the ship's hull as I moved ahead. Smooth green algae covered the entire steel surface. It was distinctively soft to the touch. There were no barnacles, corals, or outgrowths of any kind. The parrot fish must really feed on this ship, I mused to myself. Fifty years in the water and the hull looked like it sank last week.

What a chasm of contrasts. The freighter's dark topside, once the pinnacle of her pride, stood slowly rotting away above the waterline. The ship's hull and deck, once an afterthought to its imposing profile, now stood preserved as her beacon of dignity in the deep.

The fish were sparse on my side of the ship. Surely Craw must be scoring big. I wondered if I got the short straw on this hunt. In spite of this, these curative waters gave me a deep sense of peace and contentment. As I neared the halfway mark along the ship's hull, three omilu appeared swimming along the bottom nearly 15 feet away from me. Any of these fish would be a good score. My body moved downward at a slight angle as I released the safety on my gun and readied the pole spear. I continued to sink with no additional movements, advancing toward the largest of the three. When in range, I gently thrust my fins, extended my gun forward and squeezed the trigger. "Bam!" My shaft hit its mark on the big one, right below the spine, but more into his soft fleshy stomach. This was not a good shot.

Would he hold? I chastised myself for being off on my aim. The omilu fought for his life, spinning wildly up and down at the end of my leashed spear. He twisted and turned, repeatedly going down to hit the bottom, causing cloud after cloud of white sand to float up like fine powdered ash. Then, it was over. He cut himself free and vanished. I went down to the bottom around 40 feet to retrieve my spear. It was so peaceful that I decided to linger there for awhile.

I floated, gently resting on my hands and knees at the sugar-sand bottom that stretched into endlessness. The visibility was awesome, 150 feet or more. My teak long-gun floated slightly up-ward as I pulled my leader line in to retrieve the spring-steel shaft lying empty of its intended fish. The backup three-prong pole spear lay beside me resting in the sand. There was no need to rush this experience. It was too enriching to miss one moment of the parade of elaborate sensory impressions.

I looked up to the surface to admire the lagoon. The calm wa-ters above formed a clear canopy. It served as a lid that held the water down to the sand and formed a thin translucent film keep-ing the sky from descending into the sea. Broad slivers of light and soft rays of sun pierced through this film in a never-ending prism of radiant energy. It brought all the floating microscopic sea organisms to life. As I scanned the great expanse of this won-drous scene, my eyes came to rest on the wisps of fine, white sand that formed a shallow haze on the ocean floor. It struck me as un-usual to see such a blanket of haze forming a puffy cloud bottom.

In the distance, a wispy cloud of sand lay floating amongst the sand particles kicked up by the ocean currents. Waters in the la-goon migrated ever so gently out toward the channel pass. There was a disturbance of sorts, then a flicker of a menacing shadow. Out of the right side of my facemask I caught the dark move-ment. My head straightened to bring this anomaly into view.

Without warning, all tranquility was shattered. Unmistakably, charging out of the sand cloud at top speed straight toward me was a husky, full-bodied predator! It was difficult to identify the creature at first, but it was getting closer and bigger fast. I made out an elongated tail as it pushed its torso from one side to the other for thrust. The creature displayed a barrel face head, a big mouth, and a large set of side-to-side recessed teeth. The predator was none other than a full-sized grey reef shark! Oh, God! I gasped. The shark looked really mad and was coming at me! There was nothing between us except open water—no rocks, ledges, or other natural barriers.

My entire body went into an immediate emergency self-protect mode. I yanked the leader line in. A micro-second went by; I realized that my gun would never be reloaded in time to fire. This thing wasn't cruising; it was sprinting and would have no distractions. I bundled the spear, cable, long-gun and three-prong into my left hand, retreating backward as I prepared to face the menacing beast. There behind me was the partial safety of the ship's hull. I'd use it to cover my back.

I went for the 38 caliber power head holstered on my weight belt. The blaster was designed to kill dangerous fish in moments like these. It should conveniently screw onto the three-prong. This power head was my only chance for survival. Unscrewing the three-prong spear tip, rethreading the power head on the spear pole, and banging this punk's head into deviled meat was my only thought at this moment, but I needed time!

It was a struggle to keep calm as my breathing got faster. The bubbles from my regulator gushed everywhere. My situation became more desperate. I rushed to unthread my three-prong tip. Oh crap, it wouldn't unscrew! I wailed madly at my stupidity. I fumbled with the loaded 38 caliber tip in my hand. Again, I grasped the tip and applied more pressure to remove it. It wouldn't budge! It was wrenched down, frozen solid on the shaft. Suddenly I remembered. It was the Craw. He would be the cause of my death!

It was our practice to check the equipment before each dive. As we prepared for this dive, I inspected my pole spear and tried the tip. It was loose. I looked over to Craw, asking, "Hey, what do you think?" as I displayed my lance with the loose tip. He examined the spear and paused while he thought about it. I asked the ninja again, "This bugger is so loose, hand tight or wrench it down?"

Craw replied confidently, "This lagoon... 40 feet... old wreck... nah, you won't need it. Wrench it down!"

I did and we went on with our preparations. It was too late now for regrets. I clumsily unscrewed the power head safety. Jaws was so close. For an instant, I stared at the shark as he came in, ready to fire, waiting for the moment of his attack. Suddenly I realized, Oh no! I'll blow my fingers off if I fire from my hand. What was I thinking? This bullet was a hot load from the Craw's garage workbench. I've seen the results of his homemade, over-powdered loads set off in practice sessions back home. The barrel could peel open like a banana. This slug wasn't at the end of the spear, it was in my hand. I'd blow my hand apart and bleed to death hundreds of miles away from a modern hospital. There's no way anyone could save my hand or my life.

My mind raced with horrible ideas. I was so conflicted. I can't blow my hand apart. Everyone will laugh at my foolishness. I could hear them now, "How stupid could he be? He blew his hand off and bled to death." Thoughts and feelings flashed through my mind in milliseconds. I anguished. No, I would try to fend the shark off without it. Only if its teeth were in me would I lose my hand with the power head.

The predator was upon me. He came to a skidding stop about 6 feet away and hovered slightly above my head. He was huge! In a display of strength, he arched his back up and used his side fins for leverage and positioning. A white underbelly and scars about his fins flashed at me. He shook his head and moved his fins in a killing ritual. He was about to chomp.

I was so scared and confused. This shark didn't behave in a normal pattern of cruising, testing, and getting closer, instead charging me with no deviation of purpose. He was pissed off, like he wanted blood revenge. I had seen a decent number of sharks while diving through the years, mostly white-tip reefs, small tigers, and a few hammerheads, but up to this point, never an attack. This guy was scary; he had an enormous mid-section girth. Most of the other sharks I've seen were more muscular and lean. It was hard for me to imagine how much the beast must devour to keep his size. "This isn't good," I told myself. I put these thoughts out of my head as abruptly as they had appeared and clung to a pathetic hope for salvation.

These frightful feelings went through me like I was trapped in a time warp. I was surprised to see a small entourage of cleaner fish follow the creature's every move like a pack of vermin. Always at the under portion of the shark, they would wait for scraps and leftovers from their god of food. Now it would be my scraps they would feed on. A strange feeling of resentment for these fish ran through me. I hurriedly dismissed these images and refocused my energies on facing their killer patron.

Time seemed infinite, with each moment containing an endless series of feelings, yet time was so very compressed, each second seeming to be my last. My mind was stuck in an endless loop of fear, yet it was destined to end all at once at the hand of this animal. My feelings and emotions were raw...fear, regret, and hope. At this final moment, I would do anything to beat this creature. I wanted to live.

The shark vaulted over with his mouth cracked open. In one swift movement, he shot downward to the right side of my face and shoulder. The cleaner fish scattered to give the shark some room to work. Jolting backward in one swift motion, I swung my pole spear toward the top of his rounded head, just missing his snout. Moving the spear swiftly broadside was terribly difficult with the drag of dense water. My spear moved much too slowly to be accurate or effective! I was disappointed in myself and ashamed of my ability to fight. The swipe missed him by less than a dozen inches, but at least I got his attention.

My breathing continued to quicken; I was almost out of breath. So many more breaths, but I still couldn't get enough air. I was losing it!

The shark ducked backward to get away from my spear and then moved around to the side of me. This beast was clever, I thought, as I spun around to keep him in front of me. I've got to keep him in my face. If I lose him, he'll come from behind and take a chunk out of my back. I kept telling myself to stay calm. That became my battle plan: keep the brute in front of me, fend him off, and don't dare let him get behind me.

I also knew that I had to retreat farther toward the ship's hull and do a better job of jabbing with my spear. I vowed to give this gluttonous pig less of a target and inflict some damage every time he came for me. I kept moving backwards as I readied myself for the next attack.

He came at me again, this time from the right, close to my

backside. The shark dropped lower, trying to get at my mid-section. I turned and swooshed my spear wildly like a drunken roundhouse kicker. Again, the shaft missed hitting him; I was just too panicked and unsteadied. But I broadened his area of danger by marking my spear's reach. After this swing, he backed off a few feet.

The shark went up and over to the back of me while I franti-cally spun around to keep up with him. I shuttered to think of sharp teeth penetrating the back of my neck. He came again, his head twisting and hunching over like a hyena going for bloody flesh. I swung frantically again, this time even farther away and with even poorer aim. But again he got the message that there was a danger zone. He changed his attacks and moved in and out as I swung my spear in larger, more desperate circles.

I was exhausted and hyperventilating. My frantic air bubbles rose and clouded the water everywhere. I couldn't see him now. I didn't know where he was. That wasn't good!

The attack may be over, but was it over for good? Where was this vile creature? Is the animal laying in wait for another charge? Will he come at me from behind to bite me in the back? How could I defend myself from such an attack?

My vision blurred, the gauges became fuzzy, then almost sightless. I wasn't thinking clearly, so I left the safety of the bot-tom and the side of the ship. My breathing was uncontrollable as I started to the surface. Bubbles poured out from my regula-tor exhaust port. I ascended slowly but not slow enough for the bubbles to clear around me, so I rose in a sea of air and turbu-lence. Clearing the side of the ship's deck I tried to slow my ever increasing ascent. "Relax, slow down," I admonished myself.

I ascended to a position slightly above the ship's deck rail and stopped to catch my breath and halt my dangerous ascent. Craw loomed ahead at mid-ship, searching the silent grey steel deck for fish. Totally unaware of my presence, he finned forward with no clue of my near-lethal ordeal. Immediately, I set upon warn-ing him of the danger. I grunted in my regulator to get his atten-tion, and then grunted again and again with no success.

Craw looked all of the swimming ninja shrouded in well-worn aquatic battle gear. His trademark setup of a black Scubapro vest, steel 100 tank, black mask and fins, black aluminum JBL long-gun, and aluminum three-prong was hard to miss. His black full-bodied wetsuit and torpedo-like profile moved through the water in silence. I almost smiled as his thinning salt and pepper grey hair undulated to the thrusts of his movements and underwater currents. It ebbed and flowed to reveal a receding and slightly thinning hairline. I watched in an expansive view of a serial fish killer at his stalk. By far he was the most aggressive shooter in our group, always advancing the deepest, staying the longest, and producing the most fish.

My buddy Craw was self-employed and ran a marine safety company in Honolulu. He was so talented in dangerous ocean situations that he was sought after by marine film makers. Some producers would hire him to ride shotgun as the paid muscle to protect the underwater cameramen when filming shark footage. The film crew would don their stainless-steel shark suits as Craig hovered about them like a guardian angel with only two pre-loaded 38 caliber bang sticks. These explosive guns were holstered in PVC tubes attached to his tank by way of a special design that allowed for lightning-quick access.

Craw was good with bang sticks; he practiced often to perfect his technique. He drilled for the speed of the draw, precise aim, and lunging technique, just as the samurai did with their katana swords in ancient Japan. Despite all of these unusual and serious talents, Craw retained a childlike playfulness. It was his youthful years of watching samurai movies that led him to imagine himself an aquatic warrior ninja. He even aptly named his dive boat the *Katana,* the long sword of the samurai.

I hovered just above the deck level 30 feet or more from the Craw trying to catch my breath when from below and slightly behind me, I noticed another dark movement. Oh, no! For God's sake! my mind wailed. This damned devil is back. He won't let go. He's here to rip some flesh from the Craw. I just knew it. This time, the shark used a different tactic, stealth. Like a serpent crawling on its soft belly, he slithered up the side of the hull in near-undetectable movement. No energy was wasted as he slowly slid across the hull, then up and over the deck rail and into the ship.

So clever an approach I would not have imagined from any creature. He must know this ship well. He's playing it to his advantage, I realized. This change in temperament was unusual, but his scheme was brilliant. He didn't break his way on to the ship in a showy display of daring. He sneaked in like a common thief. My mind ran wild with outrage as I thought about this change of strategy.

He's going for Craw. I can't let that happen. I have to get Craw's attention now! The punk shark was following the trail of blood leaking from Craw's fish stringer. I banged my steel three-prong tip against my long-gun spear shaft. I had to get Craw's attention before it was too late. Ferociously I banged away to create the most piercing sounds of alarm. It would surely alert anyone in the area, but Craig was in his very own world of hunting, not knowing that he was the one being stalked. He intently swam forward while the angry shark snaked in for the kill. It was horrible. I screamed into my regulator and banged away, but still no response from the Craw.

There were three omilu dangling from Craig's weight belt. All were dinner size with silver skin and dark flashes of color. The fish swayed gently in an open invitation to this most devious animal. Like an assassin, the shark moved without apparent effort as he gained on poor Craw. The beast's nose took point as he honed in on the prize. It looked as if they swam together, with predator moving ever so close to become one with his prey. Meanwhile, I was still screaming, yelling, and banging the spears. I couldn't watch this, but neither could I tear myself away.

There was nothing I could do to help. I thought about lunging downward to spear the shark, but I was too far out of range to be of any aid. This damned shark was less than a foot behind Craig's fins and just about ready to complete his final lunge. Craig's body gave pause for a moment, his neck muscles tightened and his head coiled forward. Then he slowed from his forward movement. I could feel his subconscious mental energy. He knew something was wrong. Some metaphysical force told him that some danger or inconvenience was afoot. He turned his head slightly to the right and casually glanced backward. Craw finally saw the predator. He gazed openly upon this most imminent harbinger of death. The shark was now above his calf muscle. In one short pounce, those sharp saw-snapping teeth would either be in Craig's bleeding fish, arm, leg, torso, or his neck or head.

Craw did not flinch or give any appearance of fear. In a totally natural response, he moved his head back forward to an extreme twist, taking his eyes off the shark. In a head wind-up, and at the apex of this head coiling, Craw snapped his head backward at the shark with a loud guttural grunt of an ancient ninja. "Hiyaaaaaahhh!" boomed through his regulator. The grey killer stopped instantly, angled his head away, flipped his tail, and whimpered into the distance. Astonished, I stopped yelling and banging. What the hell? How'd he do that? He yelled at it! I was bewildered and amazed.

I left the scene immediately. Craw didn't need me; he could fend for himself. I continued up in slow wide circles scanning the distance for any signs of the predator shark. Where did he run to? My thoughts nagged at me. Maybe he'd come back for me, the easy prey. If another attack came, I wanted to be ready. I kept alert and prayed the dingy would find me quickly at the surface. It would be way too dangerous floating in the lagoon, bobbing like chum.

I broke the surface. My lungs exploding, I was completely exhausted and drained of any strength. The dingy attendant must have seen the massive explosions of bubbles and knew something was amiss. He was right in front of me. As the water sheeted down my facemask, I crawled over the side and into the skiff to collapse on the floor.

Blubbering in an almost unintelligible groan, "Shark... Shark... Shark charged me." I repeated in hopes of some aid or acknowledgement of my survival. The motorman smiled but showed no real concern. Maybe he didn't understand English, but he should have at least known what the word shark meant. He should have seen my eyes, the distress, and the exhaustion. Apparently not, for by his manner, all seemed in order to him. He smiled and nodded to my ranting with no emotional attachment whatsoever. I turned upward and lay collapsed on my back in the bilge water of the dingy. Unconcerned, he blasted us back to the yacht.

Hughsan, V and Gordon were suited up and waiting for the second shuttle to the freighter. They could see that I had physically unraveled. I started in with them and ranted my tale of woe. They were attentive, but each one of them hurriedly continued on with the dive preparations. They too, didn't seem to comprehend the seriousness of the attack. I was confused by their lack of concern. They could be getting ready to dive for my body parts at the bottom of the lagoon rather than diving to spear fish, I mused. They don't seem to understand that I was almost dead meat.

After the second wave of shooters left the ship, I retreated into my own world, silent and moody. All the images of the shark attack ran through my mind over and over again. I couldn't shake the mental movie of its raw horror, even on the safety of the yacht. Trying to settle down, I made my way to the bow of the ship.

Juula and his men were engaged in evening cocktails. With a plastic bag load of beers, I found the foredeck and rested against the forward cabin structure. I told the natives my horrific story. They followed my tale with interest but showed more amusement rather than concern.

It was odd, but I was no longer concerned with what anyone thought about my ordeal. I had survived. That was all that mattered to me.

The evening continued on for the divers and crew, but I would have no part of it. I sat numbed in my own thoughts. Sometime later, Craw came forward to join me. By this time, my attack was old news and we were nested at anchor for the night.

"Brynos, how you doing? Hanging in?" Craw asked.

"I'm still freaked. Maybe another couple of beers, and I'll be alright." Then he started with some advice.

"Brynos, cheer up, you're here in one piece! To hell with the shark. You should've shown him who's boss."

"Yeah, sure, Craig. He was after my ass! What the hell was I supposed to do?" Then Craig proceeded to unload more of his well-intentioned but irritating advice.

"When he charged you... did you charge back? Did you look him in the eye, yell, and tear into him head on?"

My response was immediate, "Hell no! Of course not! I was too busy struggling to get the power head on the spear. I wrenched the three-prong down, remember? The 38 was stuck in my hand, useless!

Craw passed over my comment like he hadn't heard it. That's

alright, I decided. I would go no further with this implication of who suggested the wrenching down of the three-prong. I would not put my own mistake of synching the three-prong down on him, even if he did suggest it. My thoughts moved on while Crawman continued with his advice.

"Sharks are like dogs. You've got to be firm. Put your foot down, or they'll run all over you." I listened but was not moved. "You got to have an attitude. They can sense fear! Sharks know if you're an easy target. They can smell you. You got to be tough. Look at 'em. Tell 'em, 'You screw with me, I kill you! I kill your whole family! I kill your brothers, sisters, and parents... I kill 'em all, dead!'" I was silent. "Brynos, just for the hell of it, let's go kill a couple of 'em tomorrow. You'll feel better."

I wasn't in the mood for more talking. Craw quieted down and we had a few more beers together. Tomorrow is another day, I thought.

The next day was a washout for me. After a dead sleep and a late rising, I thought I'd take a day off from diving. I made peace with the shark incident and designed a new spearfishing strategy for the remainder of the trip.

In addition to a new emphasis on extreme caution when spearing, the new technique included carrying a long-gun, three-prong spear, and a preloaded power head on another spear. It would only be a minor inconvenience to carry three spears on a dive, but it was well worth the protection. No more fumbling around like an incompetent fool hoping for a miracle from a detached power head.

The boys planned another full day of diving. That was just fine with me, but I wanted no part of it. To add insult to my injured confidence, they dove a pass where no one in their right mind should.

We motored to a small atoll entrance channel adrift in a sea of smooth, silky waters. The exceptional water clarity allowed us to see a mammoth school of sharks milling about in perfect peace. Some sharks cruised the surface with fins piercing the water, some swam a few feet below, and hundreds more were seen deeper. Looking down into the water from the yacht gave us all a ringside seat to the mother of all shark conventions. The boys were excited to have this unique opportunity to observe the phenomenon. I couldn't understand their lunacy to make such a dive, especially after they nearly lost me.

The chief and his natives observed the action and shook their heads at the idea of diving into the school of predators. The crazies–Hughsan, Gordon, and Craw–looked at this dive as a once-in-a-lifetime opportunity to swim with hundred of sharks in their natural habitat.

The only diver with any common sense was V who decided that caution might be a good strategy in light of what happened yesterday. She was only too happy to let the others do the shark-watching dive. I figured that maybe no one told them that this wasn't anything like bird watching; it was shark watching. With bird watching, when the birds get tired of you they fly away, but when sharks get tired of you they have you for lunch! Whatever possessed them to dive with the sharks I did not know.

The boys discussed their dive plan before entry and agreed on a few rules. No one would shoot any fish or shark unless there was imminent danger. No one would take any unnecessary risks of any kind. All hands and legs would be kept close to the body. There would be no harassing or instigating any contact with the sharks. With that agreed upon, into the ocean they went.

I couldn't relax while they were down, so I paced the ship like a madman. Being born and raised in Hawaii, I had a healthy respect for the damage that sharks can do if agitated or hungry. Perhaps my diver friends approached sharks with more scientific curiosity than I did, but I wasn't the least bit curious about them. My only interest was to keep them as far away from me as possible! I wanted to keep all of my speared fish, as well as my fingers, toes, arms and legs. I didn't want shark for meat and I didn't want to be meat for sharks.

Time moved slowly as I waited for the divers. After 45 minutes or so, one by one, the would-be shark scientists surfaced. The dingy picked them up and ran back to the boat in waves back and forth. Gordon was the first knucklehead to rave about the beauty of the dive and interesting shark behaviors. Soon Hughsan and Craig were onboard talking about the wonders of these beautiful animals. I listened and took a healthy interest in the conversation in spite of my opinions about their sanity.

I wanted to tell them how foolish they were but ranted silently to myself. These sharks aren't beautiful creatures, they're ocean cleaners and undertakers. At any moment, for any reason, any one of them could have turned on you, and an arm or a leg would be gone. Tucking your extremities into your body, you think that's going to help? They'll just take some of your torso with it. It would be like taking a little breast meat with the wing of a small chicken. Get real, guys! I knew they would laugh at my opinions with their adrenaline running so high, so I kept silent.

After we were settled in, the yacht traveled on to Likiep atoll where we planned to spend a few days. Likiep is a populated landmass with a tiny airstrip that landed a small plane once a week for supplies and transport. At the time, there were fewer than a couple hundred natives living on the island.

After a day at sea, the yacht slowed though the lagoon pass and turned starboard to the inside atoll where an inlet formed to shape a crescent beach with a natural harbor. As far as the eyes could see, white sand beaches sprouted coconut groves from the shore to the blue clear horizon. Just ahead of us, the village center and surrounding homes built of natural materials were nearly hidden by coconut palms. If it weren't for our guides, our group would be surprised to find the atoll inhabited.

We made our way cautiously into the cove and only then could we see any signs of life. In the distance we saw a small sand clearing with a few beached dinghies at water's edge. Just behind the clearing was a gathering area surrounded by a few buildings the size of small houses. A scraggy dog rested beneath a lazy palm, and four or five chickens roamed the village undisturbed. A few inhabitants sat on the steps of the largest of the buildings, the community center. I would come to learn that it also served as the general store, government office and hospital. By all observations, the village was devoid of any activity when we arrived at our anchorage.

Our captain dropped anchor and sent a crewman ashore to announce our arrival. Sometime later, Juula's daughter and a party of village elders came aboard. They had been waiting for their monarch to make landfall. There was a flurry of activity onboard between the elders and their chief. The natives kept to themselves.

Soon it became obvious that Juula might prefer some privacy with his people, so the divers made themselves as unnotice-able as possible by going ashore to explore the landscape. After a few hours we returned to the ship satisfied that we had seen the natural beauty of the atoll. We kept to ourselves as Juula entertained his village guests. It was late in the evening when the villagers returned to shore and the divers turned in for the night.

The next day we embarked to dive the atoll, doing one dive at the outside pass and another at a reef area just a few miles down the coast. We didn't know whether the chief stayed in his stateroom or if he had gone ashore, but he was nowhere in sight this day.

We returned to the inlet early from diving to find the villag-ers scurrying about in preparation for a big feast in honor of the chief. The nearly deserted atoll teemed with life as men, women, and children went about the preparations for a welcoming cer-emony for his highness and the royal guests.

The entire village pulled what meager resources they had to make this welcome memorable. Chicken, fish, vegetables, rice and other delicacies were prepared for a luau. Our dive group went ashore early and waited with the villagers for Chief Juula's arrival from the ship. When he made his grand entrance, the elders greeted him at the water's edge and ushered him to the front of the village congregation in the communal clearing. Every person on the atoll gathered to sit on the sand in the center of the village for the welcoming rite.

Juula paraded forward to face the villagers as their best music and dance were performed in his honor. Hugh, V and Gordon, our senior divers, were invited to sit with the chief and the village officials. Craw and I sat on an overturned dingy slightly off to the right of the honored guests.

This scene had all the makings of an old-time Polynesian movie with the white ship's captain and officers being welcomed by the natives with local ceremony and spectacle. Dark-skinned school children were presented to the elders by age groups in musical performance as other children danced to the songs har-monized by the community. It was splendid. The chief took great pleasure in their offerings.

After a great deal of ceremony and a few prepared speeches, Juula finally rose to address the gathering. All were intent on what their distinguished guest would say. He spoke in Marshallese, sprinkled with a few phrases of English. Embracing their cultural heritage and adhering to traditional values were the themes of his heartfelt oration. He stressed their rich island customs, living in harmony with the environment, and loyalty to their cultural traditions.

When Juula concluded his speech, he honored a young married couple who returned to the island after their education in the United States. They were praised for their service and devotion to island society.

Craig and I sat as casual observers, somewhat swept up in the mood of the moment. Hughsan, V and Gordon were with Juula at the center of it all. It was an ideal moment, where a beloved leader interacted with his followers with obvious love and affection.

Somehow, even with the wonders of this cultural event, I was taken aback by the reality of this spectacle. My feelings were mixed. One side of me was thrilled to witness an event of this nature in which a royal personage was being welcomed by his islanders. All the natives showered the chief with great respect and love. It was such a beautiful experience—the ceremony, the music, and the outpouring of affection.

On the other hand, it was sad to see these beautiful islanders living so sparsely on a tiny strip of sand in the middle of the ocean. With only the very basics of food, clothing, and shelter, how would any of them face a future in the modern world? How would these children adapt to a global society? Could they continue collecting coconuts, catching seafood, and making do with what nature provides them? Would their whole existence be limited to life on an atoll? I felt a great sadness for the young children. Despite all its beauty and splendor, life on the atoll was not as splendid as I had imagined.

Thankfully, the rest of the trip unfolded without incident or further life-threatening traumas. Great spearfishing dives, wonderful marine scenery, good local food, and loving friends combined together made this the most noteworthy dive trip ever.

CHAPTER TWO

LIFE ON THE WATER

Learning to swim wasn't easy for me. For some reason quite beyond my control, I wasn't very buoyant. My early attempts at swimming had me sinking and crawling along the ocean bottom rather than stroking on top. Mastering the technique of floating and moving forward on the surface took several years to perfect. Until then I got comfortable with my tendency to sink to the bottom until I ran out of breath.

Just about the time I became a decent swimmer, my family moved from the city to rural Niu Valley. Past Aina Haina, but before Kuliouou Valley, it was one of the last stops on the southeast shore of the island of Oahu before you reached the Kuapa Fish Pond and the end of the island.

A lush valley hamlet, Niu sat amidst isolating mountains spanning all three sides of its boundaries. Entrance into the valley is by a narrow beachfront coastline that travels from west to east for a distance of a mile or two. At various periods in its history, the valley was used for ranching, growing sugarcane, dairy farming, and now for settling an excess of Honolulu residents. Transportation into and out of the valley was by a beach highway via city bus or private car.

Our family moved into a new housing subdivision near the Niu stream and beach. Growing up during the mid-1950's in a wilderness valley, amidst sugarcane fields and a working dairy offered adventures beyond belief for an eight-year-old. I would find best friends in the likes of "Curt" (Curtis Nishikawa) and "Randy" (Randall Hoffman.) We three became masters of the river and explorers of the ocean bay.

Back then, we were considered active outdoor boys. Under today's standards, we'd be labeled hyperactive children suffering from attention deficit syndrome or whatever else that might apply to difficult children. In our day, the only prescription for the problems of growing up was to get out of the house and play with your friends.

Curt was a skinny kid of Japanese and Spanish descent. His father, a newspaper editor, married a beautiful Hispanic woman and raised his family in Niu. A fisherman and all-around water guy, Mr. Nishikawa worked nights, so his schedule allowed him more flexibility to teach his boys and their friends the hobbies he enjoyed. All the stuff Curt's father taught him, Curt would share with Randy and me.

The thing about Curt that made him so memorable was his highly-developed methods of agitation. He harangued his sister without mercy, drove his brother nuts, and often had my older brother chasing him with a rubber slipper, trying to teach him some respect. But Curt was fast. At about half my brother's size, he always outran and outmaneuvered him. Curt was my kind of chum, living a life filled with excitement and danger.

My other pal Randy was a quiet kid. A year or two older than Curt and I, he stood out in the neighborhood with his blond, crew-cut hair. He had a beautiful older sister that Curt and I ogled over, but she was a little too old for us. She wouldn't give us kids the time of day. She was the pretty sister of a friend we dreamed of from afar, but to her we were just troublesome pests.

Randy was really fairly levelheaded, but his ideas were so advanced that he was anything but normal. He read popular mechanical books and trade magazines like the rest of us kids read adventure novels. Fortunately for us, Randy became the brains of our neighborhood mischief. His mom, a kindly woman, allowed us free reign of the patio, backyard, and river. Randy's house bordered on the stream and from it we had easy access to the beach, bay, and swimming pier. Even if Randy wasn't home, Curt and I were comfortable taking over their riverfront like it was our own.

Of the three of us, Randy was the thinker, architect, and logistics guy; Curt the rabble rouser, instigator, and ramrod of our pranks; and I the unheard voice of reason. I was also the most timid of the three. The things that we did were so beyond my realm of experience, the best that I could do was struggle to keep up with them.

I was very happy to be the friend of these two mates, as my older brother and sister were too busy with their own lives and had no intention of playing with me. That left me alone to find my own friends. My parents were busy people, too. Dad worked long hours on the waterfront in a supervisor position. Mom stayed at home and spent a lot of time with her church groups. So unless I wanted to sit at home bored out of my mind, I had to find some excitement with my friends.

In our gang of three, leadership shifted between Curt and Randy. Randy lived on Haleola Street. At the boundary of his backyard, a rock wall embankment went upstream from the highway inland a few hundred yards past Randy's house. Curt lived across the street, and I lived on the other end of Pia Street, less than a few minutes' walk from my friends. Also living in the same community were my Mom's three brothers and their families. A dozen of my cousins were within yelling distance, but then again, all the neighborhood kids were within earshot. Randy, Curt and I were the kids that the adults made a point to keep their eyes on.

Niu Stream sits in the middle of the valley. Its waters come from the Oahu hills where its origins spring from the stately Koolau Mountains, the spine of the island. The stream is often a dry bed of eroded rocks from the mountains, but where the river nears the ocean, the creek becomes moist and muddy, turning into an estuarial riverbed. At the beach, salt water from the ocean breathes life into the shallow freshwater stream. The lower part of the river is always filled with water, but the degree to which it travels into the valley depends on the season and the rainfall.

There is constant turmoil in the stream where the river meets the coastline. During the rainy season, the river runs wild through the brown sand beach in torrents of rushing water. At flood times, crossing the river to the other side of the beach becomes a matter of sheer determination for a youngster. Then in the dry season, the river withdraws unto itself, forming an inshore body of stagnant lake water.

The stream unfolded before us each day, always a surprise of nature. The flowing waters were particularly beautiful in transition from flooding rapids to a calm drift. These were the times when sandbars formed to partially block the stream. The shifting banks of sand moved freely across the river to interrupt its path to the sea. It would make more beach or take more beach and change the path and strength of the water into the ocean. Sandbars moved like ghostly shoals to challenge the authority and to test the strength of the ocean against the river. A sand shoal formation might tame the river and reduce its entrance to the ocean from 60 feet across and 4 feet deep to a mere 2 feet across and 6 inches deep. Overnight it might choose to reverse itself and enlarge again in size. There was just no way to tell how it might behave.

Niu Beach lay on a unique lagoon. Behind a barrier reef a quarter of a mile out to sea, the pristine reef water laps its way ashore, losing more of its clarity until it becomes brown like the river water at the dark sand shoreline. Seaweed rolled along the shoreline like lumpy brown matting stacked up by the currents.

Just east of the river and only 50 yards away from the stream, the Niu Swimming Pier made its way from the shore out a few hundred yards to clear water less than halfway to the reef. At the end of the pier was a swimming platform with an ocean ladder for entry into a sandy area that became the swimming hole for the valley kids. The original land barons of Niu built the two-plank wooden pier on cement pipe pilings for their families, but somehow it became a community asset.

The river entrance, beach, and pier became a gathering place for us kids where long summer days were consumed swimming, fishing, canoeing, snorkeling, and growing up. Most of the kids walked across the highway from the neighborhood. Sometimes we walked along the river, and sometimes our gang of three would paddle downstream with our canoes.

Boating on the river by home-crafted tin canoes was our favorite pastime. The ingeniousness of the craft was impressive. Randy took the lead as inventor, but I imagine Randy's father must have aided him in the design and construction plans for those do-it-yourself creations. When Curt and I showed up to help Randy build the canoes, there were no discussions; he gave us our assignments and we went straight into production. A tin canoe is a simple and inexpensive alternative to a real boat. For us juveniles it was marine construction of the finest sort at "Randy's

Shipbuilding Works."

The canoe was fashioned with scrap two-by-four lumber, a used tin roof sheet, and tar gathered from the telephone poles and roofing sites around the neighborhood. The first step was to bend the ends of a roofing sheet lengthwise like a long sheet of paper. This was difficult manual labor. On each end, we placed a two-by-four into the folded metal and nailed the hammered-smooth tin along the edge of the two-by-four. Then somewhere in the middle of the folded tin we stretched out the top and inserted another two-by-four and nailed it into place as a seat. All nail holes and rust spots were coated with thick tar for water-proofing. Since all of the tin sheets had been previously used, each canoe had its own patchwork design of black chickenpox.

Attached to each canoe was an outrigger for stability, an out-reaching arm to keep it from turning over and capsizing. Randy's homemade outrigger was secured by two-by-fours placed at an equal distance from the front and back of the seat. For our propulsion, crude canoe paddles were similarly handcrafted out of leftover materials.

The joy of it all is that we were completely left to our own plans with no parental interference. We'd labor in the hot sun of Randy's backyard, stoking the fires of a makeshift fire pit in the middle of his lawn to melt the tar. Thick, dark smoke rolled over the river and nearby homes as we busied ourselves in boat building. It's a wonder that Randy's parents didn't mind the fire pit in their lawn. It's an even greater wonder that the lawn never fired up and burned the house down. The three of us worked with all sorts of tools without the least bit of adult supervision. Eight and ten year olds running wild–what a life.

After a few days of construction, we'd launch each canoe and test it for leaks. It took a couple of launches before we had a water-tight boat. When we were finished with our boat building, we'd canoe the river downstream to the highway bridge. Sometimes we'd travel under the bridge and fish the hau trees, and other times we'd go to the river entrance and beach the canoes so we could swim at the pier. When the river was high, we'd even make our way out of the stream to canoe in the lagoon along the shoreline. Our destination depended on our moods and how much time we had before dinner.

We never planned canoe fights; river wars just happened. Mischief followed us when we got bored. It would start off innocently enough. We'd have nothing to do, so we'd launch the canoes and paddle downstream. Then Curt, the rascal, would start something.

On one particular day, Curt let me get ahead of him as he fell behind in a "laying low" attack strategy. The river was very muddy and high from seasonal rains. We maneuvered around the canal as the midday sun cooked our skin. Curt joked nonstop downriver, laughing and teasing Randy and me. Soon Curt quieted down and only the irregular sounds of the paddles bumping against the tin hulls could be heard.

It seemed too quiet for me. Something must be in the works. Before I had a chance to finish my thought, a fast glob of river mud slapped my back and neck like a rotten fruit thrown across a harvest field.

Curt laughed uncontrollably. He was in the water holding on to his canoe, diving for more fertile muck for his next projectile. I anticipated his action and paddled in a hard sprint to put some distance between us and lessen the possibility of another accurate hard strike. After only three deep strokes, I felt a stinging thud as another river-bottom mud melon smashed into my back. Two hits to none.

This called for massive retaliation. Hastily but awkwardly, I turned the canoe around and started a ramming speed run for Curt's idle canoe. He was broadside to my bow and Curt was still in the water gathering more mud balls.

My canoe picked up steam. Curt figured it out. I stroked wildly forward like a rowing slave on a Roman warship in a vicious sea battle. I heard the thud of the guard's wooden hammer rhythmically slamming against a worn wood block, "Boom… Boom… Boom…Boom…" In my mind, the cadenced beat of the wood mallet became deafening as the merciless jailer hammered away to lead my canoe strokes. I imagined a sweaty soldier walking the middle plank of the ship. He whipped the shoulder flesh of a feeble slave as he failed to keep pace with the rhythm. The leather whip bit deep into his aged hide. My mind was filled with the spirit of these images. I dare not slacken my paddling speed for fear of harsh punishment. Then, in all the glory of a slave turned captain, I rammed Curt's canoe at full speed. A direct hit to the port quarter!

Curt had barely got onboard and was scurrying backward to move his craft when I smashed into him like a wall of rocks. Unfortunately, the boat did not sink or wobble. It just pushed backwards a distance without damage. Curt was still paddling backward to get away when I dropped my paddle and raced to the front of my canoe. "I'll teach you a lesson about canoes!" I threatened him as I launched an impromptu boat-to-boat scuttling.

I held onto the bow's two-by-four and leaned over Curt's canoe to rock his bow up and down, trying to get it to sink. Each time I pushed it lower in the water with a downward thrust, water would spill into the canoe. At this point, I wanted nothing less than a grand sinking.

Curt tried to get away by paddling faster, but I locked the canoes together with my arms and legs. His canoe bobbed up and down to an ever-increasing motion as water fell into the canoe and created a puddle in its bottom. Curt reacted fast. He stopped paddling and lobbed more mud from his stash under the wooden seat. Bilge water made his projectiles sloppy and runny. He splattered me repeatedly as I ducked to protect my face.

Next he rushed to the front of the canoe to engage me in hand-to-hand combat. Curt reached over to push me out of my canoe. I rose up to defend myself. Soon we were enjoined in a standing test of strength, Curt trying to push me and me trying to toss him. We fought hard, making fierce war faces and doing whatever it took to win. Our hands were locked with our feet keeping us balanced in our own canoes. Then Curt lifted his left leg and stomped it on the bow of my boat, pushing it dangerously down to meet the river. It only resulted in a small spill. I did the same to his canoe. It took on more water but not to the point of sinking.

It became an imagined life-and-death struggle. We were two young pirates in a boat-to-boat clash of strength and courage. We didn't need grappling hooks to make our craft steadfast; we wrestled across the water, boat-to-boat locked in a battle royal. With both of us leaning forward to each other's canoes, our boats started to part. We couldn't let go of each other or retreat to our own canoes. We were too far forward, balancing on each other

over the water. A stream of fourth grade cusswords bantered back
and forth, but that would not end this dilemma.

Curt dislodged me first. I fell over into the river, taking him
down with me into the muck. We both splashed in and headed
straight to the grimy bottom. We released each other when we
hit the mud. Then, breaking the surface for air, I was greeted
with a mud melon on my face, followed by a second. Its sting was
wicked. Curt got me good. I dove down and grabbed a handful
of muck, he reloaded, and there we stood in 3 feet of water blast-
ing each other with river mud. We splashed, laughed, and caught
our breath for a time. With our marine skirmish at a draw, we
went about the business of retrieving the canoes.

Our buddy Randy made a decision early that he wanted no
part of this, so he continued downstream to the beach. With our
moods calmed, Curt and I paddled downstream to join him.
We landed to see Randy kicking seaweed down the beach at the
Aina Haina side of the valley. There, freshwater springs from the
mountains drizzled out at the beach where the rocks met the
sand. Curt left to join Randy, but I decided to stay at the river
instead.

After sitting on the sand a while, I drifted off and daydreamed
about the far reef and Blue Hole. The round sand patch in the
reef was a natural crater the size of several houses that taunted
me into many a dream of discovery and adventure. I dreamed
about the reef all the time, especially during class at school.

To me, school was all memorization, no thinking, no feeling,
and no fun. Sister Roberta would be talking at the chalk board
while I'd imagine maneuvering my canoe on the river, fighting
fish in the hau trees, or doing cannon balls off the swimming
pier. I could live there in my own world all day, but I was cautious
enough to keep half an ear open to what was going on in class.
The last thing I wanted was a ruler on my knuckles for not paying
attention.

Here alone on the beach, I was free to create my own world
without being disturbed. I often imagined what it would be like to
see Blue Hole or to swim out to the reef where the waves crashed
in fierce lines of white foam. It must be another world out there
so far from shore. Someday when I'm older, I would swim to the
reef and see all the sea creatures. Maybe I would be more com-

fortable in the ocean then and not so fearful of sinking, losing my breath, or drowning.

I often felt torn between the thrill of our adventures and the inherent dangers of the activity itself. The river, beach and pier seemed safe and comfortable for me, but I wanted to see and do more. I wanted to go to the reef to surf and fish. I heard talk from the older kids who went there to surf big waves and spear giant fish. That would be such a thrill; I knew I'd have to overcome my fears someday. To be lost in the ocean was a terror my father drove into me. Maybe it was his way of protecting me from myself. While I longed to be at the reef, I was apprehensive of it.

My hopes and fears danced in my mind as I looked at the crashing surf. It was difficult to understand my dread of the dangers that lurked there. Curt and I talked about making a snorkel trip to free dive and spear fish in Blue Hole. We built it up as the adventure of all adventures for months before we got serious about it.

I knew it was an important escapade for me, so I accepted the fact that a time would come for me to overcome my self doubts. I kept telling myself, I've snorkeled all over the end of the pier. All I'm going to do is snorkel a little farther, a little longer. It'll be the same reef I see now. The Blue Hole in the reef is just white sand–it only looks like a mysterious cavern.

Soon the boys came back kicking up sand and disturbing my solitary pursuits. We played for a few hours at the end of the pier until it was time to paddle back up river to Randy's house.

When I wasn't on the river I went to school with all the other kids. For reasons beyond my childish understanding, school was tough. My grades were always acceptable, but I spent an inordinate amount of time at the principal's office for disciplinary reasons. I couldn't sit still in class, so I was often punished for being disruptive. I didn't have the least bit of interest in regimentation and repetitive learning. The nuns loved me, but they were always finding fault with my behavior.

Somehow Sister Roberta found out that I had fishing poles and crab nets. One day after class she asked me to talk to my father about borrowing the equipment for a retreat the sisters were having in the country. Of course, Dad was only too happy to use whatever means available to put me in a better standing with my teachers. He must have been desperate; he re-rigged all the gear, better than he rigged for us.

The idea of nuns in their white habits fishing and crabbing at the beach seemed out of place to me. My classmates and I decided that God would not allow them to take off their habits and use swimsuits, so they must fish in old worn habits kept just for that purpose. It didn't seem very religious to get their regular holy clothes dirty with fish blood and crab guts.

We also concluded that they would have to use the habits when they lay on the beach to suntan. Somehow God would let the sun through their clothes to give them a tan. We figured that's the way it worked because they were so devoted to God. We were told that they were married to God and he did all sorts of special favors for them like our dads did for our moms.

Now that I knew Sister Roberta fished, I thought she must be a real person, not just a nun with no human thoughts or feelings. Maybe because I fished, she seemed to take a greater interest in me and was a little more patient when I acted out. I started to take a greater liking to her knowing that she was interested in the ocean. I began to wonder if she canoed, surfed, or speared fish like my river buddies, even though it was difficult to imagine, considering all those clothes she had to wear. I was starting to get the feeling she might be a real fisherwoman but was too busy with God and us kids to get out to the ocean very often.

One day before morning recess she called me to her desk. I wasn't really worried because I wasn't doing anything wrong at the time. Besides, what more could she do to me? I had gone to the principal's office two days before. So what if I have to see Sister Mary Lucy again, empty her trash bucket, and sit in the corner? I was calm but quite humble in my appearance. I made my way to her fortress, the grey metal desk at the head of the class.

She pulled a book from her stack of papers. "I got this from the library for you. You might like to read it." She paused for a moment as she passed the treasure to me. "Tell me if you like it. Okay, you may go now."

Wow, that was nothing. What a relief. I took the book and thanked her. I studied the cellophane-covered jacket of *Call It Courage* by Armstrong Sperry. A Polynesian canoe flew across a stylized ocean with full Tahitian sail. There was a boy no older than me guiding the craft with a strong physical presence. He sailed an open ocean crowned with white clouds and fair skies. Gulls and seabirds flew effortlessly around and above his canoe. The young man looked like me, but he was relaxed, confident, and so content with his companion dog riding in front of his canoe.

I didn't enjoy reading the books that were required for school, but this one seemed like it would be different. The main character, Mafatu, the son of a Polynesian chief, was afraid of the sea. Never as strong or as brave as the other boys in the village, he lived a life of ridicule by his tribal peers. As I read each line, I saw myself in this discouraged soul. I understood him and felt his fear and disappointment at his own fearfulness. Some of my feelings became clearer to me, especially the self-doubts that lurked deep in my mind.

Line by line I read and hung on every word on every page. Slowly an understanding of my fears and insecurities began to emerge. I didn't have to be born brave; I could face my challenges and become brave! I just have to want to succeed bad enough, no matter what the consequences. That would be my understanding of my life's future and my new mentality. In the days and weeks that passed, I began daydreaming of how I would conquer my fears with new ocean adventures.

It became obvious to me that Curt and Randy weren't naturally brave. They did what they wanted to do, in spite of their fears, and became brave. Sure they had more experience than I did, but that didn't matter. They made a decision to do what they wanted, with everything we did. They didn't fret about the consequences. They just did it. I began to feel that everyone must have self-doubts, but the brave stepped forward to do that which they feared, just like Mafatu in the book. I was no different than Mafatu, Curt or Randy. I decided that I too would always meet my fears, just like the native boy did each time he faced a challenge.

Mafatu would become a lifelong trusted companion for me. He would be with me in my moments of doubt when I was in the ocean. I began to see myself as a young Mafatu navigating our river and bay.

Curt must have learned a trick or two from his older brother, because a summer later, he was making plans to attack Blue Hole and snorkel the far reef. He got me interested in the idea, and soon we were talking about it all the time. Of course I would go with him; it was my life's dream. There was nothing but excitement as we talked about taking a trip to the unknown. I would never let Curt know of my fears. Not even my parents knew.

The day of our spearfishing was upon us. We were at the end of the pier getting ready for our big adventure to Blue Hole. Curt hung onto the dock ladder shivering as he adjusted his mask and snorkel. His mask was foggy so he took it off and spit in the face plate to clean and rinse it before he put the mask back on. He sealed it by sucking the mask in with his nose to create a watertight seal to his skin.

I was doing the same thing, bobbing on the surface with my arm wrapped through the ladder. Small chop bumped us into each other and the ladder as we hurried to finish our preparations.

There was a real chill to the ocean, but I hoped it would warm up when the sun rose above Koko Crater. The water was clear to the bottom, with multicolor corals, rocks, and algae. An entire ocean awaited us. Earlier, Curt and I raided his father's fishing locker for dive gear, including a Hawaiian sling (a surgical tubing shooter with a one barbed steel shaft spear.)

It was very shallow at the dock's end, only 4 feet, but once we left the swimming area and snorkeled over to the coral forests, it got even shallower. It would only allow enough room for skinny young boys like us to carefully float at the surface without scraping our stomachs on corals.

Curt dragged a float line with an empty Clorox bottle floater tied to its end. Attached to the handle grip of the floater was a round wire loop that served as a fish stringer. We wanted to fill it full of fish before coming back to the dock. It was exciting to be on my first spearing trip. It was long overdue. I knew Curt and his brother Bucky spearfished with their father and uncles. I heard him talk about how fun it was for the longest time. With a tinge of fear and some minor reservations, I would do my best to keep up with my young dive master.

Curt and I ventured off the ladder and away from the dock. It was a difficult start. Curt's 30 feet of float line drifted on the surface tangled about on top of the water. It acted more like a catch line to entangle my mask and snorkel. As soon as I would get my mask tangle free, the line would snag my fins, then grab my mask again. It was provoking.

The surface chop wreaked havoc for me by filling the snorkel with water and causing me to choke as salt water rushed down into my mouth and lungs. But I didn't let a little thing like swallowing water deter me. I survived in spite of a constant stream of moist air going into my lungs. I blew out excess water through the top of my snorkel before taking any deep breaths and learned that short, shallow breaths worked better because I sucked less water into my mouth.

Curt and I didn't make any plans for the dive; we just put our heads down and flutter kicked our fins to Blue Hole. As we snorkeled along the way, we hunted for fish and other small creatures. Getting to our reef crater wasn't easy. It required a two hundred yard trek across the shallow reef.

For years it lay there before me like a flat white oyster in a dark bed of seaweed. I could only dream what such a marvel of nature would look like up close. It must be some kind of water miracle, where the prettiest, best-tasting fish lived.

We charged out of the swimming hole and made our way over the expansive reef. Slowly the pier's sand patch gave way to scattered corals and rubble, then to clumps of seaweed, which yielded to thick vegetation forming vast fields of marine brush. Sometimes I followed Curt close to his side, while other times I trailed behind in a field of fin wake and tangling float line. The view over the reef was heart-pounding. I struggled to breathe through the snorkel. My facemask leaked persistently, but I would press on, making the best of these challenges. I imagined Mafatu swimming over vast, pristine reefs. I reflected on his bravery as I did my own reef assault.

The snorkel continued to be a problem. No matter what I did or how I positioned my lips around the snorkel, it leaked. Perhaps the constant splash of the surface chop found its way into my breathing tube, or maybe the device was old and leaky, but whatever the cause, a constant stream of water kept my breathing shallow and cautious. Every once in a while I'd have to stand up on the coral to clear my mouth of water before continuing on. The leaky mask didn't bother me as much as the snorkel did.

The scenery along the reef was awesome, nothing like anything I had ever seen or imagined. Ocean currents moved the sea growth across the reef in hypnotic ripples of endless movement. The rhythmic swells massaged the reef as they traveled to shore. Our bodies floated in a mesmerizing trance with the ocean's timeless dance. Gently moving with the sea's up-and-down, forward-and-back motion, we traveled to our destination.

When the seaweed moved, bits and pieces of the cream coral floor would open itself to sunlight, revealing a diverse hidden terrain. Tiny grains of sand, pockets of pebbles, little ruts and draws, sea urchin holes, and cracks opened into other more minute worlds. I wondered if only we would stop and study each individual feature, it would be another world completely. Today we would only swim by and glimpse at its magnificence since we were committed to move forward to our spearfishing grounds.

All of this living landscape was far beyond any young boy's most vivid dreams. As I swam forward, I thought about God and his most infinite power that created all of this natural beauty. Somehow I knew in my heart that these watery reefs would be my uniquely personal way to visit someone much greater than myself.

The beauty of the terrain was inspiring yet somewhat scary. We floated inches above the seaweed and the coral formations below. There was barely any room to do anything but float. Whenever I slowed down and tried to catch my breath, my belly would sink into the seaweed and hard corals would scratch my stomach, knees, and elbows. These sensations of a hard bottom filled with sharp corals, jagged rubble, and prickly creatures concerned me. Any attempt to move around on top of the coral seemed to invite cuts and punctures.

I decided that I would not stop and sink unless there was a small sand clearing free of corals and creatures. I continued on in a beautiful trance. A few minutes later, I screamed in my snorkel with the loudest blood chilling sound. "Ahhh!" A slimy monster eel hovered before me!

The long ugly thing came out of his hole to see the commotion that Curt left and saw me coming at him. What am I going to do? I questioned in panic. The water snake was an adolescent moray eel, huffing and puffing its head with an open undulating mouth. I feared it might be waiting to bite my ear, or some other private place. I couldn't swim past; it was out of the question.

I can't do this. I have to get away! I made a sharp right turn and banked my body away from the eel. Scraping my stomach and hips would be of no consequence now, considering that I was about to get bit. Curt told me of a kid who got bitten by an eel that never let go. He had to run home with the eel latched on his finger to have his dad pry it off. What would my face look like with an eel locked on to it? What about the pain? I swam away at full speed, right full rudder.

It worked. The eel didn't come after me; it swam in place, checking me out as I scrambled away from the coral cluster. What a relief. My body calmed down and soon I resumed my path. Curt stopped ahead at the lip of Blue Hole and waited for me to catch up. Finally I arrived. We floated there for a moment to catch our breath, looking around the ring of lava and coral that encircled a massive sand depression in the reef.

It was heavenly–a sea of green seaweed opening into an oasis of clear alabaster sand as far as our eyes could see. A perfectly curved lava wall 5 feet high rose from a bed of the most inviting sand. It was an unusual type of sand, almost pure and clean, like sterile soft cotton. As I observed its unusual but peaceful nature from the outside edge, the scene created hidden, transcendental feelings deep within me. If only Mom and Dad could see this. I knew how wonderful it would be for them to experience this amazing place.

Curt and I entered the caldera and swam warily around its edges where the lava wall dropped down to the sand floor. This would be the best hunting areas where fish looked for food. Curt's Hawaiian sling was loaded, the metal shaft pulled back in the plunger with its rubbers stretched. All he'd have to do was depress the metal latch, and the thin harpoon would fly to meet any target he chose. We swam forward with very little movement so as not to disturb the prey.

Soon three goat fish cruised toward us at the bottom near the cliff wall. Curt dove down, swimming toward them to get close. He squeezed down on the trigger latch to let loose his shaft. The spear flew to hit its mark. A stunned goat fish struggled to get free. Curt came up for air, took a big gulp, and went back down to retrieve his fish on the spear. I watched as the fish beat itself against the sand trying to get free. It was only grazed below the gills back into the fleshy part of the stomach. The barb held onto a small patch of skin that soon tore, and the fish sped off. Curt picked his spear off the bottom and surfaced.

We bobbed at the surface, treading water for awhile. Curt re-loaded and we continued on with our sporting raid. There was only one gun amongst us, so I was content to watch and learn. I was more engrossed in this incredible ocean. All the colors, shapes, and sizes of things were spectacular. There was nothing in the valley, river, or beach that could match the mystery and elegance of this place.

Curt and I took our time to scout a large part of Blue Hole. More fish swam into range and many more shots were taken. Curt's misses started to stack up. It wasn't real easy to shoot a swimming fish in the wild with a gun that had no sights while be-ing bullied by the push and pull of the currents. I eventually took a turn to discharge the gun on an unsuspecting fish and missed him by at least 9 inches. It was a total thrill. I knew this was for me. I'd have to save up some money for my own gear and learn how to use it.

Curt and I eventually agreed to call it quits and swim back to the pier. Exhausted and cold, we lay collapsed on the swim deck warming ourselves in the sun. As we lay on our backs watching the clouds drift, we relived every detail of our dive and planned the next trip to Blue Hole.

I eventually got my own snorkel equipment and made regu-lar trips around the pier and beyond. I would go to Blue Hole again and again, but no matter how often I dove the site, it always remained a special place for me. It offered rare and unique op-portunities to see the real beauty of the ocean.

Some years later, when I was twelve years old, my parents took a boat ride to see the new marina development in Hawaii Kai on a long Sunday afternoon. They returned late to announce that we'd bought a new house and would be moving to Kuapa Pond. I wasn't happy to leave my friends, but the notion of living on a marina captured my interest.

Henry J. Kaiser, the famous industrialist at the time, secured the rights to develop the east side of the island from the Bishop

Estate, a charitable trust set up by the late Hawaiian princess. A powerful man of vision, Kaiser planned the master mini-city on the theme of waterfront housing, apartments, shopping centers and marina recreation. His company would take the sprawling ancient Hawaiian fish pond and turn it into a first-class marina community over the next fifty years.

We were part of the first wave of twenty-six families that bought into the dream. From the very beginning, the fish pond offered an exciting new way of living. We lived off Hawaii Kai Drive in a cul-de-sac of six homes with an assigned boat slip for each residence. At the urging of my parents, it wasn't a year later that my Auntie Vickie moved into the neighborhood with her three boys, Dickie, Jimmie, and Johnnie.

I made new friends and grew in my love for the sea. Scott Thomas and his younger brother Kirk became my buddies. In Niu Valley we made tin canoes for the river, but here in Kuapa Pond, we made telephone-pole rafts to navigate the marina. With the discarded leftover dock pilings, the kids taught themselves how to build long, sturdy rafts. Massive amounts of material were available since each boat slip required a telephone pole sunk into the mud to form the outer leg of a slip and tie-up dock. After the pile pole hit bedrock, the dock builders cut the tops of the posts off so all the poles would be the same height. The leftovers were set aside and abandoned, so the kids gathered them together and lashed them into rafts.

We used our "*Kon Tiki*" crafts to transverse the marina to a nearby spoil island created by dredging leftovers. Only the kids were allowed on this island! We had bonfires at night, sleepovers, and private fishing away from the troublesome adults. On many occasions the parents would gather at a dock party to see us off with cocktails in hand. We were so happy to have our freedom it never crossed our minds that perhaps they had motivations of their own.

The rafts were sturdy but not built for speed. Eventually the kids graduated to faster, smaller dinghies and row boats, but soon all of that was replaced with surfboards. Our close group of friends took up surfing in junior high.

Riding the waves became our primary passion for the excitement and pure physical connection to the ocean. Snorkeling and diving were always there, especially when the surf was flat, but surfing became the rage for us. We got better at surfing as our skills improved with practice. Our favorite spots included the Second Reefs, Pillars, Portlock Point, and Sandy Beach Point.

As far as we were concerned, we'd find the surf whenever and wherever it was breaking on the South Shore. Scott was the first to get his driver's license and car, so his station wagon became the surf "woody." We chipped in for gas and it wasn't long before Scott became the ring leader of our surf clan.

Later in high school I fell in with a group of surfers that formed "The Freedom Riders" surf club. The roster of members included a literal who's who of top surfers from the south shore. We were the top club in Oahu for a number of years. I was very proud to be a member of the club and served as its treasurer for a while.

During these surfing times I chummed with my Hawaii Kai boys and made new friends with a few Kahala kids. It was a fabulous life... surf, eat, sleep, and school. Soon I was old enough to get a driver's license and part-time job, so with a Red Cross Lifesaving Certificate and first-aid class under my belt, I became the lifeguard at the Hawaii Kai pool. It was a super job, working the pool and making a bundle of money at $1.65 an hour.

The pool manager knew the Director of Water Safety for the city, and after I attained a few years of loyal service, he recommended me for a city lifeguard position. When I got the beach job, my best buddy Mark Olsen from Kahala took over guarding the pool. Now he would have to deal with my Auntie's three rabble-rouser boys.

Beach guarding was a terrific step up for fun, not to mention the immediate raise to $2.65 per hour. The young college guards weren't full-time employees, instead working on a seasonal contract for the city. We were hired to supplement the regular guards and cover the beaches when school was out for weekends, holidays, and vacations. As I traveled to the different beaches for work, I became more knowledgeable about the island's surf and dive sites.

When I went away to Wisconsin for college, I kept my lifeguard job so I could return during Christmas and summer vacations. The employment helped pay for trips home to the warm weather. My usual stations were Sandy Beach, Makapuu and

Hanauma Bay, the first two spots being top-rated body surfing beaches and Hanauma a world-class snorkel beach.

On the rare occasions that Lifeguard Captain Aloha Kalama found displeasure with me, he sent me out to work the country stations across the island for corporal penance. Looking back on it now, I think he really needed the manpower out in the country and knew I wouldn't complain. That was probably his primary motivation for sending me out to the countryside so far from home.

Our lifeguard corps was filled with high-energy, cutting-edge watermen with a true dedication to service. Their special skills gave them the courage to enter the water where others would dare not, all to save the life of a stranger. This type of life guarding wasn't like pool or lake guarding; it was rough water, big wave, beach guarding, each day filled with excitement and heart-pounding rescues.

After college I returned to Hawaii to take up a career and make a life for myself. Quite by chance, I fell in with another group of water people. An ad appeared for a beach cottage rental in the Sunday paper. I went to check it out and ended up renting a 500-square-foot gardener's shack on the grounds of a Niu Valley beachfront home. The residential compound was four houses down the beach from Niu Stream. My landlord, Davie James of Honolulu Marine, was a real mentor and a wonderful person. His beach compound was a waterman's paradise, with a canoe, Hobie Cat, dingy boat, and lots of parties. I truly believed I'd died and gone straight to heaven at the Niu Beach Club!

Niu Beach was a cocoon of life. The feel of fresh trade winds from the valley, the sound of the surf breaking on the reef off-shore, and the coconut palms shuffling overhead all slowly brought me back to the Hawaii I loved. I reverted to the simple things: walking the brown sand beach, wading across the old stream, and swimming off the pier. All the things I did as a young child with nature, I did again but with an older pair of eyes and a more experienced soul.

I settled into my new digs and became part of Davie's beach house clan and discovered that the two houses next to us were inhabited by water sports enthusiasts too. It was a communal collection of surfers, Prindle Catamaran sailors, and party animals just like Davie's household. Between the three houses, someone was always doing something in the water or having a party.

Davie's company introduced a newly-manufactured fiberglass canoe based on an old Polynesian design. Honolulu Marine had the marketing arrangements and took to promoting it as an affordable and nearly indestructible one- to three-man canoe. One of the demo models lay beached at the house waiting for aggressive testing and marketing.

The sleek yellow canoe became our water taxi to the reef offshore. All of us at the beach houses were avid body surfers and skin divers who would put the canoe to its tests. When the surf was breaking, it was easy to load two or three surfers into the canoe with surf fins for a trip out to the breakers. We'd paddle out and throw anchor just off the surf line at the channel. There'd be no one but us in the water, so hooting and hollering were commonplace. Friendly rivalries for dominance in the lineup were also very frequent. But above all else, it was about everyone having fun until we were too tired to swim and limped back ashore in the canoe.

When the waves were flat, the canoe would be used to take snorkelers out to the reef for a look-see. Snorkeling and spearing were not as popular as surfing in the neighborhood, but every once in a while there'd be some interest. It was the same drill, but mask, fins, and snorkel were the ticket to this activity. Sometimes a spear or two would accompany the entourage.

The most unusual activity and by far the most treacherous was canoe surfing. Catching and riding a breaking wave with a long canoe was difficult, requiring much greater skill than just paddling the canoe into a wave. Many subtle nuances had to be employed to maneuver the boat out safely through the surf break, and another set of skills were required to steer the canoe onto the wave. Those Waikiki beach boys who took tourists for canoe rides made it look simple, but it was really difficult. It was especially tricky with the smaller, shorter canoes that float lighter in the waves.

Davie had the greatest canoe-steering ability. On regular waves, his track record for not swamping was excellent, but the problem with Davie was that he wasn't satisfied with catching regular waves; he'd purposely wait for the biggest meanest swells the ocean would dish out. If the size of the waves was slightly lacking, he'd wait until the last minute for a critical takeoff or any combination of wave size and timing for the thrill of it. That would stress the canoe and place the crew of paddlers into the most adrenaline-filled circumstances imaginable. It was always the most fun, high adventure waves that Davie looked for. It was all worth it when we survived it, and almost always, even when we didn't.

On the occasions that we didn't make the wave and wiped out, we'd crash and swamp. Desperately hanging on to the sunken canoe, we hoped to survive being pushed across the reef by the relentless crashing waves. Finally we would end up inside the surf line on the shallowest part of the reef. The crew would be glad to have made it without coral cuts or losing crew members to the surf. Then, like the scene of some shipwreck, we slowly came back to life and started the job of bailing the water out of the canoe. Captain Davie would make light of the situation, and the fun would begin again as we went back out for another wave.

I did my fair share of canoe steering, but there was no way I'd attempt to do the stuff that Davie did. My takeoffs were restricted to the more survivable waves where we'd have a good ride but wouldn't have to contend with a probable wave wreck.

Life on Niu Beach was indeed good to me. Davie and all the water enthusiasts in the compound only encouraged and strengthened my love for the ocean and the many ways of relating to it. It gave me a chance to revisit my childhood and to see the river, beach, and ocean through an older pair of eyes.

As a child, I could have never imagined that someday I would be prowling the surf line and outer reef with these trusted waterman companions. I would not have dreamed a timid boy from the river would canoe surf past Blue Hole and the barrier reef.

My life was fantastic at Niu, but renting a beach shack, as wonderful as it was, wouldn't be forever. With my career in financial planning safely underway, I made plans to purchase a Hawaii Kai waterfront condominium. It was a melancholy time for me, leaving my adoptive beach family and the joys of Niu Beach.

With the sadness of leaving one life, the joy of starting another began. This move to Hawaii Kai would put me closer to my folks and old friends on the marina. I would have to revisit old dive spots and develop new ones in Moanalua Bay.

It was during the process of finalizing my condo deal when my dad suggested I purchase the family home and they take ownership of the condo instead. They were getting older and wanted a more carefree lifestyle. We figured and refigured until an equitable but generous deal was struck. I would be home again in the house of my youth, and my parents would have a worry-free retirement in an upscale condominium at the Esplanade.

Over the next 25 years I would make a life of boating on the Kuapa Marina and diving the eastern tip of Oahu and the north coast of Molokai.

CHAPTER THREE

KINDRED SOULS

I'm thankful for having been influenced by my friends Randy, Curt, and Curt's father in my early days of inshore fishing and diving. Any fish in the inner reefs of Niu Valley were never very safe with our die-hard troop of young spearfishermen. Armed with old style Hawaiian slings and firing single-barbed spear shafts, we roamed the coral heads relentlessly looking for game large enough to take a spear. Our tools were the standard of spearfishermen of the 1960's. With hand-me-down masks, snorkels, flippers, and homemade float lines, we'd spend hours in the water spearing reef fish.

After moving to the Hawaii Kai marina, I settled into a great life of diving the beaches, shoreline cliffs, and occasionally off-shore spots on boats at anchor. But all of that changed when I met the Professor, Hughsan. He's the sensei and grand dive master who took me from the stone ages of casual diving into the modern world of advanced drift-dive spearfishing. His passion for diving led him to study, learn, and explore new techniques and perfect old ones.

One casual business lunch with Hugh Fraser would turn my diving into a new life of cutting-edge spearfish diving. We initially talked about insurance, but somehow the conversation drifted to boating and diving. I became entranced with his dive stories: the unusual spots, the shooters, and the tales of large fish and tasty lobsters. With the hope of deepwater adventure, I took him up on his offer to join the boys for a dive.

The guys were genuinely friendly and immediately welcomed me into their stable of shooters. Although I was not as experienced with deepwater spearfishing as they were, I did have my strengths: I was a decent shooter, knew the ocean well, never got seasick, was a good deck hand, and happily contributed for fuel. Oh, lest I forget, I was also easy to get along with on the confined space of a boat.

At the time I joined the group, the lead divers were Hughsan, V, Gordon, and "Smitty" (Kona Smith.) The group slowly expanded and soon included me, "Killer" (Gary Brent,) "Crawman," "Lungs" (Gerry McClay,) "Gman" (Mark Gerasimenko,) "Capt Dev" (Dev Merrifield,) and "Grant" (Grant Stoddard.)

One of the benefits of Hughsan's crowd was its treasure trove of amazing dive spots. Their repertoire was extensive, diverse, and exciting: Split Rock, Mount Terrace, Lyman's, Smitty's Reef, Shark's Cove, Chris and Jamie's Traps, Hanauma Bluff, Ulua Cave, Lava Mounds, Makapuu Flats, Rabbit Island Reefs, and Molokai Cliffs... the list went on and on.

There were so many dive spots that when they grew weary of one, they'd try another that they hadn't visited in months or years. On the other hand, my list of dive locations was short, only consisting of shallow-water bay sites and a small group of beach entry locals. Comparing their offshore sites to mine was ridiculous. There was no way that a shoreline spot could even come close to the spoils to be had on an offshore site.

Any experienced diver would take a deep-ocean dive in preference to a beach dive. Offshore dive spots aren't frequented as often as the beach spots because there are fewer divers with boats. With fewer divers on a reef, the marine ecosystem is subjected to less spearfishing pressure. That always meant more and bigger fish for those divers who ventured out to sea. To make matters even more attractive for boat divers, bigger fish naturally congregate in deeper water, only venturing into the shallows to hunt smaller fish.

Any spearfisherman knows it takes a lot more spearing to feed a family with a bunch of small fish. One large 40 to 50 pound ulua (giant trevally) would feed four or five families at one sitting. For all the time and effort, deep water spearing was always more productive. But the main reason we all continued with the dive group was not really about harvesting fish—it was about the thrill of underwater hunting with good friends.

The great rush of adrenaline that powers through your body when stalking, shooting, and fighting a monster fish, eye-to-eye, up close and personal, kept us hooked. It's an experience difficult for most people to imagine, possibly comparable to the victory of winning a life-and-death gladiator match with a fish.

Hughsan's group perfected the art of drift diving and underwater spearing. By using a team approach to hunting, one team of divers went down to its selected spot while the second team handled the boat. The second team prepared for its dive while tracking the first team from the surface. After the first group was safely onboard, the second team got a turn at spearing at a location of its choice.

If on a particular day, there were only enough divers for one team, someone from the group could be persuaded to drive the boat as a courtesy. Under this circumstance, the driver was treated with the greatest respect, often having food and drink provided by the active divers. The volunteer only had to drive; he wasn't required to help with the preparations or cleanup after the dive. He usually waltzed in, just in time to depart and drive to the chosen spot. When the dive was completed and the boat docked back at the slip, he walked away at will. If he cared to wait, one share of the catch would be gifted to him as a token of the divers' appreciation.

Boat drivers are ultimately responsible for the safety of the divers while in the water. Good navigational skills are critical to delivering the divers to their site and picking them up again. By use of landmark triangulation, dead reckoning, and depth finder readings, a spot far out at sea could be located and found over and over again. Each spot has its particular mapping idiosyncrasies. Sometimes it took lining up two trees on a mountain top, one building onshore crossing the front of another building father behind, or an irregular depth reading jumping up from the bottom signifying a reef.

A combination of spot locators made a site easier to find. But no matter who was at the helm, or how good the driver was at finding the site, there'd always be directions shouted by anxious divers to help the driver fine tune the boat's final position before they jumped in the water. No diver wanted to be dropped off in the middle of the ocean without a reef to hunt. The difference between landing on a spot and missing it could be compared to landing in a desert oasis of luscious date palms and cool water or getting stuck in a wasteland of the desert itself. In later years with the advent of GPS navigation, finding our dive sites became much easier.

The boat driver tracked his divers below through a variety of tools. He might follow their bubbles, track a float line dragged by a diver, wait for a flag placed on a three-prong spear upon surfacing, watch for a small nylon kite flown by a diver, or later, with the improvement of technology, wait for a waterproof VHF radio transmission from the divers in the water.

With this latest radio technique, a VHF was tucked into an underwater case attached to a diver's weight belt and opened upon surfacing. Drift diving allowed the divers freedom to go where the fish took them without worrying about making it back to the boat, but it put an awesome responsibility on the boat drivers. The new radio communications method was instrumental in finding many a diver that would have been lost with old methods.

The bubble method, one of the earliest techniques of diver tracking, was the least dependable. It worked well when the divers were shallow with large, extremely visible air bubbles breaking the surface. But the deeper the divers went, the more the bubbles dissipated, as compressed air expands and bursts numerous times on its way up to the surface. By the time the bubbles reached the top from 120 feet down, they were very small and spread over a large area, making it difficult for the boat driver to see. If the ocean currents were strong and the surface choppy, it was even harder to find the bubbles and track the divers. Clean, calm seas were necessary for this technique to be reliable.

The popular technique of following a float line significantly improves the success of tracking the divers. One of the divers carries a line with him below that's attached to a small float on the surface. Our divers preferred a cleaned, bright-yellow antifreeze container. As the divers drifted with the current, the float would tell the boat driver where they were headed.

When the divers attacked a ledge that held promise of game, the float line was tied around a coral head so the diver had both hands free for shooting fish and grabbing "spinies" (Hawaiian spiny lobsters.) After all was done, the diver returned to fetch the float before moving to the next ledge. For shooting fish on the fly, the float line was attached to a weight belt or held loosely in the hand.

On some occasions, the float was difficult to lug around because the swells tossed it around or the surface currents moved it in a direction counter to the bottom currents. Although no one enjoyed being attached to it, that was the price to pay for not being lost at sea.

The Crawman is credited with introducing the flag on the three-prong pole technique. That one little invention allowed us to dump the cumbersome float and streamline our operations. All of our hunters carried a long-gun and a three-prong. Craw made up a bunch of 3 by 5 foot orange flags that slipped over the three-prong and attached with Velcro. When the diver surfaced, the flag on the pole became an ocean rescue flag that any blind man could see from hundreds of yards away. Since the flag was made of parachute nylon, it folded down very thin so you could store it in the pocket of a vest or wet suit.

Hughsan discovered a new rescue whistle through his mainland connections with the diving industry. With the "Dive-Alert" whistle properly attached to a power inflator hose, this shrill alarm became the bread and butter method of finding our divers. The ear-piercing sound emitted from the device could be heard over a mile downwind and slightly less up wind. However, it soon became obvious that excessive boat noise should be avoided when the boat drivers were depending on the rescue whistle as their primary means of finding the divers.

Not to be outdone by Crawman, Gman came up with a better version of the three-prong flag. Experimenting with different nylon forms, he attached a shaped piece of fabric to a string cradle and a long line. He designed a parachute kite that folded down into a wet suit pocket and unfolded to form a workable kite that would fly straight at a 45 degree angle. When deployed, the boat driver would see it flying high in the air from a much greater distance. The invention was ingenious, but there were limitations.

Lack of wind or strong winds could hinder this technique. Without wind, the divers were apt to drift away with the currents unseen. The utility of the kite came into question one day in unusually windy conditions when Gman was pulled out to sea and away from the boat. The power of the wind turned the safety device into an uncontrollable sail dragging our diver though the water. Eventually the kite concept was retired due to its limitations.

Normally, a VHF Radio serves as a ship-to-ship and/or a ship-to-shore means of communication. It's been used reliably for many years. In recent times, technology advanced to handheld, waterproofed radio sets that could transmit from the water. The Craw went to work and designed an aluminum underwater case that was pressure tight to 300 feet. The compact round cylinder held a portable radio and attached to a weight belt. When the diver surfaced, the radio would be retrieved and transmissions sent to the boat with directions for pickup. Channel 68 became our diver retrieval channel.

The new radio system had other benefits. In addition to letting the driver know that the divers had surfaced, it allowed the divers to give directions for pickup or note emergency circumstances. On a number of occasions, our divers radioed that they were being stalked by unwanted aquatic visitors in gray suits with large jaws. Of course, the boat drivers made great haste to pick their buddies up out of the water.

When it came to diving equipment, my original gear was representative of the best well-worn diving antiques. I had a couple of steel 72's (standard size tanks) with J valves, a homemade backpack with shoulder hooks and a waist strap, a yellow horse collar buoyancy compensator, and an old mask, snorkel and fins. My regulator was a comedy routine with a pressure/depth gauge combination that was so scratched it tested my eyesight. It was a holdover from my high school days, but it did have an octopus (air sharing regulator.) I dove with cut off shorts and a wet suit top.

I was in the dark ages compared to the top-of-the-line, high-tech diving gear that most of the divers used. There were a few exceptions to this general rule, like Smitty, who purchased good equipment but just wore it out through constant use. Hughsan taught me that the best equipment was also the best safety measure for deep-diving and spearfishing. It was foolhardy to dive to the extremes and rely on outdated gear.

I decided my life was worth more than the price of a new regulator, properly serviced and maintained. As I slowly upgraded my gear, I also invested in one of the first dive computers, "The Edge," to help me track repetitive dives and avoid the bends (decompression sickness.) What a relief it was not to have to calculate multiple dives using dive tables. The increased bottom time was a welcomed benefit too.

The drift divers also taught me that great spearing is a team effort. When you constantly dive with different buddies, you're never sure of your partners or their skills. But when you dive with a steady group of buddies, you learn each one's habits and style. You become attuned to their thinking and are more likely to coordinate dive strategies for the good of the hunt. For example, when attacking a ledge with good potential for larger fish, each diver would know to distance himself and attack from opposite ends of the ledge to box the fish in for shooting. No matter what temptation presented itself, partners stuck to the best shooting strategy for group success.

On rare occasions, a fish might show himself early on a dive team's march to assault a ledge. This might be one of the few acceptable departures from the "stick to the plan" strategy. After all, "A fish on the spear is worth two hiding in the ledge." In that case, the other partner might come in to assist the diver involved in the action. Then, the attack could be resumed as originally planned. Going to the ledge alone is usually considered poor spearing etiquette. Yes, it's sometimes done, but hard feelings between partners may follow. The karmic revenge for the offending diver's bad behavior is the horror of watching all the fish swimming out the opposite end of the ledge.

Aside from the increased fish-catching potential with dive buddies, the expenses of running a boat every weekend gets easier for everyone. When boat expenses are split amongst added divers, the cost of diving becomes more affordable. In addition to saving money on a dive, there's another important benefit of sharing the work load of maintaining the boat. Oil changes, bottom painting, and minor repairs need to be done on an ongoing basis to keep a safe and reliable boat. The more hands, the better.

By far, the greatest benefit of diving in a team is the solid friendship that develops between dive mates. While the communication underwater is limited and often misinterpreted, the process of hunting together requires communication, even if limited to hand signals and gestures. As partners, we pre-plan before a dive and review our execution of the plan after the dive. While no dive is ever "just as planned," each dive brings hunters together in a bond of mutual respect and dependency.

Oftentimes one partner will speculate where his buddy has moved on a reef, mentally calculating how long it will take him to get there and back. Then, if the partner is overdue, he will backtrack to find and assist him.

Aside from the need of a partner, strong and lasting friendships develop because of shared spiritual underwater encounters. When both hunters float with the current side-by-side 80 feet down in crystal blue fluid, blowing past stark mountainous lava formations, gliding with the currents, with awesome marine life passing before them, it's an experience of wonder. To feel and sense nature in this manner is a rare moment you've shared with another living being, your dive buddy. Instinctively you know that he is, as you are, becoming a different person for having experienced this underwater world. Many years spent in the water with dive partners eventually creates deep lasting friendships between divers, their families, and friends.

Successful drift diving would not have been possible without the organization, discipline, and devotion to the cause of a leader or organizer. Some of the dive boys may object to the term "dive master" or "sensei" applied to any of them. All of our divers are independent souls, preferring to operate in a watery world with no leaders or bosses. But for lack of a better phrase and to truly describe the wonderful things that Hughsan has done for the boys, I will call him the dive master.

The man has perfected important talents that have kept this independent, diverse, and aggressive group of divers together for many years. To expand a dive group or elevate divers to a team, qualities of sharing, tolerance, and socialization are necessary.

It's often been said, "Some people give, and some people take." It takes a true giver to attract and retain top-notch marine crusaders. Sharing skills is a big part of the success that Hughsan has had keeping the dive team alive. One of the best qualities of a good dive master is the ability to share knowledge and skill without having the diver feel criticized or embarrassed. Letting a person learn for himself from a teacher's example is usually the best teaching method. This is especially true for old salts and deep divers.

When I started out with the gang, I struggled to manage larger fish at the end of my spear until I saw Hughsan use the "optic nerve squeeze" and the "gill grabber hold" so effectively. With the optic nerve squeeze, he uses his thumb and pointer finger to grab the fish by his eye sockets to control, paralyze, and hasten it to a quick death. The gill grabber hold is not as effective as the optic nerve squeeze but is better suited to controlling fish so large that it's difficult to get a hand around the bridge of the head. With the gill grabber hold, Hughsan uses his gloved hand to reach behind the gill plate and into the fish to firmly secure a grasp on the fish's gills. I learned by observation that instead of fighting with the fish to get it in the bag, gripping control was the required first step.

A boatload of fish killers all hyped up and ready to spear can be a pretty scary testosterone fest. After a full work week, the anticipation on the first dive can easily rattle nerves and flare tempers. Every shooter onboard hopes for the big score he's dreamed of all week. Sometimes individual tensions snap in the self-interest of winning. A coolheaded, tolerant dive leader can go a long way at smoothing things over between divers and maintaining a fun atmosphere on the boat. There were several occasions when Hughsan had to defuse a rough situation at sea with patience and tolerance.

Many of our divers make an extra effort to keep the group together by including the families of the divers in social activities. This not only encourages a bonding of divers but that of their families as well. Hughsan was particularly successful at bringing the "dive widows" and "dive orphans" together in friendships. Since weekend dives were an all-day activity, some divers dove only one day and kept the other day for family activities, while others dove two days and did their best to keep up with their family duties. No matter how often a diver dove, having our families mingle together somehow encouraged more diving.

Quite a few of our social activities occurred at The Esplanade condominiums. It served as a good location for all of us. *It's Time* was docked there at the waterfront, our dive gear was stored in the boat locker, and a few of the boys and their families lived there.

The location was especially good for me since my Mom, Dad, and Auntie Vickie resided there in the park building of the complex. Auntie was divorced now, her three boys grown and moved to the mainland. I'd usually stop in for a morning cup of coffee before diving and drop off fish after diving. Some of the boys, Killer in particular, were especially generous with my folks and gave them their excess fish.

When Dad had nothing to do, he might go downstairs and sit on the marina bulkhead late in the afternoon to see what the hunters were bringing home from the sea. It was curious how he showed up more often when he knew that his favorite divers would be hunting. Dad was always interested in the boys and the fishing plans. It seemed as if he'd just happen to be there waiting for us at the dock if there were divers who didn't take much fish home or if we were planning to go to the lobster grounds.

If we went to the lobster grounds, he was a welcomed partner and beneficiary of the divers. Most of the boys were only interested in the tails, so without my dad all the lobster heads would go to waste. As a lobster connoisseur, Dad was mostly interested in the heads. He'd haul them up to the apartment, freeze a bunch, and then feast on a few each day as an afternoon snack. Mom was patient and didn't mind her apartment smelling like cooked lobster for days on end. However, the neighbors may not have been amused with the lobster smells permeating through the halls.

My life of diving with the drift divers became a coveted lifestyle that brought me excitement, adventure and great personal satisfaction. It was enjoyed as a respected gift from the sea.

I had been diving with the boys for a number of weeks before getting an opportunity to apply my talents to large, deep-water fish. I was just a rookie in this group of experts, content with getting to know the guys and the dive spots. Still so new to their techniques, I wasn't alert to the fine points of hunting with their advanced methods. As in most hunting situations, just because someone goes out to shoot doesn't mean that they will bring home the trophies. It's called hunting, not bagging.

Today we would dive the Split. The boys talked about Split Rock all day long when we dove the shallower Moanalua Bay spots the week before. The Split was deep, 135 feet below the rough waves of Portlock Point and a half mile out to sea. The spot was a series of three daggered rock ledges, each the size of half a dozen small house lots that spiked out toward the deep. Separated by two large sand valleys and surrounded by the ocean's sand bottom, the terrain was barely doable in one dive. On one of the lava plateaus, the outermost part of the cliff fractured and fell off lower than the main cliff line.

I could hardly wait to tackle this challenge. Smitty was at the helm flanked by his dive partner. They finished their previous dive and now it would be their turn to drive the boat for Hughsan and me. Hughsan sat on the port gunnel and shouted last-minute instructions to Smitty on just where he wanted to be at the drop-off. His plan was to enter up-current of the spot and drill down to land on the top-current side of the cliffs. Then, we would hunt going with the current downstream. I sat patiently waiting for the signal to fall off and scramble down to the bottom. We had to be quick about it; otherwise, we might be blown away by the ocean currents on the way down.

Wonder and anticipation filled my spirit, so I tried to calm myself by taking several deep breaths. My gear was mentally checked over and over again to be sure I was prepared for anything that could happen. My three-prong spear and Biller long-gun stood sternly in my grasp.

Smitty shut the motors down and gave us our signal, "Go! You're outside a little, Koko Head, up current." Hughsan glanced at me, signaling with his eyes, Ready? I responded with an affirmative blink. He fell backward and I followed his lead. We were finally in the water. It was a perfect entry.

When the bubbles cleared I confirmed the status of my gear—all was well. Nothing had jerked loose in the free fall off the boat. I jacked-knife kicked and finned down towards the bottom. The seawater was cool on my face and body. I got lost in the excitement of the event, so the initial penetration of chilly water into my wet suit was barely noticeable. I focused on getting my bearings by referencing myself to Hughsan and where I thought the bottom might be.

The water went on and on into the distance, disappearing into endlessness with no sign of any bottom at all. The visibility was at least 70 feet, but the floating plankton and microscopic organisms kept a thin, foggy surface layer in the water. It wasn't the least bit uncomfortable, but it limited the sight distance and helped conceal the bottom from us. The floating organisms also reassured me that this area would abound with life.

Hughsan looked back at me several times to point in the direction he wanted to descend. As we hoofed it down, a dark, indistinguishable formation began to emerge out of the wispy mist. Just a dark cloud lying on the bottom at first, it slowly grew into the outline of a steep, black cliff pointing out to sea against the backdrop of boundless white sand. Slowly, another black cliff emerged like a dark cloud in the distance down current. It remained murky and far off as the first lava cliff came into focus.

Hughsan swam to the beginning of the bulging cliff and floated gracefully halfway down its lava face. He would work the upper and lower portions of the cliff from his mid-level position if any game showed itself. I was shocked at the size of this formation. Layers and layers of lava moved out to sea in tight configurations, creating a mountainous bluff covered with growth and organisms. Each twist and turn revealed more intricate detail of the geologic strata.

Hughsan perked up. Antennae peeked out of the cracks just ahead toward the end of the bluff. He continued forward then sank to the bottom and placed his guns in the sand to free up both hands. I stayed close in to back him up but didn't want to interfere with his potential lobster score.

Floating in a relaxed and non-threatening manner, he went to the front of the lobsters and slowly moved his left hand out and to one side of the spinies. The antennae followed his hand. They were on alert but had not taken any defensive postures yet. Curiosity got the better of them as they watched his hand moving slowly in a hypnotic manner. The larger one of the two stepped a few inches out to see more of what was going on.

"Swoosh!" Hughsan's right hand flashed out from his body and landed on the back of the carapace to pin the lobster on the lava ledge. Then his left hand came back down to stabilize the catch. The perfect left-hand fake, right-hand slam, it was so fast that the lobster never saw it coming.

He wrestled with the spiny for a moment as he unlatched the catch bag and carefully placed his lobster dinner in the mesh sack. The second lobster did not stay to rescue his partner but disappeared back into the cliff. I handed Hughsan his guns, and we continued on with our search.

Rounding the face of the first cliff line exposed a large sand valley with another massive black formation ahead. We swam in an arch to the base of the next ledge, only to be distracted at the sight of five or six wekee (goatfish) grazing the sand for scraps of whatever food they could find. It was the perfect setup for us.

We were careful not to spook the fish as we traveled calmly and slowly toward the school. Hughsan took the deeper outside position while I took the shallower inside station. Quite naturally we coordinated our approach as we tried to get in range. When we got closer, the school's movement became apprehensive as they sensed danger. For all they knew, we could be large wet suited fish basking in the sand with no particular interest in them, but then again we could be hungry monsters looking for fish to devour. We slowed our pace and quieted our movements. Hughsan stopped and rested on the bottom, throwing up handfuls of sand grains like he might be burrowing for food. I followed suit but continued to inch up slowly on the fish.

I was angling in for a shot but was still too far out for an effective kill. Perhaps I pushed the bounds of the fish's comfort zone or maybe Hughsan looked more like a harmless grazer, but the school shifted direction and moved toward Hugh in deeper water.

Hughsan sneakily lifted his arm and extended the Biller Aluminum long-gun forward. Careful not to tighten his muscles or exaggerate his movements, he puffed his fins to propel himself to the fish, gently elongating himself into one long spear with his gun leading the silent charge. The leader of the pack came into range, looked up, and slowly turned to move the school away from the silent running human shaft.

"Bang," the spear was let loose in a perfect shot. The shaft pierced the gill plate and went through the fish with ease. The wekee panicked and ran, taking the spear and leader line to a taut end. The fish kept running but went in circles like a kite caught in an ill wind. The struggling wekee went ballistic. He worked for his freedom, pulled back, and dove into the sand, causing the greatest hullabaloo.

I rushed in to get my shot at another fish that was swimming in a confused panic and let loose my spear at a good-sized wekee. "Bam," the spear shaft flew forward. In the last 3 feet of trajectory the spear fell 9 inches below the mark. It was too long a shot! I was too slow and too late, and the school of wekee moved to a distance where they watched in horror as Hughsan pulled his leader line in to subdue their clan elder. Using the optic nerve squeeze technique, he took control of the fish, pulled the spear point out of its head, and placed his catch in the bag.

While waiting for Hughsan, I took a moment to pause and looked up at the distant light filtering down through the tons of liquid sea above us. What a rush of emotions I experienced in this deep underwater world. It was like floating in some sort of watery heaven.

We instinctively reloaded and proceeded forward. Hughsan gave me the thumbs up success sign and signaled toward the end of the cliff line. We moved on to the infamous Split. I was on Hughsan's tail, anxious to get my fair share of game. He paused for a moment about 30 feet away from the cracked structure ahead. He signaled for me to go first, giving me the sign for ulua as he pointed to the crack. Yes, an ulua, the best predator of all. I was thrilled.

Quickly, I moved forward into position. My eyes had trouble adjusting to the darkness deep inside the black eerie crack. I paused. No rushing this opportunity like an amateur, I said to myself. Hughsan swam ahead to back me up if any fish exited the other side of the cave-like opening. My pupils were still not open enough to fully grasp the terrain. There was a swooshing motion and a dark shadow three quarters the size of my body moving pensively from one side of the cave to the other, darting in and out of the shadows. "Holy smokes, it's a monster!" I wailed with excitement. I hadn't seen anything this size up close... ever. The ulua's oversized darkened gill plate was nearly the size of my torso. The marauder was as menacing as an alleyway thug with a vendetta for violence. Now, I was about to take him down for dinner.

I double checked my gun's safety... off. Rechecked my air supply... 1,600 pounds. Checked my catch bag... ready. Then I went toward the face of the crack and took a blocking position so as not to let the creature escape. I waited there hoping to see better. The ulua moved again across the back of the crevice.

He didn't stop, but his dark, moody eye focused on me blocking his escape. He was taken aback at the thought that an intruder had the gall to lurk at his door. I saw his eye again as he moved across my field of vision. He wasn't scared–he was mad, livid that anything would dare threaten him in this manner. I floated at his den, anxiously trying to line up the best shot as he paced back and forth.

Something had to give. A good shot wasn't materializing. I was burning air. Each passing moment increased the chances that this ulua would break out and leave me empty-handed. Be calm, wait for the shot, I told myself. In a few short moments, the fish swung around the end of the cave and moved across the back wall. It was now or never! I squeezed the trigger. The spear tipped shaft exploded into the cave and cold spring steel slammed into his bony gill armor no more than 8 feet away from me.

All hell broke loose. The ulua thrashed wildly, wrecking extreme havoc in the cave. The sound of the spear shaft scratching against the rocks raged in my ears. He twisted, turned, and fought to get the spear loose from his body. I wouldn't enter the cave's tight quarters. One flip of his tail or one forceful body movement could injure me with the spear wielded around like a broadsword.

I let loose my wooden gun stock to float above me and out of the way while I choked up on the 400-pound test monofilament leader line. I didn't want to bring this big fish in too fast and have to deal with a charging bull, but I didn't want him tearing up his flesh either. My plan was to keep him firmly on line and let him cool down before pulling him out of the cave.

I also didn't want to go in there to give him a three-prong blow to his head; I'd have to have better visibility before I'd attempt such a risky maneuver. The tension on the line was fierce as he struggled to free himself. I slackened and tightened my line as the action dictated. His pull was strong.

Suddenly the line went dead. He broke free and escaped through some unseen passageway. I was overwhelmed with disappointment that I hadn't taken the fish. Now, he would become a meal for other sea creatures, not the main course for my dinner table.

I was on a high but bummed that I had the chance to score the biggest fish in my spearfishing career and ended up empty-handed. I pulled in my leader line only to discover the real power of this animal, a bent steel shaft in the form of an archer's bow and one missing spear point. I paused to look at my gauges; it was over, time to start my ascent to the surface.

Hughsan and I met at our safety stop. I used hand signals and body gestures to recount the whole story for him while we floated under the waves. He shook his head in approval with the satisfaction that comes to a teacher when a student comes into his own. At every major point in my story, he smiled and signaled, I saw you! Sensei was very pleased; he had brought another waterman into his flock of drift diving spearfishermen.

One of my earliest regular dive buddies, "Killer" (Gary Brent) was also one of the most colorful characters in our cast of notable personalities. We were certainly an unusual pair, me being the lanky, six-feet, two-inch drink of water and he being the mid-sized, beefy, muscle-beach guy. My partner reminded me of an old-time mustached boxer with a tank-top stretched tight over bulging biceps. One thing for sure, we never got our wet suits mixed up.

Although we were comfortable with our differences in personalities, we were both raised Catholic and had a common strong work ethic. In and out of the water, we got along well and genuinely liked each other. Each of us knew how to rely on the other's dive strengths to enhance our hunting strategies. I look back at our "infested grotto" dive as one of the more remarkable times we spent in the water together.

We were diving on a submerged cliff line at the north coast of Molokai, off from the northwest tip of the island. Killer and I angled our descent down to the underwater bluff below. Our anticipation was fierce as we descended through the clear water that enveloped the marine landscape. The visibility was incredible.

My buddy was always in a rush when we dove together. Killer moved to Hawaii from New York after years of vacationing here and scuba diving the reefs of Oahu. He decided on a new life in

Hawaii Kai away from the cold winters and bought a part-interest in the local dive shop where he met our group. Killer started diving with us regularly and fit in well with the boys right away. We partnered up and dove together most every weekend. Life was never dull when diving with Killer.

One look at my buddy revealed the hard-core, testosterone-spilling personality he flaunted. He carried his weight well and took the title of "Bodybuilder of the Year" in his younger days. As a concerned health nut, he was always interested in good nutrition. For lunch on the boat, he brought fruits, nuts, and vegetables and always ridiculed my fish sandwiches made of canned sardines slapped on white bread. I didn't mind, though, as joking was all part of the fun on our dive trips.

Killer was easily heated and as fast to cool in most discussions on the boat. Talking politics with him could get steamy, so it was best to talk about our wives or fishing. Killer had a heart of gold and cherished his family and friends, but there was something different about him.

It seems that sometimes he just couldn't enjoy the scenery of a dive. He was always on alert, waiting for the kill. There were numerous occasions that we'd be floating 60 feet down with reef ledges passing below us. In rapture, I'd float by like a human feather caught in a gentle current, amazed by it all. Not Killer, he'd swim through the water full speed ahead looking for elusive large predators. I'd almost want to yell at him, "Hey, slow down! Take your time!" Maybe I misunderstood him, or perhaps he found the beauty of it all in his own way.

I crowned Gary with his nickname because of an underwater brawl he instigated with a large ulua. His most unusual fish kill at Split Rock in 115 feet of water was a spectacle to watch, and its pivotal story earned him his nickname.

We were finishing a dive on a Sunday afternoon, and both of us were running low on air, so Killer and I started our ascent to the surface. Suddenly, as if he had forgotten something, Killer turned back to the ledge and swam down with his long-gun leading the way. Before I could figure out what he was up to, "Bang," his spear shaft rocketed past the cliff to an area out of my view. Immediately his barbs locked onto a thrasher ulua and Killer's body jerked away with the fish. With a low torque pull, the wounded monster ran for its life, dragging Killer downward.

The spear, leader line, long-gun, and Killer were all taken down by the power of this huge slab of animal. From my point of view, I saw them fading deeper into the blue and then disappearing behind the steep volcanic crag. Reluctantly, I followed to see if my partner needed help, all the while complaining to myself how risky that shot was. It would be a dangerous fight because of the size of the fish, even more risky with so little air remaining. Gary, you'd better have a quick kill, I hoped.

I swam over the ledge. It was unbelievable. The leader line floated about, snapped and drifting in every direction. Killer had thrust his hand and forearm up to his elbow into and through the fish gills trying to keep his hold. His whole body contorted to wrap around the predator, his legs and fins squeezing a scissor hold around its tail. The fish was locked in Killer's body grip. The fish's head and wide mouth extended above Killer's face. His sharp, serrated dive knife flashed repeatedly back and forth as he stabbed the upper torso and head of the fish.

It looked like the fish monster had clasped onto a deranged child and was shaking the life out of it. I really couldn't tell who was shaking whom; the two were welded together in a bout of extreme wrestling. From my vantage point above, it didn't look like my buddy was in the least bit of control. Killer's right hand pounded his titanium knife up and down in powerful strokes as he tried to kill the beast. Thunderous eruptions of green-black blood clouded the blue water with each stroke of his knife. Gary was lost in the kill and in the heat of a struggle. He wasn't aware of my presence although I was in plain view. He focused into a collapsed field of vision no farther than the opponent in his arms. Oblivious to his surroundings, his air gauge, or the clouds of blood that poured from the fish, Gary remained lost in this fearsome death match.

I stopped moving towards him and paused to watch the gruesome battle. Then I remembered I was getting low on air. I slowly rose to conserve my remaining stream of life. My eyes kept locked on Killer as he repeatedly stabbed the life out of the predator. He continued to thrust his knife inward toward the fish and his chest.

Then it flashed before me, what if the fish moved or his knife slipped on the slimy scales? Killer would jab the dagger right into his own chest. Oh my God, he'd kill himself. I watched in dread and hoped he'd stop before the knife would find him. Over and over again he moved his arm out away from himself in a windup before unleashing another powerful stoke toward the fish and his chest. There was nothing I could do to stop this danger but be ready to drag Killer up to the surface if he needed help.

Life slipped out of the fish, and it wasn't long before the slaughter was over. Man and fish rose out of the blood fog and drifted upward, one predator the victor and the other the vanquished. I was drawing fumes for air and knew I had to surface, so I left Killer behind with his victory.

Every now and then when I dove with Killer, it amused me to relive the scene of my dive buddy stabbing the life out of the big animal. What a lasting mental etching of an extreme fish brawl that I carried with me. Killer has been trying to live this incident down for a long time. Thankfully, he has a loyal dive buddy like me to remind him of the event by re-hashing the tale to new divers at social gatherings.

On another occasion Killer and I were diving our favorite spot on Molokai. I wondered what mischief we would get into on the gorgeous underwater lava cliffs of the north coast. We dove these ledges with Hughsan, V, and Gordon as often as we could when there were smooth seas for a safe channel crossing from Oahu. This area of the Molokai shoreline is very rugged and remains mostly uninhabited, except for the old leper colony farther down the cliffs. It's a beautiful coastline with tall, cathedral cliffs that fall into the sea from the mountain ranges above. The underwater topography of our dive site follows the same rocky geology from the coast. An undersea cliff line runs parallel along the coast at a plateau of 90 feet deep and then drops down to a 130 feet at a sand bottom. Scuba diving the face of these cliffs is like diving into the face of heaven. There isn't better diving anywhere in the world than among its recesses, caves, nooks and crannies. The marine life is diverse, abundant and challenging.

This had all the makings of a perfect dive. I floated gently downward, equalizing my ear pressure while looking for the cliffs below. The plunge into the blue was like falling through a portal into weightless space. We drilled down, finning our way to the lava cliff that shot up from the white sand belly of the ocean floor. The scenery was enthralling yet chilling in its untouched power.

We reached the top of the bluff and let the tide take us along the commanding face of the ledge. Killer and I were ready for anything that might come our way, long-guns locked and loaded, three-prong tipped pole spears ready, game bags on weight belts to be filled, holstered knives waiting for action, 38 Magnum detachable power heads securely stowed, and thick gloves for grabbing and holding. As was our usual practice, we were suited up with full-body wet suits for warmth and protection against fire corals and other sharp rocks.

As we moved along the ledge, Killer and I harvested a few lobster hiding in shallow potholes and small cracks in the cliffs. So far we hadn't seen any prized fish to shoot. It wasn't long before Killer was ahead of me and out of sight. Even the telltale trail of bubbles rising from his regulator soon disappeared. I continued on at my own pace, investigating the ledge and experiencing the beauty of my dive.

Soon it became noticeable that this part of the terrain wasn't familiar to me. I no longer recognized any of it. We were getting into an expansive depression along the cliffs that we had yet to discover.

This new environment was fascinating. The vegetation got thicker, fish life became more active, and the variety of species seemed more abundant. I didn't know it at the time, but the whole area resembled a giant stadium or a large volcanic crater half formed into the cliffs. Another miracle of nature, the recess provided a protected, incubator environment where life was teeming.

There ahead in the distance I saw Killer's trail of bubbles rise, but something didn't look right. There were too many bubbles in too irregular a pattern, like giant puffs of smoke. I could only imagine what trouble Killer was getting into, so I picked up the pace and swam forward with more purpose.

There he was, going at lobsters like a madman. The action looked ferocious. Killer floated against the wall 20 feet above the sand, wedged in the large recess of a cave the size of a small two-story house. With his arms and legs drawn and quartered outward, he clung to the rocks like a marine spider working its prey. He was buried in the thick of a strange battle.

Large Molokai spiny lobsters of every shape and size blanketed the entire face of the cave. Hundreds and hundreds of spinies were in some sort of revival or congregation. At first, I mistook them for a thick carpet of seaweed swelling with the currents that swirled gently in and out of the stadium structure. The lobster antennae, thick to the eye, crowded forward and moved like soft corals. I realized I was looking at lobsters, piled on lobsters, piled on lobsters! I don't know if it was a migration site, a mating area, or some other extraordinary event, but it was grand.

Killer was lost, mesmerized in a zone of his own. He fought the hordes of spinies that swarmed about him. His bag weighed heavy on his belt, filled with lobsters. A number of captured creatures were trying to escape through the small torn holes in the mesh sack. Antennae, legs and claws stuck out from the bag everywhere.

Legs upon legs attached to Killer's body and equipment through the catch bag. With his right hand, he struggled to pry a large granddaddy lobster from the rock while several other spinies hung on to their kin. These spinies were at least three- to four-pounders. While Killer worked with his right hand, his left hand attached to a crack in the rock face for support. His hand was overrun with lobsters crawling up his forearm picking at him in protest.

I rushed to join in on the ruckus and worked my own area next to Killer. The first huge spiny in front of me became my target as I grabbed him tight. The overgrown critter hung on for dear life. With a firm grasp I worked on prying the creature from the rock, but he wouldn't release! This spiny was welded to the rock as sure as hardened steel. As I pried and pried, it became a tug of war between us, me for the prized meal and he for his life. After near exhaustion and hyperventilation, I finally pulled him off the cliff and forced him into my bag. Then I started on the next spiny, but this one became an even greater challenge to pry free.

Killer's bag started to slow him down as it was close to capacity. Each time he tried to stuff another spiny in, all would attempt to escape. I decided to abandon my working area knowing that

Killer and I would get more game working together rather than working alone. Our air supply was dwindling, but there were still hundreds of lobsters to gather. Our adrenaline was running off the charts. I grabbed Killer's bag and signaled that I would work as bag man. All Killer had to do was pry and pass; I would take care of the spinies from there. It worked well. Killer's bag was quickly topped off, and we started to fill my bag.

He had been working at this breakneck speed longer than me, so Killer was nearing the end of a safe level of remaining air. Lobsters were still crawling everywhere. On this next lobster pry, Killer showed signs of obvious fatigue. When he pulled this spiny off the rocks, the bug inadvertently sprang forth onto his stomach. Before he knew what was happening, the spiny locked its legs onto his weight belt. He kept a firm grasp on the spiny and worked at getting it free from its accidental attachment. Finally, the lobster broke loose, but the clasp of Killer's weight belt opened, and both lobster and weight belt fell immediately from around his body down into the sand pits 20 feet below.

I saw Killer wrestling with the lobster, but I hadn't seen the spiny and belt sink to the bottom. It was only a second before Gary started to float away with a buoyant low pressure aluminum tank. Puzzled, I did not connect the circumstances or the fact that Gary was leaving me. With verbal grunting and wild hand signals, he rose up at an increasing speed. He held on to the overloaded bag of spinies, trying to use it as an anchor weight, but it didn't help. He kept swimming downward to slow his ascent, but the nature of diving physics kept him on a steady upward path.

Floating there alone and bewildered by his unusual behavior, I waved him goodbye. I couldn't figure why he departed so quickly. Killer fired off a number of additional hand signals before he vanished.

As best as I could tell, I think he said, "Lost my weight belt." He grabbed his waist repeatedly. "I'm taking one bag." He showed me his bag and moved it up and down. "Stay here and finish up." Killer pointed to me and the cliff alternately. Then the signals got somewhat erratic as he shook his fist, shrugged his shoulders and rolled his eyes. I guess he might have said, "Shit! Nothing I can do now. Damned lobster took my belt. Get as many as you can! See you up top." I did a courtesy "look-see" for his weight belt but then went straight back to the unruly lobsters.

I picked up two additional spinies of my own then headed up to check on Killer. He was safely onboard ranting to the team about the mother lode of all lobsters. What a score. From there on, whenever we made the trip to Molokai we'd try to find Lobster Grotto.

Its exact location always remained elusive to us. We hit the spot several times again and scored, but more often than not, we would miss the grotto completely. Then on the occasions when we landed on it, the lobsters never flourished like they did before. Oh, there were usually a few big spinies here and there, and the dives were wonderful, but never again would there be hordes of lobsters as far as our eyes could see.

For most of us divers, it wasn't always about stellar diving. There were scores of hours devoted to equipment maintenance and boat driving for the team. Sometimes diving wasn't all about fun and games, either. There were always calculated risks.

The water at Makapuu Point glimmered in the hot afternoon sun with barely any turmoil to support its well-deserved reputation of treacherous seas. The Point and Lighthouse marked the eastern tip of Oahu where northeastern and southeastern currents collided, only to be met by the volatile deep ocean tides of the Kaiwi Channel between Molokai and Oahu.

Gordon and I finished a Sandy Beach Cliffs dive and drove the boat for Gman (Mark Gerasimenko) and Grant (Grant Stoddard.) They selected one of their favorites, Ulua Cave, for their hunt. This site always produced a steady supply of large ulua for the divers. It was on the deep side of my diving tastes, but only in a moderate depth range for the deep divers of the group. After all, if you dive the Penguin Banks at 185 to 225 feet for monster ulua, 135 to 155 feet is nothing at all.

Gman was not a native of Hawaii but came to us by way of Northern California. He moved to Oahu in the early 1980's and adapted to the local culture as if it was his own. A strapping six footer with a football lineman's muscles, he was currently the youngest of the group. Unlike the rest of us, he ran the dive tanks around like they were feather weight jigs, not the weighty bottles they were. It was often commented that we needed more divers like the Gman, with strong backs and good personalities.

Like the Craw, Gman had an inventive spirit. He used these technical and mechanical inclinations to make our diving easier and safer wherever he could. Gman created a low-tech, foolproof method of gauging the currents before a dive. It was a most practical and useful invention.

He deployed his new current meter to test for current direction and speed. The indicator was built with a six-foot-tall, inch-and-a-half PVC pole floating on a sturdy orange bullet float. A small but very visible pennant flag attached to the top of the pole. Under the float, a 12-foot length of galvanized chain was used to hold the flag upright and to catch the drift of the currents. We dropped it off at the dive spot when we arrived, took marks, and came back to it after the divers finished suiting up. Then we'd adjust our drop off positions to account for the current speed and direction gleaned from the float's movement off the spot.

The float would always move with the current because it dragged the length of chain in its direction and at its speed. The surface wind direction never affected the reliability of the "current meter." Finally, with this device, we always knew the direction of the current and the speed of its movement.

Gman and Grant were almost ready for the drop. We shouted directions back and forth to fine tune the boat's position for the exact location that would put them up current of the underwater site. Ulua Cave was simply beautiful with two jagged mountains that formed the left and right plateaus of a lovely sand valley between them. The sheer rock bluffs, from the plateau top to the sand bottom, fashioned a cliff wall of well over 20 feet in height for excellent hunting.

The real jewel of this spot was the four-foot undercut at the end of the ledges that went back into the bluff like a flat cave. In some places it scooted back nearly 20 feet into the cliff. The unique fish den served as a sanctuary for large schools of ulua that hung out to escape the strong currents. It was a shooter's paradise.

To maximize their fish kill, both divers tried to hit the spot from the cliff top, not from the sides or valley. This hunt was all about stealth and surprise. If the divers came from the sides or valley, the fish would hear and see them coming from a long distance. The school of fish would bolt from their lounge like an overworked congregation from a Sunday morning church service hungry for brunch. The best plan for the shooters was to drill straight down from the surface, hunt the top of the plateau first, and then drop down the cliff face at both ends of the cave to surprise the fish in their den. If the divers worked together and came at it from opposite sides of the cave, the fish would be boxed in. What a fish kill it would be.

Gman was torn between shooting movies and shooting fish. A man of tremendous talent, he worked for various movie producers as cameraman and eventually would work his way up the ranks to artistic director. He was overcome by the need to capture the underwater action on video for the boys to enjoy. Although a great shot in his own right, he spent most his time trailing the shooters and documenting the beauty of the undersea hunt.

Gman was easy to get along with on the boat and quite a hard worker. Some boat mates would fade when the work piled up, but not the Gman. He was consistently on the spot and cheerful to pitch in to get things done. It was always a fun time diving with Gman. Fortunately for him, his flexible schedule allowed for as much diving as he desired when he wasn't on a shoot.

Grant, an airline pilot, was also blessed with a flexible schedule and was available for diving during the week as well as weekends. He was in and out of town but dove whenever it didn't interfere with his flying. Here was another man of extraordinary diving ability and very capable boating skills. A big tall German with an eye for spotting good fish in the distance, he shot plenty of game.

Most of our divers loved the Ulua Cave spot. It gave them access to the nesting place for schools of deep water ulua and the unbridled beauty of an imposing, mountainous underwater seascape. Divers were always excited to see the bluffs rise from the sand knowing that it sheltered hoards of ulua awaiting the carnage of their spears. Grant and Gman loved to work this spot and knew they would probably score if the opportunity presented itself.

After our divers finally went off the side and down for their hunt, Gordon and I set about stowing our gear and tidying up the boat. I turned the motor off for some peace and quiet, so we drifted with the wind down to the southwest toward Hanauma Bay. We had close to an hour to kill since the divers took 20 minutes of safety decompression as part of their excuse to hunt for surface ono (wahoo) on the drift. During slack times like these, my buddy Gordon always amused me with his verbal skills. We'd chat about the news of the day. It gave him an opportunity to flash a few elongated words from his extensive vocabulary. I'd play along with him and act like those fancy words were my best friends, even if I hadn't a clue about their meaning. He must have known I usually bluffed on my knowledge, as he constantly defined his chosen words with the most complete definitions that one could imagine, just because he could.

There was no doubt that he was well-traveled and very well-read, but I didn't hold that against him. I treated him like any of my other dive buddies. Oh, I did tease him often about his love life during his brief periods of being single, but that never brought us to blows or anything close to it. Gordon was my senior, so I always gave him the run of the conversation.

It was time for our divers to surface, so we motored back to our drop off spot to start our search. Gordon kept a keen eye out for the boys just in case they drifted south of the spot, while I kept an eye toward the north. We usually headed back to the original spot where the divers entered the water to start our pick up since there was no absolute certainty of where the divers would drift. Gordon and I paused at the drop off site and scanned the ocean 360 degrees on the compass.

"Gordon, anything?"

"Nothing!" he replied.

Several minutes went by as we moved about the boat for different views of the ocean. There were no heads floating in the water, no flags on pole spears, no signs of our divers. They didn't carry a marine radio; it was down with a dead battery. After some time I went back to the helm and drove the boat north into the direction of the known current while Gordon scanned the horizon standing on the gunnels holding onto the roof of the cabin. It seemed obvious to me that they had drifted out past Makapuu Point.

I figured where they might surface relative to their time in the water given the strength of the current and turned the motors off hoping to hear an emergency whistle or see a red flag waving in the water. Gordon and I continued to search the horizon for our divers. Zilch. I moved the boat farther out to sea and searched in an arc toward the Point. We took on a mood of silence and concern.

A half hour passed from the time Gman and Grant should have surfaced, and still nothing. Nothing appeared to indicate that they were in the area. Another half an hour passed as we drove in larger and larger circles, moving farther out to sea. It started to concern me that as time passed, the divers would drift away from the shoreline and out into the Kaiwi Channel, only to be taken by an even larger ocean current. That would surely not bode well for our guys. As my worries mounted I decided not to share them with Gordon, lest it encourage the both of us to worry.

It was over an hour now, and the divers weren't in sight. The thought that Gordon and I were responsible for finding our divers weighed heavily on my mind. How would their wives feel about us losing their husbands? I shuttered at the very idea. Here we were scouring the ocean with nothing in sight. Where were they? As time passed, Gordon moved more erratically from port to starboard looking, searching, and hoping. I became more agitated as I went back and forth from the helm to the back deck praying for a sudden sighting. I thought about their wives again and again.

Daylight was burning–it was now late afternoon. We had to find them before nightfall; otherwise our search would be near useless in the dark. I contemplated calling the Coast Guard for help but decided to put it out of my mind. I kept reassuring myself: the boys will show any minute now. They'll be pissed off it took us so long to find them, but they'll be happy to see us!

I drove the boat faster and made wider circles in a search pattern farther off the Makapuu Lighthouse. They can't be sucked out into the Molokai Channel and swept out to sea, I prayed. Gordon and I weren't helping each other as both of us became more nervous and agitated. There was an awkward silence, a building emotional tension, and grave frustration, but neither

Gordon nor I would admit it. We were getting nowhere, as miles and miles of empty ocean stared back at us with nothing on its surface as far as we could see. Finally my indecisiveness came to an end and my emergency lifeguard instincts kicked in. I need to alert the Coast Guard. They need to get an early start finding these guys.

"Gordon, what do you think, should we call the Coast Guard? It's been over an hour and a half, and it'll be dark in a few hours." I looked for his approval.

"Yes, good idea!"

"Okay, one last run at it and I'll make the call." We did a final circle on the outer edge of our search pattern and then went back to our diver drop off point. Nothing, a complete void!

Picking up the handset of the VHF radio, I called out, "Dive vessel calling Coast Guard, come in Coast Guard." There was a pause.

"Coast Guard Honolulu Group, come in, dive vessel."

"This is dive vessel, *It's Time*, requesting assistance. We have two scuba divers in the water. They are overdue one and a half hours offshore near the Makapuu Lighthouse. Do you read?"

"This is Coast Guard Honolulu Group, read you loud and clear. Please switch to channel 22."

"Switching to channel 22, over." I hurriedly dialed in to 22 and hailed the Guard again. "Coast Guard, we have two experienced divers in the water. They are probably floating out of sight some distance from our boat. Would you put out a notice to boaters in the area to be on the lookout for our divers in the Makapuu and Sandy Beach area?"

"*It's Time*, will broadcast public notice immediately." Then the guard operator went through a list of questions similar to the interrogation one gets before admittance to an emergency room.

We kept searching while I answered the Coast Guard's questions. While we were tied up on channel 22, the Guard put out the bulletin on channel 16, the emergency hailing and distress channel. As soon as we were done on channel 22, we switched back to 16 to monitor what was going on but kept automatic scanning on channels 16 and 22.

It wasn't but ten minutes later we heard a strange transmission. It came from a local boat operator with a thick Pidgin

English accent. "Cos Gard, dis da Parasail boat frm Hawaii Kai." There was a long pause as he seemed to collect his thoughts. "We see one red wetha balloon, or som flying red stuff above da wata one mile pas Hanauma Bay."

"That's it, Gman's red nylon signal kite." I yelled in relief. My spirits instantly went from worried despair to the heights of jubilation. That had to be them. Gordon and I looked into the sun toward the Bay some six miles away but could see nothing. I knew we were still too far away to see his kite.

I jammed the boat in gear and blasted toward a general position offshore of the Bay. We radioed the Coast Guard. "Coast Guard, that's our divers with the red signal kite. We're on our way to pick them up. Thank you, and thank the parasail captain for his help."

We rushed down to Hanauma at top speed. The kite became visible flying some 30 feet above the water. I honed in on it, dead reckoning to our boys. In no time we were on them and slowed upwind for a pick up. Both Gman and Grant looked up to acknowledge us but stared down in the water, breathing through their snorkels. Something's wrong, I feared. They should be bitching at us for not finding them. Both Gordon and I knew looking down toward the bottom during a pick up is not normal. Our moods changed to one of concern.

Gman moved positions in the water with some twists and turns, never taking his eyes from the water below. He repositioned again and spit the water out of his snorkel, "Visitor!" Grant hovered over Gman with guns cocked and lowered. He took up the task of guardian angel. Gman's only weapon was a movie camera, and no matter what kind of visitor was threatening him, his camera was no real weapon. No other words were spoken.

Gordon and I knew immediately it was a shark. I quickly maneuvered the boat closer to the boys and turned the motor off. The wind blew us to them in less than ten seconds. Both Gordon and I went to the swim step to help. Gman was first to take his eyes off the water and passed us his camera. Grant kept guard, intent on following whatever was below. Gman passed up his dive gear and soon jumped in the boat. Grant was next; it was all very quick, and both were safely aboard.

Gordon and I prepared for a tongue lashing and a ration of

grief. None came. We shared all of what happened on the surface with our divers. They told us of the unusual cross currents that were split at depth levels and how the currents changed during their dive. I went back to the helm relieved and thankful for having found our divers. We motored home to Hawaii Kai as Grant and Gman went about stowing their gear and talking about their dive. I overheard Gman smirk to Grant, "Lost at sea by two Mr. Magoos."

Most of the time our dives went off without a hitch. While there were the occasional mishaps that caused concern, our safety procedures and years of experience helped us to avoid most of the dangers of deep diving. However, there were times when we became a danger to ourselves.

Smitty (Kona Smith) was one of Hughsan's original buddies who dove with the drift divers for many years. I was new to the troop when Smitty was at the top of his diving-spearfishing game. A successful business owner and retail medical device salesman, he made the time to dive when he could, usually at least once a week and sometimes more when family and business conditions allowed.

A medium-framed man with a ready smile and fine humor, Smitty was loved by everyone. He was a man of immense spearfishing talent, but he was a happy-go-lucky type who never took himself, or diving, too seriously. There were a few divers in our group who took their shooting too seriously for their own good, but it wasn't that way with Smitty. He was there to have a good time and hang with the boys while catching his fair share of fish. Some of the guys were so obsessed with scoring that their moods dampened if they didn't do well. Not Smitty... he was always up socializing with everyone, making the day pleasurable for all.

When Smitty's wavy dark hair blew in the wind, it showed slight signs of graying and the beginnings of a receding hairline. That didn't seem to bother him in the least. His physical appearance only showed him to be maturing, but his dive gear dated him many years older than his age. Each of the divers had his preferences of gear, but Smitty's choice was old and well-worn.

It started with his wet suit. It was new at one time, maybe ten years ago. The long pant bottom and over-locking vest jacket combination showed all the signs of fatigue and disrepair. The once dark blue outer color faded to a light grey with unusual stretch marks, tears, nicks, scrapes, abrasions, and areas of worn rubber throughout. Major areas of wear and various small holes showed at the knees, elbows, and butt. Sometimes when he bent over on the boat, the shredded rubber on his fanny became an embarrassment. For some odd reason, he refused to part with this old suit, his loyal best dive buddy.

Smitty dove with old steel 72 tanks and used the ancient style backpack of a hard nylon tank base and a confluence of nylon straps. His regulator was worn chrome, revealing the brass sub-structure that told its own tale of use. I shuddered to think of the condition of his hoses and gauges whenever I washed the gear and took a closer look at his stuff. He was a devoted horse-collar buoyancy compensator guy and would not hear of the emerging styles of modern vests.

His most modern piece of equipment was his self-named, "Bend-O-Matic." Actually, it was one of the first dive computers sold by Scubapro back in the 1970's. God only knows if it functioned or how it worked, considering the first real consumer computers came out in the early 1980's. Nevertheless, Smitty strapped it onto his arm and followed the gauge to many a safe dive. To the uninformed, his gear may have looked a tale of woe, but to see him dive with it was awesome. He was a leading shooter and an even better lobster harvester.

On this particular warm December day, Smitty and I were dive partners. I always felt honored to be diving with him. We used an underwater scooter to cover more ground to scout the reefs for lobsters. The holidays were upon us and there was no better Christmas dinner than juicy lobster dipped in lemon butter sauce.

It was a somewhat difficult task for two guys to dive together with spear guns and one scooter. Each diver would hold on to a handle with one hand and grasp his spears with the other. One man controlled the throttle while both tried to adjust their positions on the scooter to travel in a straight line. To turn, body positions were altered "just so" to bank into a turn. With a scooter, we could cover six times more underwater ground and gather more spinies. What a blessing for us to be able to employ these devices to gather food from the ocean.

Whenever anyone would spot game on the scooter, he would jerk on the handle to get the other partner's attention. Then both divers would adjust their positions to go to the new target. Once there, the driver would tie the scooter to a coral head and both divers would go about the business of hunting. When done, they'd meet at the scooter and move on to the next reef.

On this particular dive, Smitty and I splashed into the water on the inside of Rabbit Island off the northeast coast of Oahu. The terrain varied between 40 to 70 feet deep with lots of exciting low-lying rubble and minor coral formations, the perfect lobster grounds. Somewhere in the middle of our dive we came upon a large coral cluster the size of a car. Smitty spotted several pairs of antennae sticking out of the reef holes and immediately jerked the scooter to move in its direction. I looked to my left and saw the coral head and arched my body in its direction.

When we got there, Smitty rushed over to the lobsters while I tied the scooter down. When I swam over to join him, he was already engaged in a fight. Smitty stuck his hand into a small reef hole and grabbed onto a big-husked hard-shell lobster. With his hand extended around the lobster's body, the total size of both his hand and spiny was larger than the hole. He struggled to squeeze his expanded fist out, but it wasn't working. The hole was too small. The pace of Smitty's hand movements picked up as he kept trying to force his hand out with the spiny. I peeked under a small opening at the sand bottom and saw the huge prize. He and I both knew this was a trophy that would make a great holiday meal.

Every time Smitty tried to pull his hand out, it would jam against the narrow sides of the hole. There was no solution but to let him go and move on to another lobster. But my buddy Smitty wouldn't swim away from this one, so he was stuck in an awful, "damned if I let him go and damned if I don't" dilemma. Without some intervention he could be stuck there all day burning air without ever bagging the spiny.

There was always a slim chance that somehow he could get

the lobster out in an alternative fashion, maybe chipping the hole a little larger with his knife, looking for another bigger hole close by and passing the lobster to his other hand for removal, or some other miraculous solution that he hadn't considered just yet. It would be pitiful to release an epicurean meal of this size.

I hoped that Smitty would get on with it and bag the lobster or release him so we could work the coral head for more lobsters. We had not fully explored this site yet, so who knew what was hiding deep in the cracks along the other side of the coral. Letting this one go would also allow us to move on to another spot if this one proved empty or if the lobsters took positions so deep in the nest that we'd never be able to catch them. But it was easy for me to think like this—it wasn't my spiny.

Smitty was frustrated and couldn't make a decision other than to hold on and continue trying to get the spiny out. By this time, I was at the other side of the coral head looking for lobsters that might have scooted away from the ruckus.

I lay flat on the sand along the edge of the mound. There were small gaps where the coral head hadn't grown into the sand; I peeked inside one of them. It revealed most of the inside of the reef formation to be hollow. There were a few smaller spinies on the inside roof safely tucked away and hiding. But there it was, plain as day, Smitty's gloved wet suit hand moving in and out in the open space only to be stopped at the hole. No wonder he was having so much trouble—this spiny was giant! It was hopeless for Smitty. I lay in the sand at the bottom observing, working my brain for a solution to his problem.

I rose up to see how Smitty was doing. No more than 9 feet away, he gestured to me for help. His hand motions were erratic and sweeping. I couldn't make them out as they flew through the water wildly. I floated there trying to read his eyes, as his body language was unreadable. He wanted help. He seemed to be determined about that. He must have a plan, but what was it? I looked at him and opened my arms, shrugged my shoulders, and cocked my head in response. "What do you want me to do?" I asked.

He continued with fresh signals as he tried to respond to my inquiry. I hastily considered a list of potential options: does he want me to swim under the rocks? Tunnel in through the sand?

Demolish the reef to make a larger hole? No, I don't think so. I was confused. He saw it in my eyes.

Then he gave me a slow, desperate gesture with the back of his hand, "Shoot the spear! Shoot the spear!"

What? What a horrifying thought. Impossible! You're out of your mind. I signaled him with my index finger pointing to my head making circles in the water. In a state of disbelief I asked myself, He wants me to use my three-prong spear to shoot the lobster out of his hand? I paused. You're freaking nuts! It's against the regulations to spear a lobster. Spiny lobsters are only hunted by hand; no spearing allowed. We never speared lobsters.

Besides, what if I miss the lobster and spear your fingers? Are you crazy? No way! If I missed at this depth, your hand would be fragments. I looked at him straight in the eyes and shook my head, No! No way!

He kept motioning to me to shoot, each time with more desperation in his eyes. Something was wrong. Again, I kept shaking my head to say no. There we were, arguing and burning air. Hell, no! I kept telling myself. I'm not going to be responsible for a shot like that. No, I'm not spearing your fingers. It's only a lobster. We'll find another. I'm not going to be the object of your wife's anger when you come home short a few fingers. No, I won't do it.

Smitty kept insisting. His demanding grunts through his regulator got louder. He ordered me to shoot the lobster out of his hand. I deliberated. Impossible! How could he expect me to pull off a miracle shot? How could he think that I'm that good to put these three-prongs between his fingers and into the spiny? No way! It's too hazardous!

I went back down to check on the situation again. I peered through the small, tunnel-like opening. Wait a minute. The squirming lobster was firmly stuck on Smitty's cotton glove, snagged by its sharp, barbed carapace. Smitty was trying to dislodge the creature, but his tight-fitting glove was firmly welded to his hand. It was a critical situation. Smitty had to dump his glove and the lobster; otherwise he'd be stuck there until he ran out of air. He contorted his hand every which way, but the glove and the lobster would not budge. I came up from the sand again and looked at him from across the coral head. I began to understand the gravity of the situation.

Smitty looked at me sternly and gave me the repeated signal, "Shoot! Shoot the damned lobster!"

After burning all this air, I was angry that he would put me in such a maddening position. Something must have snapped within me, and out of desperation I yielded into my regulator, "Okay, I'll shoot!"

I knew this shot couldn't be made with me lying on the sand. The back of my cocked three-prong spear might hit my body or loose gear and not travel true. There was only a tiny passageway to shoot through, but if I turned myself sideways and near upside down with my head in the sand, I could use my arms and shoulders to keep myself stable as I flapped my fins gently to keep my position. The cocked spear lay horizontal 6 inches off the sand to angle upward to the lobster. The spear was close to my head as I used my eye to sight a trajectory to Smitty's hand. I took my position. I was getting comfortable with the shot and began to think that it might even be doable.

I calculated trajectories, angles, and the very short distance my spear would travel. I tried to adjust my thinking to shooting sideways, upside down, and a spear angle that wasn't quite normal. It would be a difficult shot. I calculated and recalculated. As I studied the situation, I began to believe that just maybe I could shoot the lobster out of his hand. It might be a stretch of my imagination, but his hand was only 6 to 7 feet away, and there was some room there between his fingers to fit the spear points. Time was not on my side.

My confidence grew. I checked the position of the sleek, stainless steel prongs and twisted the spear to line them up to slide through Smitty's fingers and into the spiny. This was a big lobster, and Smitty's fingers were spread wide. I thought about it with a more accepting attitude of my task.

I took one final pause to peek above the coral and check with Smitty again. He didn't wait for me to ask, shaking his head, "Yes!" and signaling, "Shoot! Shoot!"

I put my head back into the sand and repositioned myself, looking intently up into the hollow of the reef head. I used my body to stabilize myself between the sand and the coral and consciously took inventory of where my body was, lest it float off balance. With the rubber band pulled tightly, I asked a higher power to guide my spear and do no damage. The millisecond before I let my spear fly I mentally put my energies into being one with the spear. "Whoosh!" Away it went.

The snapping sound of the spear point hitting the spiny was deafening. A thunderous, blood-curdling scream came from Smitty up atop the coral. Instantly Smitty's fingers retracted backward into his hand as it exited the coral head. There, dangling at the end of my spear was the large granddaddy lobster. The sound of Smitty's regulator was overpowered by his long, continued, high-pitch muffled scream of disbelief. It soon died down, and then foul obscenities muted by the mountains of air bubbles came pouring out.

I removed the spear from the coral head with the spiny lobster proudly displayed at the end of my lance. Smitty was free from the coral without so much as a scratch. He floated there physically shook-up and examined his fingers and forearm. I waved the lobster upward in triumph. But Smitty was not happy. He yelled riotously and waved his hands madly in an outpouring of disbelief. He swam to the scooter; it was all I could do to keep up with him.

Smitty untied the scooter and we headed topside together. He broke the surface and immediately started in on me. "Are you f'ing crazy? How could you shoot at my hand?"

"You asked me to. I told you no! You kept signaling me to shoot, shoot!" I yelled.

Smitty yelled back, "No, I asked you to grab him, grab him from underneath." He gestured with his hands in an open fist-grabbing motion.

"No, you insisted I shoot, you wouldn't let go of the lobster," I said firmly.

"You were supposed to get into the coral head and grab it." He motioned again and again with an open fist grabbing signal.

"No, you gave me the signal to shoot. I saw your hand from the backside, not the front. From my eyes, it looked like, 'Let the three-prong fly.'" I yelled back.

"No, this is a 'grab it' signal."

"Okay, that's a 'grab it' signal, but when you give it with the back of your hand, that's a 'let the three-prong fly' signal."

Again he came back at me, "No, no way..." We were both right and wrong.

We floated in the middle of the ocean discussing hand signals while we waited for the boat to pick us up. Was it a miracle or just dumb luck that guided my spear? With a clear mind I must say it was mostly dumb luck that guided the spear to a safe landing of a spiny and an unscathed hand.

I later came to realize that one can always learn something new from a dive buddy, even if they have been diving together for some time. A supposed signal may not be the real signal at all. So, the next time a buddy gives me a signal to shoot his hand, I'll give him the spear so he can do it himself.

CHAPTER FOUR

DIVING WITH THE BOYS

Gman was on a winning streak of capturing unusual underwater footage. The boys welcomed his ongoing metamorphosis. Before Gman's filming obsession, we captured our underwater action only in our minds. Each fish kill became a part of our collage of memories. The visual images of the fish fighting at the end of our spear, the thrashing struggle of life and death, the feel of being pulled through the water, and the emotional high of capture were all welded into personal mental movies. All were locked in our personal memory vaults for instant replay, but how do you share the miles of images locked in your head? How do you enjoy these wonderful experiences with your family and friends? It just can't be done, unless you have someone like the Gman.

When Gman dove with his video camera, he'd suit up like he always did as a full-fledged shooting partner but without guns. Then in the water with his camera he'd become a ghost, trailing behind the divers to capture all the best angles for the perfect recording. He was a hardened spearfisherman, so his videos were set to the best views since he could predict the probable fish action of each incident.

His good friend "Dev" (Captain Dev Merrifield) was Gman's primary dive buddy. Anytime Dev called with an offer of an after-work dive, Gman was always thrilled to go. Dev kept to a regular schedule as a working diver who ran a dive tour business off the south shore of Oahu, but he loved to shoot fish after work. Needless to say, Dev was a crack diver of serious proportions. Young, aggressive, and extremely skilled, he often hung out with

Hughsan's group when he wasn't serving his visitor clients.

Dev got his start in the dive business with a dive boat he ran out of the Hawaii Kai boat launch. He bought a blank 26' Banana Patch hull and meticulously finished it off to commercial-grade status in his garage. Dev chose a diesel Volvo Penta aft drive to power the craft and put it into service soon after its launch. Word around the dive shops was that with his patience and persistence, Dev could teach even the most fearful of students to dive.

Dive masters are far different today than the teachers I started with back in my day. Back then, the teachers were older, macho, navy frogmen that put it to us straight, "You'll learn to dive my way, or you won't be diving!" There were no interactive student-teacher relationships; our teachers were the ocean masters, and we students the lowly dirt people, wannabe deep divers. After thirty hours of class instruction and grueling sessions of pool work, we had to pass the final open-water boat dive, and only then, we became certified.

All students who passed certification were encouraged to join a club. Dive hobbies were started with beach entries, lava ledge jump entries, and every now and then, an open-water club dive from a boat. Part of the dive master's job was to tear us down, so he could toughen us up into safe diving habits. But that was then, and now diving is a more recreational sport, easily practiced by most anyone.

Dev dove for the pleasure of spearfishing and the friendship with the divers. He and Gman partnered regularly, so it was natural for the Gman to catch a good deal of Dev's antics on film. Thankfully for the rest of us weekend warriors, Gman's videos gave us a good source of homemade video entertainment of our underwater triumphs and failures.

The fearsome twosome went diving late one afternoon after Dev's dive tours were completed. It was another beautiful Hawaiian summer day. Dev and Gman floated 25' under the ocean's surface, while Dev consciously scanned the waterline for game after an unproductive deep dive. Drifting with the currents in the blue waters off Koko Head was a relaxing way to stalk unusual fish that they didn't get to see diving the reefs below. These surface drifts consumed very little air, extended the dive time, cleaned the nitrogen out of the body, and made larger sport fish accessible to our spearfishermen. Mahi, wahoo, and large uku that came up from the bottom offered the best thrill.

There was a trick to the operation, a technique that made this type of fishing much more productive: baiting the water. A five-pound block of frozen squid would be cut up into fine chunks and placed in a tiny mesh bag to be worn like a purse hanging from the diver's weight belt. Some divers find this an objection-able practice as it makes them part of the chum line, the main course for sharks, but that didn't seem to bother anyone in our group.

Gman drifted lower in the water about 40 feet away from Dev, using his hi-tech camera to video record his buddy. The visibil-ity was endless far out in the ocean and away from the noxious runoff of civilization. The duo drifted for some time, leaving a long trail of diced squid-like breadcrumbs dropped in the woods. Then, 2 to 3 feet below the surface, a beautiful bull mahi worked the chum line in perfect harmony with the ocean's upper sur-face. The fish drifted up and down with the swells and nibbled here and there, finding every bit of squid that floated on the chum trail.

Dev spotted it and immediately went into an alert mode for shooting. He checked his gun, brought it closer to his body, streamlined his posture, and relaxed with as little movement as possible. Gman took sudden notice of Dev through his lens and spun ahead to Dev's area of focus. There it was. Gman realized that this could be a fabulous video as he steadied his camera and adjusted the zoom. The camera recorded the action as the mahi took no notice of either diver. He was too busy enjoying the feast.

The mahi continued to get closer. Another 15 feet, and it would be in range for a long shot. With some luck, the fish might continue on into range for a sure shot. It kept swimming for-ward, moving ahead to see Dev in its path. The fish slowed, then hesitated, tempted by the idea that there was more food ahead. Dev noted the fish's new stance, pulled out a handful of chum, and released it quickly to lure the mahi forward. The area soon wallowed in chum. Caution kicked in, and the mahi scooted away, surfing the underside of the waves. Damn it! Dev thought, shaking his fist to release his built-up tension.

A few moments later, while chum still floated freely, out of nowhere, an attack suddenly materialized. It was not predator fish from the sea, but hungry fowl from the sky. Gulls rained in from above like fat arrows falling from the heavens crashing into the water. With a swift splash they plummeted 4 feet down and their wings exploded open to swim for squid. They swam like they were flying, going deeper and deeper, scavenging for edible squid. Gman and Dev were without words. It was such an unusual sight. Dev's hunting ceased, as there would be no fish feeding on chum through this feathery bombardment.

Gman kept the camera rolling. Soon the birds got comfortable with his presence. The birds were taking the liberty to swim longer and deeper distances. They looked like fish, Gman noted. Doing odd twists and turns, the diving birds checked on each piece of potential food. If it was squid, it'd be gone with an inhaling suck from their beaks. They swam in the oddest fashion, flapping their grey wings for propulsion, using their elongated head and necks for searching and grabbing while they streamlined their white bellies for speed... going here, stopping there, and going back there again. It was their crazy darting movements that caused such a visual shock to the divers. They had the comfort and flexibility of tiny seals, but they were birds–birds flying through the water.

Faster than the divers could imagine, the bait was consumed and the feeding frenzy ran its course. In less than three minutes the locust swarm of birds scrubbed the water clean of all bait. It was time for Dev and Gman to surface. There was a lot to talk about on the boat. But for all the fun and excitement, they had not achieved their goal of landing a good fish for the grill. They would have to come back tomorrow for another attempt at fresh fish after Dev finished work.

As one might imagine, there were always rivalries between the top shooters. The deep divers even had a separate score card based on total fish weight tracked on a calendar-year period. The boys had lots of fun with bragging rights. Each got a chance to boast as his results changed with the moving tides. Almost all the divers had a chance to brag at one point or another, but Crawman remained a most formidable competitor in the "tonnage" match.

They did not know yet that Dev had stumbled upon a new approach that would give him an advantage.

The primary problem with spearfishing is that a shooter can only handle one or two monster fish on a dive. By the time a diver found a fish, lined it up, took the shot, wrestled it for control, strung the fish on the stringer, and then reloaded, the other fish would have come and gone, leaving their friend behind to his own funeral.

Dev and Gman were still desperate for fish. They were at the dock preparing the boat for their departure when an idea occurred to them. Since Gman would be toting the camera and wasn't using his gun, why not have Dev take Gman's gun, dive with two loaded guns, and see how doubling the fire power might work out. This hadn't been tried before, so it presented some interesting logistics, but if the new method proved successful, Dev might increase his catch and really show up the other diving ninjas in the group.

With their new attack strategy settled, Dev and the Gman motored off to the Sandy Beach Arch for spearing. The Arch is quite unique, featuring two enormous, long, coral-encrusted lava bluffs that parallel each other out to sea. Resting in 150 feet of water, they rise up 35 feet from the sea floor separated from each other by a 20 yard plot of sand. In the middle of the westerly finger, a giant regal archway lay carved into the massive ridge. A massive structural overhang that blocks the current and reduces the sunlight, the arch is the perfect vantage point where a diver can see all the fish, but the fish can't see him. Continuing on through to the other side, the passage empties out into a big open sandy bowl, much like a small amphitheater. Looking backward to the entrance, a grand black coral tree can be seen as it sways in the eddying current. It was a feast for the eyes.

Dev and Gman splashed into near-perfect conditions. Soon they approached the open water of the Arch. Gman followed closely over Dev's shoulder to record any action that might unfold while Dev cautiously maneuvered himself into the open water to enter low in the lava archway.

They hit it big. A massive school of ulua congregated along the inside of the lava bowl formation, free from the ocean currents to play in their protected theatre. Dozens and dozens of big ulua inhabited the bowl undisturbed and unaware of the spearfishermen's presence.

It was a moment before Dev swam guardedly down into the sand patch, the perfect open-water gathering place for schooling ulua. One curious fish sentinel, followed by several guards, swam toward the divers to investigate the intrusion. Dev waited patiently for a target as the fish swam closer. He set the second gun down on the sand bottom so he could ready his gun with both hands for the approaching ulua.

The first bulky black ulua that led the pack swam within a shooting range of 12 feet from Dev. With some luck, this might turn into a broadside shot. The ulua inquisitively moved in closer to check things out. Dev eased his long-gun forward toward the target, moving it up to an eye-aiming position. When the fish finned in, front and center, then started to turn away, Dev applied the lightest pressure to the trigger. "Bam!" An explosion of the contracting rubbers propelled the spear forward directly into the ulua. Great shot! The ulua made one brave run and then floated subdued at the furthest reaches of the leader line. He didn't continue to show much life. With the butt halyard of his long-gun clipped to the right side of his weight belt, Dev let the gun float free. The pressure of the fish kept the leader line taut and the long-gun extended away from the shooter.

Dev then picked up the other gun from the sand and moved it into his favored hunting hand, temporarily abandoning all worries about his ulua securely attached to his first gun. Dev's field of vision broadened wide to see all the ulua that swam in the circular gathering. He hastily glanced back to recheck his first catch, calculating the odds of him getting loose. The ulua exhibited a lack of fight and might just die there without further incident. He looked again to the school of ulua that swam around him, confident that he had great options for an additional kill.

In short order, another 40-pound black ulua swam into the outer reaches of a prudent targeting distance, just close enough for a far but noble shot. Dev quickly set up for a chance at this new ulua coming in to investigate the upheaval. The cocky fish was followed by an entourage of supporters not far behind.

Dev pulled his gun up for sighting and without hesitation launched his spear into the big fish. "Slam!" Right into the gill plate. The ulua bolted away like a marlin on a screaming run and hit the end of the leader line desperate for life. This fish had a fierce reserve of energy and fought boldly for its survival. It bolted forward only to reach the leader's end and then retreated backward, swimming in a desperate arching circle. Then, the frantic fish went down toward the sand and hit bottom before doubling back around to an upward reach like a kite trying to run a string line. After this one big spurt, the ulua settled down to a more manageable fight.

In the center of this shooting spree, the two-gun killer floated weightlessly with his knees in the sand beholding his marvelous fish. Clipped to his right side was the first gun fully extended with his fish swimming slowly into lifelessness. Dev clipped the second gun to the left side of his weight belt as it extended out to hold his second ulua. He looked back again at the first ulua and realized that he didn't have the strength to rush away, so he turned his attention to the second fish. He pulled the leader in and readied his three-prong for the final paralyzing shot to the head. The ulua regained a breath of life and swam for freedom again, the line tightened, and soon the creature was making a close pass in front of the Gman's camera and away from Dev.

After a struggle, Dev finally got control of the second ulua and inflicted a killing blow with the three-prong. With both fish tamed, Dev started up to the surface, keeping a keen eye on his two spearguns dragging the prized uluas to the surface. He worked the inflator hose on his vest to add enough lift to counteract the excess weight of lugging these heavies from the bottom. He rose to his safety decompression stop with the two fish on the spears just as they were shot with the Gman filming the notable event.

There was ample time for celebrating and clowning at their decompression level. Elated with his feat, Dev felt it was time to enjoy his success. He slipped his fists into the gill plates of each fish and swam the uluas around in front of him for the camera. Moving his catch in short tight circles, he brought them close together for a finale of a romantic fish kissing pose: a Hollywood moment.

Dev had set a new spearfishing standard: two guns, two speared ulua. No one in our group had ever achieved such a feat. Not only did he bring in two great fish for the weekend, he was bestowed with unsurpassed bragging rights.

The astonishing creativity of our divers never seemed to diminish through the years. New equipment technology, better boating skills, and greater field-tested knowledge all combined to make this band of divers the most envied on the south shore.

In each individual's quest for a score of fish, personal rivalries and friendly competition played out in a number of ways on and off the boat. If the divers weren't trying to invent new tools or techniques, they might be attempting to squeeze out an advantage on every opportunity to bag a fish. Lungs (Gerry McClay) and I tangled up in one of those competitive situations at the underwater cliffs of Molokai's north coast.

Lungs and I were on a hunt winding down a cliff line hoping for a slaughter of spinies and fish. We cruised with the current, on the lookout for any signs of crawling delights or swimming fillets. The imposing 30 foot cliff face ran along the sand bottom rising up from a depth of 135 feet.

Lungs took special care to balance our hunt, alternating his depth level to complement my movements. As I finned along the lower portion of the ledge, he'd work the higher parts, and as I moved up the ledge line he'd adjust to move down to hunt the lower ledge. He was a natural hunter and used such techniques without much thought or consideration.

The Gman was also on the dive, but neither of us would have known it. We'd see him every now and then, usually back in the distance, camera in hand, away from his subjects.

We finned along the bluff to look up and down the silhouette of the cliff line. Lobster antennae peeking out from the cliff showed up easier against the backdrop of the white sand or the sunlit surface above. At this depth, looking at a dark red spiny against a black cliff covered with brownish-green algae wasn't the easiest way to spot a lobster. For my less-than-perfect eyesight, I'd almost have to be on top of them to see the crawlers.

As we drifted, a few parrot fish grazed the cliffs using their strong jaws to snatch food from the corals on the lava walls. They roamed freely and undisturbed as we moved forward waiting for bigger game. Under most circumstances, the mid-sized females would be fair game and good shooting, but Lungs and I weren't interested in these fish, at least not until we got desperate. It was the start of our dive, and this territory was noted for large ulua. We were itching for a high-value target. After all, today of all days, we had the cameraman with us. We'd much prefer to be chronicled with a monster fish rather than a few wimpy, barely-edible parrots.

The sun pierced down past the cliff line to light up the sand like high noon in the desert. The visibility seemed endless, perhaps a 150 feet looking across the bottom seaward away from the cliffs. The clarity of the water was so different from our splash in at the surface where floating organisms clouded the top layer, reducing our initial visibility to 60 feet or so. It was also much warmer at the surface, while noticeably cooler near the bottom.

I kept telling myself to relax and extend my air supply. The problem was that the scenery was so awesome and the hunt so exciting, it was easy to burn air in the enthusiasm of it all. I had to remind myself that there would be lots of time to get excited about the dive later, up top on the boat after the dive was done. Sometimes purposefully timing my breath to a cadence would help, while sometimes just the mental suggestions would do the trick. It's not that I was an air hog; on the contrary, my air consumption was excellent, better than most. But I was always hoping to stretch my bottom time by squeezing more air out of a tank.

My black web 14-pound weight belt, made up of two 3-pounders and two 4-pounders, slipped out of place on my waistline, distracting me momentarily. I switched my gun and pole spear from my right hand to the left so I could use my dominant hand to adjust and tighten the chrome metal buckle. The belt normally fit perfectly on my waist to become unnoticeable, and that's just where I wanted to reposition it.

It was a good time to check on Lungs, so I cocked my head over my shoulder to see him trailing slightly behind and 15 feet higher on the cliff. I shot him an okay sign, which he flashed back in confirmation. Lungs was a fearsome spearfisherman with lots of bottom time. With his twin super eighty tanks and connective yoke, he looked like a stocky underwater projectile of deadly force. The boys gave him the name Lungs because he carried more air than any of us single-tank divers.

As a self-employed contractor, Gerry was in high demand around the neighborhood for his quality work and meticulous craftsmanship. Prior to managing his own business, he ran large construction projects for a developer. With this wealth of knowledge, he went into business to work on small remodels and repairs. He wanted to do the jobs himself for the variety and satisfaction of doing the work ...carpentry, painting, plumbing and light electrical. He was always my ace when I screwed things up around the house trying to do it myself.

I had a water leak at the house a few weeks before, and after cutting holes in half the living room wall the source of the intermittent leak remained elusive. Lungs came over right away and tracked the problem to a leaky drain pipe in the kitchen. He fixed it in a few hours and I was free to repair the wall later. I owed him big time for the help and wanted to make it up to him. I thought about putting myself in a position behind him for a first shot at an ulua, or maybe I'd hold back so he would see the lobsters first. Repaying him in such a gracious manner would be quite noble. I thought about it ...no ...we're hunting. He's on his own. It was my selfish hunter side that made the decision. I promised myself that I would take care of him later, some other time. I felt a little guilty about my attitude but would have to live with it for now.

Soon we came to a recess in the cliff line that went backward into a hollowed bowl 120 to 180 feet in diameter. It was beautiful where the cliff went back inland and bloomed with more geologic structure and hidden nooks and crannies. A sand and rubble bottom curved irregularly upward, forming a nest-like arena for marine creatures to congregate. What a pleasant surprise. There were more corals, a few jagged lava slabs on the bottom, and all sorts of small reef fish throughout the area. It was a visual feast for the eyes. As we rounded the corner of the cliff, more of the nest came into view as our eyes labored to grasp all of its bounty. It was a mini version of the Lobster Grotto.

Yes. Three of them, I shouted to myself. Ahead, at the very back of the crater were three ulua having fun and fooling around. They were swimming a few yards in front of a recess, playing a game of tag. The largest one chased a smaller ulua, trying to intimidate the other into a type of submission. The smaller one would dart up to get away and then move around behind the bigger one. Then the game would repeat again in an unpredictable skittish chase. I wondered for a second if it might be a mating ritual or some bonding event.

I was ecstatic. One fish for me, one for Lungs, and the last one for me again. The fish sparkled as their scales caught the rays of sun and reflected it in the most unusual angles. Caught up in their game, they seemed not to notice us at first. We drifted into the middle of the crater. All three of them were out in the open but remained close to their protective nest.

In the excitement of the moment, I forgot about Lungs. Gone were my thoughts of owing him for his skilled labor. There was nothing in my mind but the fish. My years of training went missing; the attack sequence of working together was forgotten. I was on my own, with no consideration for my partner that I left behind. At this point, it was exclusively about killing a fish. Lungs would have to find what he could after I took my trophy.

I sank down carefully toward the fish at a shallow angle. Gun checked, safety unlatched, I moved the three-prong to my left hand and kept the long-gun in my right where I put it into the trigger grip handle. I carefully slipped my index finger into the trigger guard but waited for the perfect moment to extend the gun forward for a shot. Then my hand moved to line the gun's sights up with my eye to block out a target on the fish's gill plate.

The largest of the three took notice and moved in to investigate what this large, wet-suited diver might be. It must look unusual to a fish to see a big, swimming human leaving a trail of bubbles streaming from a regulator. The ulua was too curious for his own safety. He came forward to see what I might be. Soon he would know that I might be a force best avoided.

He started at me straight away and then moved in slightly to an angle. I waited for him to turn for a broadside target. He came forward, hesitated, and then turned to head away. I slipped the long-gun forward, placed the gun in a position where one sight blocked the other on a mid-gill plate spot, and then gently squeezed my finger down on the trigger to fire. "Bam!" Lung's gun went off next to my ear. I jerked my gun trigger down and in a matter of a millisecond, two stainless steel shafts exploded into the mark. "Slam!" Two spearman's javelins struck deep into the ulua.

The force of the impact knocked the fish from its intended course and away from us. Two shafts lodged deeply into flesh and bone and attached us to the creature with high test leader lines. The fish's death run began in its panic. The leader lines tightened as the injured fish flipped his big tail in desperation to extricate himself from us. The other fish scattered in a frenzy, moving away to a safe distance.

The run began! I held on to my gun as the fish dragged me through the water to trail in its wake. A few feet away Lungs held on to his gun, as he too, was being pulled though the depths. I balked at the idea that Lungs was on my fish. What the hell? This is my fish. I was in the best position, I fired! The rant went on for a few seconds. Then doubts came to mind. Did he fire first? Was it his fish? No, I reassured myself again. He shouldn't have taken the shot, it's my fish. I was ahead of him and closer to the fish. He must have seen me lining up for the shot.

By this time I was breathing hard and my mind started to play tricks with me, so I moved on and figured we'd hash it out later. Lungs held onto his gun for the joyride. He smiled wide, with his white face framed by a full beard. I saw it in his eyes–he challenged me.

"I shot this bad fish, what are you doing here?"

I returned his challenge with a smile and a mental retort, "What the hell are you doing on my fish?" I don't know if he got my message, because we were both in heaven with this fish ride.

The power of the ulua was awesome as he pulled both of us through the water. He was mortally wounded and bolted away from the cliff and out to sea like an ox. The fish had literally turned us around and struggled with our weight as he headed out toward the end of the cliff and to deep water.

Moving out to sea, Lungs and I rounded a small arch. The ulua hit the bottom and dragged our spears, entangling the leader lines. Spears clashed, lines tangled, and then with a blunt thud, Lung's spear fell to the bottom. My spear continued to hold; this prize was now my fish! But how much longer would the spear hold with my dead weight on it? I crawled up on the leader line, hand over hand, hoping to get a paralyzing head shot with my three-prong. He kept flipping his tail, wiggling his body to free himself from the spear's grasp.

The desperate fish swam toward the upper ledge of the cliff. My leader line snagged and ran across a rock on the cliff, getting trapped by its grip. I prayed that the leader line wouldn't fray. The line slid on the rock to slow him down and served as a pivot point to hold him close to the cliff. It forced him into a small rock depression where he beat himself up from side to side in the confined space. I quickly saw my opportunity and rushed over to block his escape. I pushed the three-prong deep into the fish's head. Blood spilled out from the its gills more profusely as it slipped from consciousness.

What a thrill! What a fish! I thought. Lungs watched as I slowly rose. He smiled and flashed me the thumbs-up sign which I returned with great joy. He stayed deep and reloaded his gun, hoping for a return of the other two uluas. Unfortunately, that did not happen.

Lungs and Gman surfaced shortly after me. I was helping Lungs with his gear on the swim step when I started to mess with him. He wasn't even out of the water as I went on the offensive. "Shot my fish, huh?" I asked in a teasing but accusatory manner.

"Your fish? Where do you get, 'your fish'?"

"I was in front of him for the best shot," I said.

"I shot first!" Lungs protested.

"No, I squeezed my trigger and you interrupted me while I was shooting."

Lungs came right back at me. "No, no, no, I had the first shot."

"It sure felt like I took the first shot," I said.

"Mine was the first shot!"

"But I had the better shot." I would not concede.

"How do you know you had a better shot? I could have been above you and shooting down," said Lungs.

"Nah, you were behind and to the side. You fired your spear next to my ear," I retorted.

Lungs wasn't giving in. "The fish were getting away. Why didn't you shoot earlier? Were you asleep? Couldn't you see them in front of you? Do you need a new face mask prescription?" Lungs continued.

"I waited for the classic profile shot!" I defended myself.

"You weren't shooting, so I shot," Lungs insisted while he continued stowing gear.

Lungs and I bantered back and forth the rest of the day in good humor. It was quite irrelevant who shot what, except for the bragging rights that came with the kill. We shared all the fish onboard so each of us would take home the same portion to our families. Sometimes the right to lay claim to a fish is more important than a fish dinner.

Lungs and I agreed to disagree on our interpretations of who did and who should have done what. Even when we reviewed Gman's video onboard we couldn't tell who shot first or who was in the very best position for the shot. I think Lungs knows my position was proper, but I don't blame him for not admitting it. I would probably do the same, just to keep the sparks going.

Aside from the friendly competition, our family of divers had a great affection for each other, and we went out of our way to avoid any conflict. Diving together took all priorities in making the team concept work. The frequent use of each other's distinctive nicknames was a way of bonding experiences into the fabric of a relationship.

Killer gave me a nickname which stuck for a few years. It was later replaced by a more appropriate tag as our diving experiences played out. I was not particularly proud of "Rocky" but accepted it as appropriate at the time. On one of our dives, I caught up with Killer to find him with his spears full. He pointed down to two rock fish that I might take for myself. One was huge, the other of average size. Obviously I speared the larger of the two. Well, being nearsighted, my eyes deceived me, and the rock that I speared blew up into dozens of pieces. I would not hear the end of that incident for some time. I could not distinguish a rock from a rockfish.

The christening of a diver-fisherman by his nickname is neither required nor requested. In fact, many offshore fishermen
go through their whole lives without ever having been dubbed.
Sometimes an angler comes to a boat with a nickname already
given to him. Usually the name is graciously accepted by the boys
and all is well. On most occasions an event or extraordinary circumstance might dictate that a new name be tried, to see if it
sticks. If the boys take to it, and if there is no objection to the
new moniker, it then becomes a welcomed addition to a diver's
handle.

Cousin Hooks (Jimmie Alves) was a regular offshore guest on
our boats when he returned to Hawaii to visit his family. Jimmie,
the middle son of my Auntie Vickie, took to track and field as
his passion. A high school high jump star and record holder, he
spent most his time in athletics. However, he was still a part of our
water-oriented family and held his own in the ocean just as well
as the rest of us.

Jimmie's numerous and unusual fishing incidents warranted
such a naming of his offshore persona, Hooks. It started at an
early age of seven or eight when he began hooking himself and
others with the simplest of fishing gear... hook, line, sinker, and
cane pole. In one of the first incidents, he hooked himself in the
finger with a rusty hook at the Hawaii Kai fish pond. Fearful of
what he'd done, he tried to remove the hook by throwing the
pole in the water, but of course it was attached to his finger by
hook. He ran home to his father for removal by an over-the-kitch-
en-sink surgery.

Then there was the regular routine of hooking his brothers
on fishing trips in the marina. Soon he developed a technique
for speedy removal on site, rather than dragging himself or his
brothers home for an emergency visit to his father. This saved a
great deal of fishing time and avoided the ire of his dad. There
was an occasion where he hooked his younger brother in the back
of the head while casting with a treble hook. Brother Johnnie was
pretty tough, so not much skin was lost in the removal. In no time
at all, there was a full recovery and all was forgiven amongst the
brothers.

Early one summer when Hooks was in the fourth grade, he
and his family came to visit me at college on the mainland. We

traveled up to Lake Michigan and went fishing at a local resort. The brochures looked like it would be great fishing, but we didn't realize that spring arrives late in the North. Our fishing trip was a complete bust! We spent most of our casting time in the rental car trying to stay warm, rather than fish out in the cold. But not Jimmie–he scored! He hooked a bird in flight. It seems that on a particularly long cast, a loon or some similar bird dove down from the flock and grabbed his bait mid-air. Unfortunately, the bird also grabbed the hook. It was an awful event with the bird squawking in pain. Brother Dickie came to his aid and cut the line close to the deranged bird's beak, and it flew away almost as if nothing happened. The "Hooking the Bird" story is still told at family gatherings.

Years later, when Hooks was much older with a wife and two girls, he continued to visit the family and vacation in Hawaii. As a mature angler, he still possessed the talent of hooking strange and unusual things.

On this particular summer day, we'd planned a family adventure of snorkeling the reefs and fishing out at sea. We started at Niu Valley stalking parrot fish for spearing. A cool offshore breeze cut the sun's heat to comfortable tanning weather enjoyable to all. After all the laughs and giggles, and with no fish to show for our efforts, we blasted out of the shallows for a fast sightseeing trip to Waikiki. Touring the tourist shoreline by boat is a fascinating experience. Seeing the mountainous spine of the island skirted by the vast expanse of concrete high-rises was an unusual contradiction of a modern city and ancient nature that strangely coexisted and complemented each other.

Our tour of the offshore surfing spots of Queens, Canoes, Pops, Kaisers, and Ala Moana was most enjoyable. We even threw anchor and took a dip to cool off outside of Queens. After a few hours, with my visiting family nearly drained by the sun, it was time to head home.

We set the fishing lines in an abbreviated spread of two poles and two teasers. Since we'd be going into the waves, it would be slow punching our way home, but it would be an ideal trolling speed of 7 to 10 knots. Hooks ran his favorite lures with blue, purple and green skirts. It was his turn at the poles since he was our visiting guest. Mainland guests are usually known for having a hot hand at blind strikes. Hugging the reef line for calmer seas and less chop, I hoped for a strike of anything edible. A blind strike is called "blind" because that's what happens: a fish bites without any warning signs that there are fish in the area... no birds, no breaking of surface waters or other telltale signs of fish. The angler is blind to the possibility of a fish strike. We'd all be happy just with a drag clicker going off, even if it wasn't a hookup.

There's a noted windsurfing area along the coast that's frequented by locals and visitors alike. Located at the base of Hawaii Loa Ridge, it has a quaint neighborhood park and auto turnaround for access to the mountains above the beach. We navigated by the offshore reef with our fishing poles set and four lures splashing. We hoped for dinner. Our poles were clearly visible, and the lures churned up the water like a ski rope pulled at the back of a speeding boat.

Jimmie was in charge of fishing, so we paid little attention to the parade of windsurfers crossing the seas to and from the beach park in broad reaches against the wind. Dickie and I talked about tomorrow's adventure without much concern for the activities at the park or what was going on behind the boat. Many of the windsurfers timed their cruising out to sea by cutting in front of us with a comfortable distance for safety. We had no idea that one of them would be so stupid as to cut close behind us.

Out of nowhere and in a startling surprise, "Slam." The spool of line screamed out, the rod bent over, and all anglers went into immediate "hook up" attention. Instantly, we looked at the rod and reel to gauge the condition of the strike. Then we looked behind the boat to see where the line played out for the fish to make his run. Oddly, there was no fish on a tear. A windsurfer was down behind the boat with his board dragging in our direction. Our eighty pound test monofilament line suddenly snapped back to us and the windsurf board popped free.

A young blond male floated in our wake, shouting at us with fists blazing and obscene gestures flying. The windsurfer was uninjured, but his board took a 9-0 stainless steel hook. The gash must have been near critical to the surfboard. We paused for a moment to watch him maneuver around to his board. It would serve us no purpose to drive back and apologize for his error or argue with him about who had the right of way. I only hope he learned a new lesson about the dangers of crossing behind a fishing boat on a trolling run. We were disappointed about losing the expensive lure; we didn't even get to have fillet of windsurfer.

A few years later, Hooks returned again to visit our family. On this particular day, we planned a boat ride down to Waikiki for another offshore adventure. Lightning struck again–unbelievable!

As we hugged the reef line home, another windsurfer was offered up to Jimmie's lures. As if by some twisted happenstance, a windsurfer came shooting out from the reef with a stiff sail of wind. It was a small unsuspecting female, a Japanese tourist. When her sailboard hit the lure, the frail young thing flew off the board as if the board had crashed into a rock wall. She went up and over, then backward, down into the water with the greatest force. This time, when Hooks snagged the second windsurfer, we wondered if it was an unfortunate accident, random coincidence, or some haphazard devilish occurrence? No! No one had ever hooked a windsurfer before, yet he hooked two without trying. I imagine Hooks may hold a record: Hooks, the man with the magic hook. "If you need it hooked, and it flies, sails or swims, Jimmie's your man!"

A few summers later, Hooks called to tell me that he and a neighbor were coming to Hawaii for a short vacation to fish and dive. By a stroke of bad timing, I was scheduled for a financial planner's meeting on the mainland. I set it up with Hughsan and Killer to make sure my cousin and his friend got to do some diving while they were in town.

All was pre-arranged: Killer and his airline pilot buddy would take Hooks and his friend for a late afternoon dive at Smitty's Reef. The plan was to let the two friends bottom fish while Killer and Hooks attacked the reef spearfishing. By the time the boys got started it was well into the afternoon. The winds picked up during the day and the seas were in the 3 to 5 foot range. That didn't pose a real problem since the boat would be in the bay, not in the open ocean.

After a twenty minute boat ride to the dive spot, Killer threw anchor. They were securely positioned slightly inside and up-current of the reef. The anglers got settled in for fishing as the divers geared up for spearing. Hooks took his time since he was rusty at scuba and wanted to be sure his gear was well-positioned and in good working order. Killer helped him along to speed things up. When they were ready, Killer gave the pickup instructions to the crew, "Forty minutes! Look for us in around forty minutes." With regulators in mouth and thumbs ups flashing, both were off the side and on their way down to the reef.

Killer took the yellow float bottle so the boat could track them from the surface. He carried his usual three-prong, long-gun, and catch bag. Jimmie carried a three-prong only. This was good practice for divers who have been away from spearing for awhile, at least for the first dive. With everything that can happen at the bottom, you don't want to be wrestling a monster fish without having used your dive gear at least once.

Killer served as the dive guide and led the way down. The duo landed slightly inside the reef where three rock formations started the rubble patch before the main reef. The current whipped strong toward Diamond Head. The divers had to swim a little harder, but it wasn't anything that would deter them from reaching Smitty's Reef.

Hooks re-acclimated himself to the scuba gear, and his years of diving experience came back to him immediately. He shadowed Killer, following his trailblazing path, but soon paused to investigate what looked like a shell. Sure enough, it was a large helmet shell, a gastropod of the cassidae family, laying a travel track in the sand. The large outer lip of the shell boasted a high sheen pinkish color and was sometimes used for cameo making. Hooks stopped and picked it up, thinking what a score it would be for his daughters, Beth and Karen.

Hooks deposited the shell in the bag. It lay heavy on his weight belt as he swam on. There ahead of him he saw another, this one slightly larger than the first. Now he was really excited. Each daughter could have her very own shell from Dad. Killer had no interest in shells but played the patient guide. He knew how beautiful those shells would be all polished up on a desk or bookcase.

They finally got to the reef and skirted along the ledge line looking for game. Hooks took a few small goat fish with his pole spear. That got him back in the game again. Killer kept his gun cool as he waited for a larger deep-water fish to come his way. That's always the risk with spearfishing: if you wait for something big and pass up the small fish, sometimes you end up empty-handed. Each diver played the angles on the dive based on the gamble he was prepared to take. Each dive's chances were different, based on the dive spot and the diver's skill and luck.

Time disappeared and soon the divers were running out of reef, being blown down by the currents. Killer checked with Hooks to discover that he was down to 500 pounds of air. He signaled Hooks for them to leave the bottom and start their slow ascent to the surface.

Soon Killer and Hooks broke the surface to find very rough seas and their distance from the boat a lot farther than they would have imagined. Both of them could see the boat at anchor, but it was too far to swim to. It soon became obvious to them that for some reason, the anglers couldn't see them at this distance.

Unfortunately, sometimes finding divers is nearly impossible if they drift away into the setting sun. The sun on the water was blinding as the boat drivers looked directly into it. This was the case for the two bottom fishermen; their divers had blown out toward Diamond Head at sunset, so the anglers were staring directly into the sun's glare on the water. The only solution for the boat drivers would be to pull anchor and look for the divers in ever-larger search patterns until they got the sun behind them and the divers, but the boat drivers decided that they wouldn't leave the dive spot for fear of not finding it again. They were apprehensive that if they left the site they would be lost in relation to where the divers went down.

It was a standoff. The boat sat parked on the reef while the divers drifted away west into the sunset. Killer and Hooks inflated their vests and remained calm as they were roughed up by the increasing size of the waves. They hoped that at any moment the boat would pull anchor and drive over to pick them up. The divers bobbed about from wave to wave, up and down to a rhythm of the ocean. Hooks made small talk about his family and the grocery business while Killer listened as he tried to show a cool face.

Time passed for both men blowing out to sea in the salt spray. Hooks began to tire. The helmet shells weighed heavy on his belt, creating a strain on the vest's flotation ability. He was using the guest BC which didn't have a lot of lift, unlike my larger

Scubapro vests. Hooks struggled to stay afloat with the excess weight. Killer became concerned as Hooks swallowed more and more water and consequently kept spitting to clear his mouth. As time progressed it became obvious to Killer that Hooks should dump the weight belt and the shells. It kept him too low in the water for his safety. Hooks was losing steam fast, and no one knew how long they would be in the water or how this would end.

"Hooks, why don't you drop the weight belt?" Killer asked in a suggestive manner.

"No, the shells are for my girls," he responded. Killer backed off, not wanting to cause a stir.

A few minutes later, with things not getting any better and Hooks still taking on more water, Killer tried again. "Hey, you're tired, it's okay, drop the weight belt."

Hooks shook his head, declining the suggestion. The scene could have easily gotten worse, but it wasn't very long before Hooks realized that these souvenirs could end up costing him his life. Reluctantly, he loosened the clasp of his weight belt. The fourteen pound lead belt and the shell anchors raced to the bottom. Hooks rose up like a cork to bounce up through the blue troughs of the waves with the utmost of ease.

With each passing moment, the dive boat got smaller and smaller and soon faded in the distance. Killer and Hooks were being swept out to sea past Diamond Head. Hooks started to think about their fate, bobbing like chum with their dangling legs awaiting any predators below. He wondered how he might fare in the water when darkness fell.

Killer began to calculate various survival strategies. His one and only game plan, aside from a boat stumbling upon them, was to start a slow and deliberate swim toward Diamond Head for land. Even though they would blow past it, if they kept swimming, they might end up somewhere in or past Waikiki. There would be lots of boats out in the water at night. Any one of the tourist dinner cruise boats would surely see them floating, Killer reassured himself.

They floated silently for quite some time. Killer was nearing his limit of drifting away from the island. It was regretful, but there was no other option. They'd have to attempt a swim ashore. Maybe they would get lucky and the currents might slacken.

It started as a faint hum and grew to the noticeable sound of helicopter rotor blades. Both men flagged their arms in an erratic fashion above their heads. They knew that this could be their one and only chance for rescue before total darkness. Yes! The chopper saw them immediately and hovered 500 feet above without leaving. In less than ten minutes the Coast Guard's red inflatable hard-hull rescue boat with six guardsmen raced to the divers' position. The chopper flew away when the divers were plucked out of the water and safely onboard the launch.

The rescue craft took Killer and Hooks back to their boat, still anchored on the reef with the boat drivers in obvious distress. Then, the Coast Guard boat sped off to Waikiki as quickly as they came. Yes, our divers would live to fish and dive another day.

Several months later Killer and I were having a few cocktails with our wives at the house. We were laughing about the rescue incident. It happened to be a time when the national media fielded news stories about the Coast Guard initiating fees for its rescues as a way to support their budget. This controversial issue was getting a lot of press.

Someone had the devilish idea that we should call Hooks impersonating the Coast Guard dispatcher and make some trouble. We all agreed it would be a terrific idea, so after a short rehearsal Killer's wife called on speakerphone to Hooks' home in Texas.

By chance, Hooks answered, "Hello?"

"Is this the Alves residence?"

"Yes, it is." Hooks seemed suspicious, like it might be a sales call or something.

"Is this Mr. Jimmie Alves?"

Hooks took caution. "Who's calling?"

We could tell by his tone of voice that he was getting annoyed.

"Mr. Alves, this is Chief Petty Officer Maggie Rockland from the Coast Guard Honolulu Group. I just need to verify your address for mailing."

"Mailing, what would you be mailing me?" Hooks asked.

"Mr. Alves, we have an invoice for $2,632 for a rescue on August 19th."

An immediate shock appeared in his voice as he stammered for a moment, "Two thousand... What? What's this about?" he asked.

"Mr. Alves, this is an invoice for the operating costs of your rescue in Moanalua Bay on the 19th of August."

There was a silence, then fear and panic played into his voice as he shouted to his wife, "Lisa... Lisa... Take the phone!"

Killer's wife held on the line and kept her composure as Killer and I laughed uncontrollably with cupped hands over our mouths like a couple of barstool monkeys. We quieted down just in time for the second performance of the most skillful actress. She replayed the same dialogue as businesslike as she did before. There was a deathly silence from the other line.

I was the first to crack. "Lisa," I started, but couldn't continue as laughter filled the kitchen. I hushed the trouble makers for silence and then continued, "Lisa... It's Cousin Bryan. This is just a prank, we're kidding! Killer and I were messing with Jimmie. There is no Coast Guard bill!" Finally, I could feel the tension released from the other end of the phone. We all laughed and joked for awhile with Jimmy and Lisa then said our goodbyes.

The following summer, Hooks' older brother "Bugs" (Dickie Alves) made his way to Hawaii for a few weeks visit with the family. Most of us called him Bugs since he was the best in the clan at finding lobsters, also commonly referred to as bugs. The Hawaiian Spiny and Hawaiian Slipper Lobsters were no match for him. He had a particularity good eye for locating lobsters hiding in ledges, nests, and holes only to extract them with the greatest of ease. It was a talent that landed him bags of lobster tails that his family and friends enjoyed so dearly. Dickie was indeed the grand master at finding and catching bugs, so the name stuck with him through the years.

As usual, we were out diving with the boys. Weather conditions were perfect for a day at sea. We hoped the ocean would be generous with its gifts so we could have a family seafood dinner. Bugs and I drove our underwater scooters across Smitty's Reef at mid-water level to conserve our air supply. I had no idea of the awesome encounter that was about to play out on this dive. Smitty's dive site usually produced a variety of harvestable game. It's also an attractive dive spot because some of the boys maintained fish traps on the reef which needed regular checking.

This spot was discovered by accident many years ago by our buddy Smitty. It was added to the repertoire of sites and remained a favorite to all. Smitty's Reef is especially handy for a second dive after a deeper first dive. On the days when the ocean is too rough for the deeper spots, it also serves as a terrific first dive because of the variety of its terrain.

The reef's sighting started with Smitty taking his newly-certified diver wife for an easy dive in the bay. For some reason the others divers were too busy to join in, so it would be just the two of them. Rather than anchor dive, Smitty decided that "riding the anchor" would be a fun experience for his bride. Anchor riding is a better alternative to diving at anchor but by no means as good as drift diving. With only two divers and no boat driver, this anchor riding technique was their best plan.

Riding the anchor is when the anchor is placed on a short line with almost no scope so that the anchor flukes never have the optimal angle for a secure grab at the sea floor. After deployment at the dive site, the divers follow the anchor line down to the bottom to dive and explore. When they're ready to move on they pick up the anchor and let the boat pull the anchor away, carrying the divers with the currents to wherever the seas take the boat. Then, when the boat drifts to an area of interest, the anchor is dropped or physically placed into a new anchor spot. It's great fun to be pulled along the bottom in a game of chance and discovery.

On this particular day, Smitty passed on his usual spearing spots in favor of the open sands of Moanalua Bay for a grand tour of anchor riding. After a lengthy preparation, the couple hit the bottom to a strong Diamond Head current with an endless horizon of sand dotting an occasional coral head or two. Both hung on to the anchor and bounced the bottom in leaps of 20 yards or so in visibility over 100 feet. They were traveling at a good clip and enjoying their dive.

Soon the sand bottom changed. Expansive runs of white sand gave way to patchy sand and partially-exposed slabs of lava running like flat blocks of natural stone. A few additional bounces on the anchor revealed a rock and rubble area similar to a rock quarry with a shallow linear trench forming a ledge line that ran parallel to shore. Then the rows of lobster antennae appeared from the crevice of the ledge line. Smitty dropped down, jammed the anchor in a crack, and went to work for their dinner.

When the harvest was completed, Smitty carefully ascended without dislodging the anchor. He triangulated their position for marks and noted the depth levels of the top of the reef and the surrounding sand bottom. For this most spectacular find, the boys christened the reef in his honor.

For most boaters motoring over the surface, the coral en-crusted slabs of Smitty's Reef are barely noticeable. If someone has advanced knowledge of the site and knows what to look for, it's an underwater scene of endless reef in perfect visibility. Loads of tropicals and parrots frequented the area. Often there'd be good-sized wekee or uku, and every now and then a few omilu might swim though the reef. Now that this site was on our list of regular dive spots, in addition to the spearing, we'd check on our buddies' fish traps that were placed on the scene.

I knew Bugs and I would have a great time at Smitty's Reef today. My cousin Bugs was a lifelong dive buddy and all around "gung ho" diver. He left Hawaii after high school and went to work in the Gulf Coast oil industry as a rig diver running a dive crew laying pipe, fixing valves and doing whatever was necessary to keep the underwater operations producing oil. Specially trained and at the top of his class in dive school, Bugs was snatched up by an offshore diving company right away. Although he worked for a living in dangerously deep and dirty water, he still loved to play with the boys in the shallower, clear waters of his youth.

Bugs and I started our dive off the side of the boat in a per-fect drop that put us at the up current side of the reef line. We planned to start out together at the top and separate to work the opposite sides of the large oval reef. Then, we'd finish up togeth-er down current at the end of the reef. If either of us got ahead of the other, we were to continue working the ledge back around and up the other side to join forces wherever we ended up. The whole territory was the size of twenty small house lots.

We were finishing our drive of Smitty's Reef. With scuba scooters we covered lots of ground fast. Bugs soon came around from the end of the ledge with a few parrot fish to join me up current where I had taken a modest wekee and one small parrot. I signaled Bugs that we should head into the shallower reef line that was toward shore. As we motored in, there in the sand rubble ahead, I noticed a small outcropping with a few nooks and crannies with some promise of game. I leaned to steer my scooter that way and looked back at Bugs to make sure he was following.

A calm exhilaration filled my spirit as I felt the cool water brush against my face. Speeding on a scooter gave my body a beautiful feeling of piercing through a thick, clear, weightless gel. A modest pressure against my physical being gave me more of a feel that I was moving through a soft, fluid-like substance rather than swimming through pressurized water. Gliding through the water with the faint hum of a low rpm motor took me into a complete state of euphoric pleasure but reality kept a firm hold on me as I consciously bit down tightly on my regulator mouthpiece to keep it from blowing back out of my mouth. I also become more aware of my facemask with the force of the water against it. What a grand feeling!

I slowed so Bugs could catch up. It was always best to work together when assaulting a reef, ledge, or outcropping. Bugs and I arrived at opposite sides of the formation, tied our scooters down, and started our search for fish and lobsters. Methodically we peeked and poked through the 3 foot ledge overhang. The ledge face formed a fish haven, honey-combed with holes, recesses, and sub-ledges. The reef fish were plentiful and unique corals everywhere, but we were looking for just the right fish for a good dinner: small ulua, omilu, parrot, kumu (white saddle goatfish,) and wekee. A short time later, Bugs and I ran into each other, both empty handed. He shrugged his shoulders saying, "Nothing here, let's move on."

I nodded in agreement. We saddled up on the scooters and drove away. Since I was more familiar with the terrain, I took the lead toward the inside ledges as Bugs followed. I arched the scooter slowly upward to conserve air and leveled off about 20 feet above the sand rubble. Bugs and I drove onward, looking for any signs of lobsters or other game fish. Every now and then I would look back at Bugs to see that he hadn't dropped off to shoot a fish or pounce on a lobster. It's a common bad habit to drop everything for game, so it was a good idea to check on my dive buddy every now and then.

As we continued our journey, I was intent on making my body glide through the water as streamlined as possible. The sun shined deep through the shallow layers of clear salt water. A shadow of a cloud or something moved from behind me and enveloped me in a soft shade. Sometimes, you can see the clouds moving through the sky as they cast their shadow on the sand bottom below. It's quite beautiful. I thought it must have been a small cloud as ahead and around me there was bright sunlight shining through the water. I was relaxed and soaking in the spirit of the moment when I noticed it odd that the shadow was so small and not moving past me. When a dark cloud passes overhead it usually races across the bottom; it doesn't stay in one place.

A feeling of curiosity came over me. I was intrigued by the darkening phenomenon. Bugs is up to one of his tricks, I suspected. I bet he's racing above me so I'll be eating his exhaust. No, I will not fall for this prank! I told myself as I sped up. After a second or two a strange awareness grew in my mind. I finally turned around to look for Bugs. My breath stopped. My finger slipped off the scooter throttle and I glided to a stop in neutral buoyancy.

Unreal! There, 20 feet above and a little behind, right between Bugs and me was the largest female humpback whale anyone could have imagined. It was the biggest living creature... ever! I was oblivious to all else; my dive buddy, the fish, the water, it all faded away as I was drawn to the presence of this creature. I was stunned, not knowing what to think or feel. I experienced a flash realization that I was such a small man; being so close to this tremendous animal was scary. Soon a feeling of bliss took over me as I felt a spiritual upwelling. After a moment, with the whale barely moving, I realized that there was no danger here.

Sensory impressions flooded my mind as my senses sharpened for this once-in-a-lifetime event. My body relaxed and I was left to float there in motionless awe. My mind recorded every detail with absolute precision. My spirit elevated nearly to an out-of-body consciousness. All other phenomena faded except for my connection to the whale. For the moment, I had *become* this experience with the whale.

My eyes tried to take everything in all at once. I saw the living thing in all of its age. This giant was so close to me she could have put me in her mouth without moving. If she wanted to, she could toss me like a ball in play. I knew I was in the powerful presence of the ultimate untamed marine mammal. She must have been 40 feet long. Incredible! The tonnage and length of this creature caused me some caution. I could hardly believe I was under this massive whale witnessing the power, yet grace of it all. She barely moved to keep a constant space with me, using an effortless gentle stroke of her elongated fins. We floated together like the most unlikely partners.

The whale's mouth stretched across the whole of her relaxed, ageless face. A thick oversized lip remained firmly closed and separated the top of her head from the lower part of her jaw. The lip line traveled back down her body toward the belly. It was an awesome sight with the rich, dark blue body silhouetted in the sparkling light of clear water. As the lower jaw turned under into her lighter colored underbelly, the dark hue faded in to the color of soft cream. It was all so natural, one portion of her anatomy flowing seamlessly into the next. Even the large skin lines that streaked back from the mouth seemed to be a sculpted part of her physique. The humpback lay clad with heavy wrinkled skin that armored her shape but it was so natural a part of her graceful features.

As the creature glided closer, she tilted herself over to me in curiosity and casual observation. The large eye, about the size of a coffee cup and saucer, stared into me with little emotion. All of the skin lines angled and curved around her eye. It was a focal point. It looked like the knot on the tree of an enchanted forest. I was hypnotized by her gaze, unable to move. I felt the animal's caution and distrust for a moment. Perhaps it was centuries of breeding that caused her to be careful. I showed my deep compassion for the creature as best I could through a benevolent stare. The whale seemed to pierce my thoughts as she quickly judged me to be no threat. Of course I was no threat. I was just a little mouse of a man that could have been swooshed away with one flick of her fin or tail. In this environment, she was my superior, I not hers.

I basked in this unique moment of nature between the whale and me. The humpback remained very gentle, almost motionless. I was at peace but yet so excited. Then she moved her tail and drifted slowly off to continue her journey. I floated mid-water as all came back into my field of vision. Bugs drifted back in the distance as he, too, experienced an inspirational moment.

A whale calf a quarter of the size of its mother frolicked over and around Bugs with no fear of his presence. The curiosity of the youngster had it doing twists and turns near Bugs as he tried to maintain a motionless posture. I was lost in my own world and didn't notice my dive buddy was having his very own epiphany. Soon the calf scampered off to join its mother, and there we were looking at each other in disbelief of our chance encounter. It was totally unreal.

CHAPTER FIVE

LIFE CHANGER

The long Labor Day weekend couldn't arrive fast enough for the dive boys. Every ocean opportunity was taken seriously, and three whole days of diving were always treasured. Sure there were family gatherings, social events, and other necessities we accommodated, but they'd have to be important events to drag us away from our boats.

Hughsan was the master at juggling family duties with diving needs. If it was a birthday party for one of his kids or grandkids, it would have to start late in the afternoon so he could get a dive in before the party. If guests were visiting, somehow he would coordinate with V to cover for him and then pick them up by boat for a harbor cruise–after the diving of course! If there were kids to watch, he knew they'd be better watched on the boat. As far as V was concerned, being both a diver and boat driver, she preferred to be on the boat with Hughsan and the guys.

The wives of the other divers seemed to adjust to their husband's absences too. Killer's wife believed that Gary should have hobbies with his friends. She was very encouraging about his diving and kept busy with her home-based cheesecake baking business. Crawman's wife Susie was also very patient, as she understood the deep passion Craig had for diving. She kept occupied with their son Travis and her fellow school teachers. Lungs was a committed family man with two young girls to raise, so he limited his diving to allow for more family time than the rest of us. Gordon, our senior diving statesmen, had self-granted unlimited diving privileges because of his current status as a single man. Diving had always been a big part of life since his youth.

Although many of the boys had their own boats, it was often easier and more fun to jump on Hughsan's *It's Time* for a day of diving. *It's Time* was always in the water at the Esplanade dock where we kept our dive gear in a locker for quick getaways. We used our own boats for the overflow of divers and those situations that involved our friends and families.

The wind and waves were cooperative today for an around-the-corner adventure to Rabbit Island and the Sandy Beach Bluffs. Hughsan, V, Gordon, Killer and I made a day of it where perfect ocean conditions greeted us at the backside of the Rabbit. Hughsan, V, and Gordon cleaned up on the 135 foot ledge line as Killer and I manned the boat. When it was our turn, we dropped into the other side of the ledge where we worked another reef the first team hadn't hunted.

Killer and I finned the reef together, overwhelmed with the fish activity. We felt like hired gun-slingers that had come to a wild western town to shoot up the place. We kept busy loading and firing, reloading and firing, over and over again. It takes a lot of energy to pull those three 5/8 inch diameter, custom-length, long-gun rubbers at a depth of over 100 feet. Killer and I finished our dive and surfaced with near-empty cylinders. When it was all said and done, we came aboard with our bags and stringers full. The weekend was off to a great start.

It's Time tucked into the inside shore of Rabbit Island where we had lunch and rested with two hours of uptime. Then we headed to Sandy Beach where Killer and I would do a dive on The Bluffs. It was one of my favorites, with three mountainous lava fingers jutting out into the sandy depths. If I wasn't careful, I could spend the whole dive drifting along the cliffs and floating from one cliff top over the sand valley to another. At the top of each of these towering plateaus, I could lay in wait watching the valley below for free-swimming game as I held on to the rocks to allow the up-drafting currents to massage my face.

Once Killer and I hit the water, we separated. I floated with the current and took my time in meditation on the plateaus while Killer went on a hard-charging hunting mission. Being separated didn't worry us much since we'd catch up with each other later down current. This dive proved to be very productive for Killer, with him getting the lion's share of game and me getting my fill of the most beautiful underwater scenery imaginable.

The next day unfolded with near-perfect weather for a trip out to sea. Hughsan suggested a Makapuu Point lobster ground assault, followed by a Sandy Beach inside sweep of the Lava Mounds. There was a last-minute crew substitution as Smitty joined in on the action since V took leave for family tasks.

The offshore Makapuu dive involved scouting the 120 foot bottom, looking for telltale signs of spinies along the rubble and rocks. The preferred technique was to stay high off the bottom to save air and limit nitrogen intake, while going deep enough to see the bottom detail clearly. When antennae, carapaces, tails, or signs of a lobster colony were spotted, the plan was to drop down, investigate, and grab as many as possible. Two teams and two dives later, we were quite content with more than a half dozen tails.

When all was settled, we motored to the shallows off of Sandy Beach to drift, snack on lunch, and get some uptime. After a boatload of laughter we prepped for the Mounds dive. It was good territory, with an expanse of sand fields spotted by a number of lava mounds the size of multiple small homes that sheltered all sorts of marine creatures. Uku roamed the sand bottom, omilu played between the mounds, and parrot fish ate the coral on the mounds. This place boasted great all-around potential for both fish and lobsters. All divers did well on these dives, so with our coolers full, we headed back to the Hawaii Kai Marina for a diver's dinner out.

These two days of successful hunting made dinner out with the wives this Saturday evening a must. These feasts were good times for the spouses as they visited with each other and caught up on community news.

Hughsan was a regular at The Royal Garden Chinese Restaurant in Kahala Mall. Hutton, the owner, was quite fond of Hughsan. I'm not sure how it started, but years ago Hughsan made arrangements to bring his fish and lobsters in for preparation by Hutton's chef. The restaurant charged a preparation fee and cooked our game per our requests. It was a fabulous arrangement. No better seafood dishes were to be found anywhere. We dined like royalty on every occasion at the eatery.

Hughsan and V drove by themselves, as did Smitty and his

wife. Killer and I carpooled with the fruit of our dives, iced down in a cooler. Most of the fish were distributed equally after the dive, but we held back a few goodies for the feast since the ocean was very generous to us. Killer carried the cooler while I escorted the girls. As chance would have it, Hughsan and V arrived at the same time, and we all went together into the restaurant's entryway. The Smiths were waiting there for us where the girls exchanged greetings.

On these special occasions, the boys were always well-showered. Liberal portions of aftershaves were employed to cover the fish smells that sometimes traveled with spearfishermen.

Our women dressed themselves very well. So as not to degrade their own outfits, they tried to dress their husbands in the most appropriate "going out" clothes. Hughsan and Smitty didn't need any help with that; they were fashion naturals, especially Hughsan. Killer and I took more direction from our wives in the dressing department since we weren't interested in clothes. More than anything else, these dinners were an opportunity for us to give our wives the freshest seafood dinner on the island.

There were only a few tables unoccupied, as was usual for a Saturday night at Kahala Mall. Hutton came forward from the back of the restaurant impeccably dressed and smiling to greet us, "Mr. Fraser... Mr. Fraser... so good to see you again!" Hutton glanced at our group. "How many in your party, eight?"

"Yes" Hughsan nodded.

"Ah, I see you have special catch for me." With that acknowledgement, he motioned the head waiter forward. Speaking in Chinese, the waiter nodded to Hutton's instructions and took the cooler to the back of the kitchen. "Mr. Fraser, just one minute, Li set a special table for you. Just one minute, please." In no more than 45 seconds he was back to escort our group to a large round table in the middle left side of the restaurant that several waiters had made ready.

We traveled through the crowd and took our seats, careful to mix the seating up in boy, girl, boy, girl order. Li waited on us and took our drink and pot sticker appetizer orders. It was a round of Tsingtao beers for the guys and various tropical drinks for the ladies. A moment later, as we were in conversation, Hutton came back to the table. "Mr. Fraser, your catch, excellent! You bring very big lobsters tonight." With those comments, Li returned to our table to assist his boss. Hugh and Hutton discussed the menu, special sauces, and preparation techniques while the boys ribbed each other in front of the wives.

Hugh and Hutton came to terms, and Hutton briefed Li on the special arrangements. Then Li took over notating the order in Chinese on his notepad. Ordering completed, Hughsan joined in on our lively conversation. By this time Smitty was teasing Killer about how he surfaced half an ocean away from me, the dive buddy he deserted. Of course Killer blamed it on me, refusing to take the rap for his longstanding dive habits.

There was another round of Tsingtao's and more laughter. A waiter brought out our pot sticker pupus with red sweet and sour sauce, followed shortly by a course of hot and sour or bird nest soup as each of us selected. Sometime later the appetizer plates were cleared and white or fried rice was set at our place settings.

Then Li made a grand entrance from the kitchen with another waiter running interference. With all the ceremony of a religious high mass, a gigantic white china serving platter held up on high made its way to our table. The presentation was remarkable. Six large lobster heads surrounded the edge of the tray with antennae hanging over the side in a neat arrangement for decoration or dining. Split lobster carapaces lay open in the center of the tray with the tail fillets butterflyed and sectioned on top of the ornamental shells. Scattered atop and about the juicy white meat was a most generous soaking of black bean sauce and special spices. All patrons in nose distance stared at this royal dish suitable for a celebrity's private party. Li placed the banquet in the middle on the lazy-susan. We watched the steam rising from the island of lobsters, all of us held captive by its spicy aroma. We became the focus of attention from the nearby tables.

Hughsan asked Killer's wife to start by serving herself. Those waiting to be served watched each of the others take generous servings of succulent lobster like it was in endless supply. To the rest of the restaurant, we may have looked like high-roller diners. We knew we were only weekend warrior spearfishermen, but tonight we felt like celebrities as the patrons envied our extravagance. We became the entertainment as each of our special dishes was delivered in the utmost ceremony.

The special house noodles appeared with little notice as we continued with our self-entertainment. The Kahala version of this noodle dish is a medium crispy cake noodle lavished with pieces of fish, crab, squid, scallops, snow peas, and Chinese vegetables strewn with straw and shitake mushrooms. By most standards, this would be considered a connoisseur's meal in and of itself. We ate it like we expected nothing but the very best for our palates.

The blue male uhu (parrot fish) was prepared stuffed with Chinese sausage. The chef was very generous with the black beans, water chestnuts, garlic, and ginger. Oils from the sausage mingled with the stuffing to baste the fish in a tasty seasoning of sweet spicy sausage and wine. The whole concoction bulged over from the stomach cavity onto the platter. While the fish was "to die for," the stuffing was nothing short of irresistible.

The large kumu was steamed whole. Presented on its final resting place in a deep china platter, it floated in a hot, shallow broth of dry white wine, soy sauce and sesame oil, seasoned with minced fresh ginger, sprinkled garlic, and garnished with generous sprinklings of fresh cilantro. The aromas were a delight.

We honored the lives of these fine fish by savoring the exquisite tastes they bestowed on us. When a spearfisherman eats the life he takes, it naturally encourages him to appreciate the fish he dispatched to its end. It's the gift of nature that allows us to nourish ourselves. I have always been respectful of marine life that I have taken for nourishment. This is how many fishermen and hunters feel.

Our elegant fish dinner utilized the very best of carefully-hunted, prized local fish, not easily ordered at just any restaurant. It would be a shame to waste any part of them, but none in our group would eat the head and eyes. It wasn't in our culture to do so. Many Asians and old timers in Hawaii would feast on just the heads as a delicacy. Since we would not eat these parts, we'd return them to the kitchen well kept, so any of the kitchen staff would have a clean head to banquet on if they desired.

We talked and ate through dinner. As was our custom, Hughsan was in charge of figuring the bill, and we all chipped in for our respective shares. We were stuffed! The only solution for us was to head home and lay on the couch to digest our dinners. We all agreed on a soft nine o'clock in the morning for our dive time.

The next morning, the divers gathered at the Esplanade boat locker. It would be a light crew: Hughsan, Gordon, Smitty, and me. Killer had some work to do at home, and Crawman was busy with family activities. The weather had turned and roughened up the ocean, so we'd stay in the bay to work our spots closer in to the island.

One of our spots, Shark's Cave, provided a terrific scuba dive for its varied scenery and the potential for fish. This combination of features made this locale a regular on our dive list. Unlike some of our deep divers who prefer hunting for trophy ulua, I considered myself a reef harvester. It's amusing how each diver sees the ocean through his unique vision; it makes for a diverse group of individuals.

Located out in the bay toward Diamond Head, the Shark's Cave area is an underwater ledge the size of a dozen small house lots resting in 85 feet of water. The top of the ledge varies between 65 to 75 feet, and the sand bottom rests in the 85 foot range. The best dive plan was to drift from one end to the other, always working with the current for ease of movement. It's the opposite strategy of anchor diving, where it's best to start off going against the current and then drift back toward the boat to finish the dive.

After doing a current check we had a pretty good idea of which way the current was going and how fast it might be. If we were wrong and the drop was off the mark, we had the option of terminating the dive and re-boarding for another go at it. Sometimes, if a diver landed close to the site and the current wasn't extreme, he'd work with what was given and do a little more swimming.

Today, Hughsan and I would be diving together. Smitty, the boat driver, tweaked our position with the aid of Hughsan calling final instructions for our precise entry. "Ready?" Hugh asked me, sitting on the side rail combing ready for a splash down.

"Ready!" I replied, mumbling with my regulator in my mouth.

We were over the side and angling down to our spot in 100-plus feet of visibility. Beautiful, warm, clear water invited us to the bottom. We landed on the G Spot section of the Shark's Cave located on the Koko Head side of the ledge. After a perfect drop, we'd use the current to help stretch our air and lengthen the dive.

Killer named this spot on the occasion of a lucky streak of repeated uku slaughters over multiple dives. For some of the boys, the name had a sexual reference of sorts, but as far as I was concerned, it stood for G, "Gary's spot," Killer's given name. That's all there was to it.

Hugh and I drifted along the ledge as we worked it together. High and low we searched for Hawaiian spiny lobsters and other edibles that might come our way. We looked for any telltale movement of game fish or spinies that would trigger hunter alarms in our consciousness. Hughsan worked the top and upper side of the reef while I hunted the lower side rubble and sand bottom. Out of the right side of my mask, I noticed Hugh stop to place his speargun at the side of a small coral head. He found a spiny and prepared to pin the lobster in the hole to remove him from his nest. I continued on to the sunken barge just down the way resting atop the edge of the lava ledge line.

A few years ago the barge was sunk there in the state's continuing efforts to bolster marine life through its artificial reef program. Closer to shore from this site was an old tire reef and father towards Diamond Head a discarded concrete piling reef. The smaller fish overran these artificial reefs in a testament to the program's great success.

I came up over the ledge and swam toward the back of the angled rusting barge hull. On occasion there would be ulua and omilu lurking under the hull for protection from the current. My gun was ready but to no avail–no one was home.

Up and down the barge I swam hunting for fish. Nothing. Soon Hughsan was at the scene asking if there was any action. I gave him the thumbs down sign and noticed two large spinies in his bag. I pointed at them and gave him the thumbs up sign for my congratulations.

With the barge covered, we finned away to work the ledge until we came to Turtle Cave. This was one of Hugh's preferred spots, so I gave the Master the courtesy of having it all to himself.

It was always a generous producer of lobsters hidden deep within the cave, an occasional ulua, and oftentimes a couple of resting turtles, thus the name.

Chances were good that Hughsan would be busy for at least five minutes if the cave was empty, longer if he tangled into something. That was ample time for me to swim to the upper ledge for the two-foot rock ridge that ran the length of the reef some 25 yards inside. When the small lava line hit the end of the cliff structure, just near Shark's Cave, it circled back to form a natural depression on the flat plains like a wash-out or draw. The depression was noted for a variety of tropicals and one of Hughsan friends' traps. We always checked it as a courtesy to free the larger fish into our bags and to relieve any overcrowding.

A contemporary Hawaiian fish trap looks much like a mainland hog or varmint trap. While lighter and easier to construct, it is usually assembled with an iron frame box the dimensions of 4' wide by 4' tall by 6' long. The skeleton is made from concrete rebar, and chicken wire mesh is attached to the frame to form a fish-tight enclosure. A funnel-like wire scoop is fashioned into the front of the trap, and a convenient fish removal hatch is constructed at the back or top of the trap.

The trap is usually placed in a strategic location along the reef where fish normally travel, the best areas being where the fish would conveniently funnel into the mouth of the trap along ledge lines. The devices are set in place by divers and could be pulled to the surface to be unloaded, but more commonly the fish are retrieved underwater by the divers.

From over 25 feet away I could see the trap tucked into the ledge where the rock line cut back into the lava. The catcher was squeezed in between two sides of a crack. I moved in fast to see if there were any fish we might want. Yes, there was one lone parrot mixed in with a cage full of tropicals of every shape and size. I went to work. Positioning myself at the front of the trap resting on both knees and extending my head into the mouth of the entrance, I readied my three-prong for action.

I lined up a shot as the parrot ducked for cover in and around the crowds of smaller fish. I let loose my first jab. It grazed two or three small fish and went into the wire mesh at the side of the cage. Damn! I missed the shot. The shooting procedure was repeated again and again with no luck. This clever parrot moved wildly about, darting for cover, making it difficult to track and keep my spear on target. At last, the next shot proved successful. Slowly I backed my spear out of the trap with the dinner-sized parrot fish and threaded him on my stringer.

I looked up to notice Hughsan floating slightly above and a few yards away from me. He caught a ringside view of the silly circus of missed shots and smiled in amusement. He motioned he was going on to Shark's Cave, so I waved him on, as I needed a few moments to set the trap back in a good hunting order. When all was completed, I swam down to the main ledge and dropped down to the right side entrance to Shark's Cave.

I liked to be heavy on my weight belt. Just two pounds extra made dropping down on fish a little easier. It was effortless for me to float downward off the cliff and to the base of the cave. The cave was a recessed underwater grotto with a white sand bottom and a fallen part of the cliff line forming a five-foot partial wall to the left of the entrance. It gave some protection from the currents for the sharks and turtles that used it as their home.

Hughsan was at the back of the 15 foot cavern face looking for more spinies. I started to swim in but figured he had it covered, so I swam out to continue my dive. To save air during the 75 yard swim to the next ledge down current, I slowed my breathing and angled my swim path up shallower to cross the sand valley. Finning slowly to enjoy the view, I would also give Hughsan more time to finish up his hunting. The water was crystal clear. I took pleasure examining the minute marine floaters that waltzed trough the ocean waters. They were almost unnoticeable, except for their outer jelly shells. Some of them had long, thin, spaghetti-like strands and others flat, odd-shaped pancake formations, but most of them came in every conceivable shape and size floating freely with the tides. It was an incredible scene filled with the mysterious diversity of life. Such creatures were always there to some degree, but when you're hunting there's less time to pay them any attention.

When the next ledge line came into view, I started a gradual trajectory down to the intended spot where Hughsan's friend kept another trap. Hughsan would be headed here to harvest the goodies, but he'd really have to hoof it to catch up with me.

A turtle startled me as he swam by 20 feet below going out to sea. They must know they're protected; they're not the least bit concerned for their safety. In the distance, I could see the familiar trap tucked into a recess atop of the tiny bluff. This whole area was a subtle reef complex, less than a third the size of the Shark's Cave site.

Eventually crossing over this shelf area and swimming across the plateau would place us at the University of Hawaii underwater research site. The dive spot is a collection of concrete blocks assembled in a manner to attract reef fish; it was also a good place to catch uku and other good-eating game that frequented the protective structures to feed on the smaller fish.

Casually descending to the trap ahead, I was amazed at what I saw. There, in the seaweed encrusted cage, hoards of panicky reef fish were trapped and jammed in tight with so little room to move. I approached by the front of the cage to block the entrance. A number of parrot fish flittered about, trying to hide at the back of the box. They darted between the tropicals to cover themselves from the giant intruder with a spear. Hiding in the back of the trap was a large moray eel. He slithered from side to side with his jaws open, his scary face intently staring me off. As long as he was at the back of the cage, I wouldn't worry about him.

I counted and recounted the parrot fish, getting my numbers confused as they darted in and out of the shadows and behind the tropicals. They all look so similar, all females, not one blue bull in the pack. I assessed the situation for a moment and realized that this was going to take some work.

Placing my long-gun at the side of the trap, I got myself into position with three-prong in hand. There at the front, I put my head close to the opening and lay my left shoulder against the wire entry. I let fly my three-prong through the mouth of the trap and to the frightened parrots hiding at the back of the cage. Bingo! I scored a hit behind the gill plate and into the spine. The parrot wiggled wildly for his life, so I shoved the spear forward to pin the fish into the back of the trap, pushing him up on the three-prong.

The eel darted in for a bite. "The nerve of that punk," I grumbled to myself. I shook him loose and pulled the parrot out through the trap's entrance and threaded him on to my stringer. For me it was easier to push the stringer through the gills and out the mouth of a fish. Some of the guys preferred to take the stringer the other way, through the mouth and angling it out the gills. I soon realized that I'd never get the job done without running out of air. This is a job for two divers, one spearing and one bagging. Just as I was figuring it out, Hughsan arrived on the scene.

I saw the excitement in Hughsan's eyes and felt the energy of his sharp body movements. I moved back and motioned him to the trap entrance, he being the senior diver. Hughsan gave me hand signals, "No, you proceed."

Undeterred, I continued moving out of the way and give him a barrage of gestures, "no, no, you shoot and I'll bag." But he refused. I insisted, waving my hands to show him to the entrance and shaking my head, "No." We continued to waste air as we politely argued in signals, you first, no, you first, no, after you... Then finally he accepted my offer. Hughsan unclipped the green mesh bag from his weight belt, handed it to me, and got his head into the face of the trap.

He cocked his pole spear and cranked down the rubber three quarters of the way down on the fiberglass shaft. The rubber was pulled taut, killing energy stored for release. Shooting a three-prong takes a great deal of skill developed by years of experience. Like firing a crude sling shot from the waist, it demands excellent hand-eye coordination.

Half of Hughsan's torso crowded the mouth of the trap with his head at the entrance hole. He was lined up for a shot, but by this time the moray eel was getting agitated. He slithered his way to the front and tried to stare Hugh down as he had done with me. Hugh was not intimidated by the eel's behavior. Since the stare didn't work, the moray took a few open-mouth jabs at the trap wire close to his Hughsan's head. The eel's clacking jaws were too large to get through the wire mesh, so he was no threat at the moment.

Hughsan moved his spear over and lightly poked at the eel to show the creature the three teeth of stainless steel he packed. It was a necessary distraction from the task at hand which had to be done to get some control over the eel. There was a series of spear jabbing and jaw biting between the two, but the eel eventually withdrew back into the nest of tropicals for cover. In the meantime, all the fish were swimming like crazy hoping for some salvation.

There at the opposite side of the trap were a few parrots hiding behind the swarm of tropicals. Every now and then, their skin would show through the brief spaces of panicked reef fish. "Slam!" Hughsan's spear flew and whacked the first parrot. After the solid shot, the fish held fast at the tip of his spear. He wiggled and squirmed but the shot was forceful and direct. There would be no escape. Hugh pulled his spear out and moved it back to my awaiting bag opened wide for the precious parrot.

Hughsan settled back into the cage and tracked another parrot that left the cover of the school. His spear moved from side to side, tracking the fish and its erratic movements. Just as his spear closed in and mirrored the fish, movement for movement, the shaft was let loose and the spear met its target. Pandemonium broke out as the fish tried to shake himself free. The spear was slowly withdrawn to the front of the trap and Hughsan reached in to secure his game. He brought him out into the open to my awaiting bag. Ah, it'll be like clockwork, I thought.

We followed a routine in times like these. The shooter would place the speared fish into a quickly-opened bag, the bag man would rush to close the bag tightly, the shooter would jerk the spear backward to free the fish from the spear, and the captured fish would remain in the bag. Then, the shooter would go on to the next shot. After one or two fish, the dive team would develop a rhythm that made the job easier.

The first fish was always easy, but it got harder as each new fish was added to the bag. When the sack was open for each fish, all of the previously-bagged fish got a whiff of freedom and tried to make a break for it. The slightest crack of the bag's opening caused a rush for the front. The slipperiness of these fish didn't help, either. The natural slime on their scales allowed them to fit through the smallest of places. Hanging on to them was even harder. Holding them by the inside of the gills or using your thumb and index finger to secure them by the eye sockets was the only workable solution.

Hughsan quickly moved on to his third fish. His experience paid off as his spear quickly found a mark and another nice parrot went in the bag. In no time, he was back into the wire mouth searching for the next fish. There, at the left corner of the cage, he saw a nice-sized grayish-red parrot. He moved the spear to aim at it, and the smaller fish scattered from his spear tip. "Slam!" the fish was skewered by a good, clear shot.

Meanwhile, at the other end of the trap, the eel had been watching his food disappear. As one might imagine, he wasn't very happy. He saw another dinner entree about to exit his dining room, so he lunged for the struggling fish, nipping at it with short bites trying to get small pieces of flesh with each darting movement. Then he went for the kill and took a whole mouthful by locking his jaws down on the parrot.

Hughsan took control of his catch and attempted to pull the fish through the front of the cage with the spear. The eel didn't let go. A tug of war ensued; back and forth it raged. Hugh thought about putting his hand into the cage to grab the fish from the eel, but, thankfully, he resisted the idea. Then, he considered bringing them both out to put in the bag. Thankfully, he nixed that concept too.

All the while, I was on the sidelines just waiting to bag another fish. The eel must have known he was going to lose, so he let the fish loose. Then, disappointed with his loss, he suddenly got brave. This huge thing slithered around like a small anaconda, lunging back and forth at the entryway for Hughsan's face. I didn't see how Hugh was going to put his hand in to stabilize the fish and pull him out. Then he took a gamble, rushed his hand in and pulled the fish out.

Somehow I didn't think the moray was done with us yet. I sensed he was going to be more trouble. The eel started up again and repeatedly stabbed at Hugh's face, but he continued to get caught on the wire mesh. I wondered how long before the eel would find the entrance hole and take off a chunk of Hughsan's ear. I figured I should put a stop to this and teach this punk eel some respect. I'd give his menacing head a taste of my stainless steel three-prong and back him off with my spear.

Hughsan was unaware of my plan and worked the trap, lining up his next shot. I moved up to take a position floating above the trap and Hughsan. Slipping my three-prong through a small wire hold, I took aim for the back side of the eel's head and cranked my rubber back... aim, steady, and release, "Bang!" It was a great shot. The spear slammed into the eel's head and securely anchored itself there. The eel went ballistic, sliding, curling, thrusting, and flailing all over the inside of the cage. Each undulation parted the multitude of panicked fish as his tail crashed into the cage at every angle and in every direction. The force of these movements shook the trap violently, and clouds of sand started to stir. Hughsan's head and shoulder went every which way in the mouth of the trap.

He squeezed off another shot in duress, managing to crack another parrot in spite of it. Hughsan pulled the fish out and waited for his bag man. I could see by the look in Hugh's eyes and his accompanying facial expressions that he was not pleased.

I tried to hurry it up but struggled to free the spear from the eel's head. I realized my mistake—too much force. The eel was stuck on the spear. Again and again, I quickly thrust my spear in retreat, pinning the eel to the top of the chicken wire.

The force of the last thrust pulled the spear from the eel. He swam to the back of the cage wounded but more respectful of the intruders. Finally, I was back in position and Hughsan put his fish in the bag. The parrot was slightly tattered but slipped into bag without further incident.

The reef fish were really in a ruckus now with all the life-and-death drama played out before them. Hugh set up for another shot with a slightly bigger grey. I waited. Out of the corner of my eye I saw a small squid. He came out from his rubble lair about 6 feet away from the trap next to a small collection of rocks. While he wouldn't make the main course of a meal, he looked like the perfect pupu snack, "Hawaiian tako poke." He was just a curious fellow out to investigate the cause of the pandemonium. I thought maybe I could bag him before Hugh was ready with the next fish. No, not a good idea, it would take too much time, I told myself. I moved my attention back to Hughsan.

Like the craftsman he is, Hughsan took his next shot with not one wasted movement. At just the right moment with a slight clearing in the swimming hordes, a small brown patch of a parrot's gill plate revealed itself. "Swoosh" went the sound of the spear leaving Hugh's hand, and almost instantly a thud came from the spear hitting the parrot against the cage. Another ruckus ensued. Hugh pushed on his spear to pin the fish, then slowly moved the speared fish back to the front of the trap. The sulking eel stayed in his corner coiled in a protective ball.

Hughsan turned the fish back to me for bagging. I opened the clasp as he moved the parrot into the tiny open crack of my mesh bag. Damn it! One fish tried to make a break for it. No, not on my watch, I decided. I pinched the wire mouth of the bag closed and pushed down on the mesh to move the occupants to the back of the bag. Hugh waited for me to get settled then tried again.

This time I was more careful with the opening. Hughsan shoved the fish in the bag and quickly withdrew his spear. It wasn't exactly as we planned, because the force of the hasty spear withdrawal put an excessive pressure on the fish, which slid through the clasped opening to float free stunned before our eyes. He drifted at eye level between Hugh and me. I dropped the catch bag and lunged for him, grabbing him for a second, nearly knocking off Hugh's facemask.

He was so slippery. I grabbed him again, and in an instant he was out of my hand. The fish tried to regain his wits and headed for the sand between us. Hughsan dove down with two hands stretching for a grab. Yes, he got him, but in a moment he was free and floating up and to the side. I lunged again and grabbed his tail, the very worst spot. I got him. Well... almost got him, then he shook himself free and floated in front of me. Hugh came in with both hands and lunged forward to pin the fish against the chest of my wetsuit. One of his hands held the fish fast against my body, while the other one moved closer to the gill plate and into the gills for a firm grip.

Finally, I opened the bag while Hughsan manhandled the fish into it. I shut it as he withdrew his hand out of the bag's mouth. It was done–the parrots were all harvested.

Then we set the area back to normal. I looked at the air gauge and noted only nine hundred pounds left, not a lot for everything I wanted to do before surfacing. I signaled Hugh that I saw something and motioned him to continue on to the University Blocks. He swam on knowing I would soon be behind him. I wanted to see if the squid could be coaxed out of its hole, or if he could be bagged with a clean shot. It would be a great complement to our catch.

Squiddy hid in a small borough under a rubble of rocks, peeking out from under the shadows, with its elastic skin constantly changing to shades of dark, darker, then light, and lighter as a natural means of blending into its surroundings.

Concerned about wasting air, I weighed my options fast. A head shot like this wouldn't be good for me or the squid. It would be a struggle to bring the speared squid out of the fissure with its tentacles locked deep into the nest below. Sometimes squid only come out by being pulled free with all their tentacles attached to rocks and habitat, bringing their whole nest with them. If I shot the squid in the head and couldn't bring it out, it would be certain death, anyway. It would be wedged deep in the hole only to die a slow death. The final winner would be a hungry eel.

I would have to finesse the creature out of its hole with Bugs' trick, a technique used to urge the squid to roll over to protect its head. Then it would show the attacking predator that it was prepared to use its mean, nasty beak. It was a very delicate maneuver, but I was sure it would work. I moved my spear close to the squid's head with great care and gently rubbed it with the dull sides of the spear point, almost tickling it. I didn't want to harm my prey, only scratch its head. It took a few moments, but it rolled over to protect its vitals, withdrawing its tentacles from deep cracks and crevices and drawing them up to allow him to roll over, exposing his beak. I placed my three-prong on the white underside with only a slight pressure. One by one the tentacles crawled up my spear trying to control the shaft and its movement. Soon all of the squid's eight legs had captured my spear. Then, thrusting the spear into the squid's body, it was over. I pulled it out of the hole and slid it off the spear into the bag. I was on my way to catch up with Hughsan.

It was a bit of a swim to the University's experiment station from the trap, but with the moderate current moving my way, I figured I had one last shot at the blocks before having to surface for lack of air. Getting any spare air from Hughsan wouldn't be practical, as he would be low on air, too. It would be wonderful if I speared a omilu or uku before calling it quits. I kept a constant lookout for fish as I swam, not knowing when a game fish might come my way.

After swimming a distance, there ahead of me I saw Hughsan out in the open taunted by a school of uku keeping a safe distance from him… just out of shooting range. I put more zest in my kicks and planned to circle around away from Hughsan to herd the uku closer to him. Once he took a shot, the school of fish would flee from him and unknowingly rush over to me. It would be a two-for-one shooting strategy.

The University blocks lay between us, slightly off to our sides. This was a unique area, with a multitude of hollow concrete blocks piled on each other, forming an underwater mound rising from the sea floor toward the surface in the shape of a pyramid. The structure had a height of 15 feet but was still 45 feet underwater so as not to hinder boat navigation. A secure underwater float rose from the center, serving as an anchoring device for the research vessel.

All of our divers were careful not to interfere with any of the experiments that were conducted in the blocks and stayed away from the areas that were roped off. I'm sure that if they didn't want any spearfishermen in the area, they would have posted an underwater sign. Anyway, the area surrounding the blocks was very good for shooting.

There were two separate pyramids in close proximity to each other; the bigger one was the size of a large house, the smaller the size of a tiny cottage. Like other man-made underwater structures, these were not well maintained and left to nature. Each resembled a cluster of ransacked blocks tossed in a pattern intended to form a pyramid. The structures were separated from each other by 100 yards of sand and rubble with a small series of ledges that rambled on in no particular direction.

Hughsan and I would have to take whatever fish we could find at the larger pyramid, and fast. I was down to 400 pounds of air. I found a good spot to lie in the sandy rubble, free of sea urchins, and got into position to make noise by clanking my spear and three-prong together.

Before I could really give it my best, Hughsan lined up for an impossible shot on one of the leaders of the uku pack. Nah, he'd better wait for a closer shot, I told myself. It's too long a distance for his spear. But against the odds, Hughsan shot. The shaft flew away and across the 12 foot span without dropping an inch to hit its mark smack in the gill plate. Impeccable shot! The fish made his run; the spear's barbs extended, trapping the fish on the spear and leader line. The uku moved up, down, and around in desperation.

Hughsan immediately started a slow ascent, dragging the fish with him as he rose. He didn't bother to manage his game at the bottom in order to save more of his precious air. I looked at my gauge: 300 pounds. I'd better take a shot fast before I'm down to fumes, I told myself. The school was spooked and moved away from the lethal action, but they did not like the looks of me lurking in the sand with guns resting at my side. Perhaps they'd seen this type of ambush before. I knew I didn't have a lot of time left to chase them down; I needed to draw the fish in somehow.

Ah, the Grant Stoddard dying technique might work. While I've never actually seen my buddy perform his magic, I've imagined it and tried to duplicate the ritual with the few details he divulged in an unguarded moment.

Some years ago after a dive off of Sandy Beach, Grant was on a high, exhilarated with his score of very skittish mu fish (porgy.) In a jubilant moment, he told me the secret of his catch. There was a school of large mu hanging over the lava mound and surrounding reef. They would have nothing to do with him and kept their distance out of gun range. No matter what stalking technique he employed, the fish shunned him. Finally, Grant collapsed in the sand and played dead on his back, gun in hand. Ever so slowly they came in for a look, and Grant came to life with gun blazing. "Bang!" He took out the king of the clan and one mu was in the bag. The scene was often repeated, quite successfully. I was so impressed with his story and the dying technique. I could only imagine how it might have looked.

I tried to make Grant's technique my own and took to improving it where I could. I preferred dying on my stomach rather than my back, so there I was lying on my stomach in the sand trying to get the curious fish in for a look. The fish knew I was there, but they showed no interest in coming any closer. I changed my tactic. Without warning, I feigned whole-body convulsions with my hands and legs twitching like an electrocuted cartoon character out of control. I rolled over on my side and brought my tank to rest on the sand gravel.

My convulsions gained strength as my hand moved erratically, except for the hand that cradled my gun into my stomach with the spear tip well above my forehead for safety. I moved my fins back and forth, stirring up the sand to create the dust cloud of a dying predator in his last gasp of life. My fins made traction with the sand, and I started to move in a circle to get my head away from the school. In that position, when they come in to look, I'd rise up and draw my gun to let loose the spear.

I was doing great, stirring up the sand, grunting in pain, shaking uncontrollably, and finally balancing my back on the tank in the sand. I put the last touches on my death throes with a few grand jerks of the lower legs and a twitching of the head and neck. I blew a massive burst of bubbles from my regulator, as my last spent breath. It was then that I went limp and fell back on my side in the sand. I opened my closed eyes, and slowly peeked to see if the fish bought my charade. My air gauge lay there before me, one hundred pounds! Wow, what was I thinking? Immediately I cut the foolishness and went straight for the surface. I'd have to give the fish an encore performance some other time.

I could see the startled looks of the uku as they swam in closer, almost into shooting range. It's a miracle; the human predator is alive and going to the heavens, the fish must have thought. I slowly made it to a safety stop before the fumes in my tank expired. Hughsan was already on the boat drifting 50 yards away from where I broke the surface. What a productive dive it was.

The last dive of our long weekend found us doing some reconnaissance work. A few years ago, we regularly dove a beat-up old barge in the bay. It fell from our most favored list since it stopped producing enough fish. This sometimes happened whenever we overfished a productive site. The only effective remedy was a reduction of fishing pressure, thus giving the spot some time to recuperate. This break allowed the fish to repopulate free from their worst predators, fishermen.

The ancient Hawaiians had similar issues with over-fishing. Throughout the centuries a system of "Kapu" was established by tribal chiefs. It was a specific law of restriction regarding the use, access, or taking of a resource levied by royal decree. Violation of a posted Kapu could lead to severe punishment or death, depending on the offense. When a certain reef was overfished, or some species of fish became scarce, the chief would put a Kapu or ban on taking fish from the reef, or restrict the fishing of certain species in a specific area.

As a matter of fact, a good number of our dive spots were rotational to some degree. We attempted to check on this barge a couple of times during the last few years, but somehow the spot moved from our location marks or we remembered the marks inaccurately.

A number of large ocean storms had hit our islands during the last two years. We wondered if these unusually strong currents moved the barge from our recorded location. Our dive plan would use the underwater scooters to explore the area using the natural terrain as a guide for our search pattern. If we found it, we'd work the barge and stay on station. When we were done diving we'd surface so the boat could mark it on the new GPS system.

Soon we were on location where the barge should have been. Hughsan and I stepped off the swim step with a forward entry, holding the scooters in one hand and our spears in the other. After a moment of organizing, we descended to the mid-water level and started our scooter search in a high speed motor setting. We'd use this midrange depth level to conserve air while allowing us a broader field of vision.

While our primary mission was to find the barge, we would be perfectly happy to put our search on hold if we spotted fish and hunting interrupted us. Hugh and I were more anxious to drop down to the bottom and shoot fish than we were to cruise on our scooters looking for the sunken craft. Hughsan lead the way forward with me flanking him by a 100 feet or so.

We covered lots of ground using our scooters. Whenever I used this terrific vehicle, I felt like an underwater motorcycle racer. With the muted hum of its motor and the steady forward movement, the aquatic machine took my direction and did all the swimming for me. I just relaxed and rode above and slightly behind its black nylon propeller housing, very practical and most pleasurable. We traveled over undersea hills, wash outs, draws, coral reefs, lava slabs, desert sand patches, scattered mounds of rubble, and ribbon lava ledges searching for our wayward barge.

We moved through an unfamiliar sand draw followed by a long patch of rubble and rocks. There ahead was the dark, crusty outline of the old barge. I was amazed by how far this steel ghost had journeyed. The awesome power of storm currents undoubtedly blew it in toward shore. I put the phenomena out of my mind and prepared for an assault on the massive fish collector. Checking my gauge revealed that I only had 900 pounds of air to work the barge.

Hugh slowed down a bit, and I sped up to close the gap between us. We immediately headed to opposite ends of the structure to coordinate our attack like a wolf pack. The fist signs were positive; it was full of tropicals and reef fish of every type. It was promising ground, but no game fish. Soon I glanced at my dive computer and noticed the pixels were close to the edge of the decompression line and my air supply was too low to be safe.

My dive computer was one of the earliest models on the market. It had a pixel screen for viewing the nitrogen intake and dissipation graphically on the screen. I never pushed the limits unless I had to, so I rose up toward the surface for a safety decompression stop. Hugh was just about done, so we met at 25 foot level and talked with hand gestures.

As we floated above the barge, Hughsan saw two omilu come in from behind me. He lunged forward past my right side, and without hesitation, fired his gun for a direct hit in the gill plate. More fish for the boys.

I rose to 15 feet and checked my dive computer again. It read clear with two pixels worth of safety behind the line. All my dives were tracked in the computer, accounting for multiple dives during multiple days. I floated in safety decompression scanning for game fish. Gazing up at the surface, I could see the waves dancing under the sun's piercing rays. It was mesmerizing. I fell into a peaceful trance. A slight muscle pain developed in my left shoulder. I wondered if I had over-exerted my arm working the scooter.

The scenery from below the skin of the ocean's surface was enthralling. The waves crested with the wind, splashing little beards of foam down their tiny troughs. All was so beautiful. My shoulder still bothered me, so I exercised it doing some exaggerated movements to shake any stiffness out of the extremity. The unexpected sensation changed from discomfort to real pain.

I squeezed my forearm and knew then its slight numbness

wasn't a good sign. It was a suspicious indication that the nitrogen in my blood may be coming out of solution and forming bubbles to block the circulation in my shoulder and arm. It was unlikely that I would be hit with decompression sickness, as my computer was clear. I tried to ignore it, deny it, but the pain would not subside. I floated down a little deeper to 30 feet and continued with my breathing. It didn't make a difference–the pain continued.

Moments later Hughsan and I went up together. The boat had followed our bubbles and was waiting for us. I climbed onboard, removed my gear, and tried to keep the shoulder pain to myself, but I needed help. "Hughsan where's the oxygen? I think I want a boost."

He immediately took an interest. "You okay? You alright?"

I didn't want to alarm anyone, "Yeah, I'll be fine; I just need some ox to give me a little lift. I overworked my arm. I'll be fine!"

He pulled the oxygen pony bottle rig and passed it over. I sat on the motor box and used seven minutes of pure oxygen to flush my system. Each breath brought a slow and gradual reduction of pain. What had built up to a jabbing ice pick in my shoulder socket reduced to a flat butter knife, then to a spoon, and finally down to the pressure of a heavy hand on my shoulder. Within 10 to 15 minutes I was back to normal, my cheery but somewhat shaken self.

We traveled back to the boat locker to clean our gear and prep *It's Time* for storage until the next weekend. Those tasks required an extensive fresh-water cleaning, not just the quick rinse off we used for diving the next day. With everyone doing a certain job, 45 minutes later the boys were heading back to their families with a share of the catch.

The knives returned when I took a hot shower at home. This time they were back with a vengeance. It started as a mid-level grinding of sharp blades in the joint, then escalated to a full force constant knife stabbing. I took three aspirins, skipped dinner, and went immediately to bed. My shoulder burned hot and tingly, but my skin alternated between erratic itching and pin-prick numbness. The pain never subsided. It grew, relentless and unending. I was struck with "the bends," decompression sickness.

In and out of bed, I drank lots of water, ice-packed my shoulder, and took several cold showers in the course of many hours.

This would pass, I thought. It will work itself out, I kept reassuring myself as I lay in bed with throbbing daggers of torture.

Sometime just before midnight I couldn't take it any longer, I hopped in the car and headed to the boat locker for the bottle of oxygen. We always refilled the cylinder and stored it with the other tanks next to our wetsuits. Hunched over, I opened the padlock and turned the lights on. What? There was no oxygen bottle. I paced the locker wondering where it could be. Did someone take it home? Was it misplaced? My first thought was to call Hughsan, but that wasn't a good idea in the wee hours. I went home to take more aspirin and thin my blood. I kept telling myself that a few more cold showers would break it.

Back in bed, I tossed and turned for hours. There would be no relief; the demon was in my shoulder and would not leave. Heat and numbness took over my arm while sadistic knives twisted in my joint. At 3:15 a.m., I went into the kitchen, closed the bedroom door, and called 911 for the recompression chamber. I just have a few questions to ask, I reasoned. Once on the phone, the officer on duty took immediate control and asked question after question... pain, location, dive profile, and on and on.

"Mr. Enos, you must come in now to be examined. I am alerting all personnel to open the facility. Do you know where we are located?" By the seriousness of his tone, I knew there was no escaping this ordeal on my own. I changed clothes and told my wife I was going to the chamber for a checkup.

In the black of night, hunched over the steering wheel of my Jeep Cherokee, I drove to the state decompression chamber at Kewalo Basin Harbor. Alone with my thoughts, I whimpered as I drove and prayed for relief from this unshakable curse. No matter what happens, I'll beg them to rid me of the pain or cut the shoulder off.

The recompression facility was located in an industrial area of the harbor. It wasn't the kind of place civilized people would knowingly seek out in their evening travels. The whole place reeked of fish, diesel fuel, and boat paint. I drove through the twisted terrain of the underbelly of our marine industry desperate for help. In the midst of this darkened chasm, one building stood out, a beacon of hope with lights ablaze. There were a half dozen cars in the parking lot and several people rushing into the facility, "The Bends Chamber." I deserted my vehicle in the parking lot and dragged myself into the building.

A burly fellow, the chief technician, welcomed me and started the interview in the chamber room. I took a seat on a folding chair facing him and the two imposing iron lungs that nearly filled the room behind him. He asked me to describe the particulars of my pain, the intensity, and an endless series of questions on my general health. Then he interrogated me on the profile of my last dive, and worked his way back to the previous dives. Notes were scribbled, erased, and re-scribbled on scratch paper. I assumed he was figuring my dives and how they did or did not conform to the Navy dive tables. Yearning for treatment and impatient for help, I struggled to be cooperative. I felt embarrassed and broken, but I was in too much pain to be concerned about my humiliation.

From one of the medical cabinets, the technician pulled out a small round stainless steel wheel with sharp spikes sawed into its circular edge. It looked like a mini pizza cutter with razor filed teeth. "I'm going to check the feelings in your arm. Tell me if you feel any pain." He moved the wheel freely up and down my forearm slowly and gently. "Anything?" he asked.

"I know you are moving it, but I don't feel any pain or pressure. It just feels hot and numb."

"Okay, let's try it again." Then he continued to roll the spikes with more pressure as the instrument moved up and down my arm. He looked at me for a response.

"No, no pain yet," I sheepishly admitted.

"Well, let me see if the doctor is here yet. I'll be back shortly." Then he left to the office area down the hall.

Chamber technicians continued to arrive and moved in silence as they readied their equipment for operation. It all seemed very exciting as each new arrival was greeted by the crew on station. About 25 minutes later, a medical coat walked into the chamber room. "Hi, I'm Dr. Anderson. How are you feeling?" He read my file as he asked me all the same questions in confirmation of the written record. Then he pulled out his own wheeled instrument from his coat and did his own version of the rolling needles test. I still felt no pain or pressure. When he finished, he got up, turned to the chief and gave him a nod, to which the chief nodded back in approval.

I had to ask, "What's the verdict?"

"You have a case of decompression sickness. We'll see how the first treatment goes." With that I was given a hospital gown and instructed to remove my clothes, watch, and wedding ring, and prepare for the chamber.

At last, I'll get some relief, I hoped. I asked the chief, "Can someone call my wife and let her know I'm in the chamber?" He nodded that he would.

It only took me a moment to undress and exit the changing room in my boxer shorts and a breezy hospital dress that smelled of fresh laundering. The head nurse escorted me to the massive white steel tank. I had all the mystery of a modern sacrificial altar for divers gone astray. It towered above the smaller chamber and stood in the center of this big, barn-like chamber room.

The recompression hatch swung open on a giant steel hinge. The perimeter of the door was encircled with closing levers like you might see on old ship hatches. A series of stair-steps allowed for patient entry from the concrete floor to the elevated unit. The foundry-thick steel door of faded white told the tale of many years of service. I surmised that this must be a surplus navy unit given to the state to help establish the civilian hyperbaric medicine program. As the diver-tech and I started up the stairway, he asked me if I got claustrophobic. I told him I did not.

He motioned me forward. "Crawl in and go past the inner lock of the first chamber to the very end of the second chamber," he said. The massive unit was divided into a main treatment chamber and a smaller transit chamber for pressurization of personnel going in and out of the unit. I crawled in and positioned myself at the very end as instructed. The other attendants closed the hatch behind us as the tech closed the smaller hatch separating the primary chamber from the smaller air-lock.

Once shut in by the double hatches, our only communication outside the metal coffin was limited to a thick glass porthole and a communications counsel with a headset and microphone. After a brief conversation and a few hand signals between Dr. Anderson outside at the control station and the diver-nurse in the chamber, we were slowly pressurized to a depth of 220 feet.

With this mixed-gas recompression treatment, the nitrogen

bubbles that floated in my body and shoulder would be crushed. The goal of the ten hour session would be to eliminate all harmful nitrogen bubbles by re-pressuring them back into a nitrogen solution of no consequence. Through calculated treatment formulas, various gases, decompression times, varied depths, and careful rates of ascent, Dr. Anderson would see how my affliction responded to his treatment.

The hiss of compressed air entering the chamber made for a mental tension of sorts. Loud sounds of metal valves clacking and the screeching of equipment outside the tank overpowered me as we descended to the depths of increased pressure. Out of the observation port, no bigger than the width of a dinner plate, the technician signaled our progress with a diver's okay sign. As we went deeper I felt a consistent reduction in my pain as the knives slowly withdrew from my shoulder. I'm not sure at what depth it occurred, but at some point, there was a grand re-stabbing of pain in my shoulder so acute that I screamed out in agony. The nurse signaled my distress so the tech stopped our descent, took us up a bit, and then started down again with a slower rate of pressure. The re-stabbing of the shoulder was the grand catharsis of pain. Relief! They continued to run the pressure down in their treatment plan. Within a few minutes, I was at depth, physically drained, relaxed and peaceful.

After a short time at 220 feet, they started a gradual and exceedingly slow ascent up to shallower depths. At some prescribed depth level another technician entered through the airlock and the first one left to decompress in the entry chamber before exiting. Their operating procedure was to never leave the patient to decompress alone, so they rotated nurse technicians in and out without exposing them to dangerous levels of nitrogen. By the time the third technician entered the chamber, I was relaxed and feeling euphoric.

At this change-out of personnel, when the hissing of redirected air subsided, a petite brunette entered the main chamber. I don't know if I was goofy from the gases, strung out after the ordeal, or if I was inspired by not having to cut my shoulder off, but this wonderful angel with a bikini body and a pixie haircut took my senses away. She was young, beautiful, and so compassionate; I surrendered myself to her immediately. I was like soft powdered sand waiting for her current of charm to take me away. This young lady seemed so innocent, bubbly, and full of understanding and patience.

From the moment she crawled into my tomb I was intrigued. She asked very personal questions and wanted to know everything about me and my life. Somehow, this angel was naturally interested, and yet so intense on everything that we talked about. I felt totally at ease with her. She must have had some spiritual connection to injured divers, or as I imagined, just me in particular.

I was entranced as we rambled on and on about everything imaginable. Here I was locked in this metal enclosure with a heavenly guardian from another time and place. As romantic ideas surfaced, I resisted and suppressed every one of them. I was married and infidelity was out of the question. I kept telling myself that I was delusional and misinterpreting her kindness for signs of affection. After a while when there was a natural pause in our conversation, she turned again to the topic of diving.

"How long have you been diving?" she asked.

"Since I was 16, but 18 with an open water certification. Are you a diver?"

"Oh yes, the whole team, we're all divers. Is this your first time in the chamber?

"Yes, of course," I replied indignantly. She seemed somewhat amused with my attitude. It puzzled me. "Why do you ask? I'm getting an odd feeling from you," I said.

An unhurried grin came over her face as she tried to phrase her words carefully. "We get a lot of locals who've been in here two or three times. There's something about divers. They keep coming back with the bends. They think they're invincible; it's part of the disease!"

I was quick to respond, "You won't see me back. I'm not getting bent again."

She just smiled.

I kept my silence, contemplating the implications of her statement. I didn't ever feel like I was invincible in the water, I only felt at peace–sometimes exhilarated, sometimes relaxed, but more often than not, at peace with myself and nature. It was more of a spiritual thing in the water, like the understanding of life and God that I felt when I was a youngster at church. It was a whole different attitude than one of power and invincibility. There was much to think about and lots of time to do it being locked in this metal room.

Sometime around 8:30 in the morning my dive buddies started arriving at the chamber on their way to work. The coconut telegraph must have quickly spread the news of my injury. All I could do to greet them was press my face to the glass porthole and smile with an okay hand signal. Every now and then I would lean over into the porthole to see what was going on and who was coming and going in the chamber room. It was uncomfortable leaning over in a squatting position, but it was the only way to see out beyond my pressurized lung.

Crawman was the first to roll in with a giant box of pastries for the staff. He knew most of the technicians from his wife's diving accident several years earlier. It was a very serious incident that required three weeks of hyperbaric treatment. Everyone agreed that she was lucky to survive and lived to walk with only a slight limp. Craig was a lovable character. I watched him entertain the medical technicians with his great sense of humor and animation. All the smiling faces gathered for coffee, doughnuts, and conversation.

Five or ten minutes later, Killer made his way through the door. He and the Crawman chatted as Craw introduced him to the staff. Soon Killer was engaged in conversation with the chief tech, while Craw continued with his joking. Gordon arrived soon after to join the social. Gordon seemed to know most of the people in the room and those he didn't know he was making an effort to meet. Not far behind entered Hughsan and V dressed for work. They all greeted each other and soon they were visiting with the nurses and technicians.

There must have been a great deal of laughter and party noise coming from the room, for a few moments later Dr. Anderson and Dr. Blankenship came out of their offices to check on the merriment. They, too, ended up joining in on the reunion. Other diver friends came to visit, and soon there was a small crowd in the chamber room milling about, telling each other dive stories over morning coffee and doughnuts.

From my lockup, I couldn't hear a word of what was said. I just saw their lips moving, animated facial expressions, and changing body movements that told me there was a party going on without me. They were having a fun time; every once in awhile someone would step up to the porthole to check on me. I'd tell myself, it's about time someone remembered I was stuck in here.

Our local dive community was small; it seemed that everybody knew each other and their diving preferences. The festivities at the chamber reminded me of an early morning family reunion breakfast. After some time, the boys went off to work, only to return late in the afternoon to check me out of the chamber for an early dinner with the hard-core divers. By the time we were done at Kanoa's Restaurant, I drove home exhausted to a waiting bed.

The next morning I checked into the chamber without formal procedure at the civilized hour of nine. There were the familiar faces of the staff, but my brunette nurse was nowhere to be seen. I was very disappointed but figured that it must be for the best. My thoughts moved on to the treatment. Today's session would take me down to the 120 foot depth level and then a slow decompression up for eight hours. The technicians came and went without much conversation or incident.

I was released late in the afternoon free of all pain and scheduled for a physical with full body x-rays. The results would be sent to Dr. Anderson for analysis. An appointment was scheduled for late the next week to go over the results.

When I got the reminder call for the consultation, the arrangement seemed suspicious. The scheduler was specific: the doctors requested that my wife attend. If for any reason, she was unavailable, the appointment would be rescheduled. This seemed very curious to me. It was my body, why was it so important for her to attend? It didn't make any sense. Her doctors never asked me to attend her medical appointments.

We both showed up for the doctor's meeting the following week where my wife and I were escorted to the conference room. Dr. Blankenship, the director of the facility, and Dr. Anderson, the case physician, both entered the room and were quite cordial. While they seemed relaxed and friendly as we exchanged greetings, both had a serious manner about them. Dr. Anderson asked me how my recovery was progressing. Of course, I reported that all was well with my shoulder. I was free of pain.

The doctors went into a synopsis of my condition and then

moved in for the kill. Dr. Anderson blurted it out, "You have to give up diving." I was stunned. Without taking a breath, Anderson went into a description of my decompression accident and built his case for the necessity of his recommendation. Both doctors were careful to direct their comments to my wife, while they looked at me only occasionally to keep me in the discussion.

Why are they talking to her? I wondered. Did they expect her to be the enforcer? Their tactic was misdirected. I'm the patient, not her. Dr. Anderson explained that I suffered an unusual bone hit, not the normal nerve or tissue damage. When he put it in layman's terms, I began to understand my injury. As the nitrogen was sucked into my body over the days of diving, it was absorbed throughout my tissues, muscles, and over time into my bones. For whatever reasons, my body held the gases longer or expelled the gases slower than the dive tables. My body physiology required more time to safely dissipate nitrogen. When I surfaced "clear" according to my Edge Computer, I was never clean. Dive after dive, I was accumulating more nitrogen and expending less than the computer tables accounted for. At some point, the nitrogen that went into my bones came out of solution and tried to break free through the bone joint.

They repeated the "no diving" over and over again throughout the conference. I might have been in denial. "How could this be?" I asked Dr. Anderson. "I'm a safe diver. My computer showed me cleared through multiple dives, never any decompression time!" I was bewildered and depressed.

Dr. Anderson elaborated. "It just happens. Each body is distinctive and reacts to nitrogen and pressure differently. The dive tables used in computers are based on data gathered from the Navy diver population, all young, physically fit, healthy people. Your body may not fit the table profile; you may have other medical issues that we don't know about."

What a disaster. What a bummer! It was obvious that my life had been changed and would never be the same. My thoughts drifted in and out of the conversation, which by this time, was between my wife and the doctors. What would I do with my weekends? What would become of my friends, my dive buddies? These questioned plagued me as I gave the doctors a put-on look of attention. I was in disbelief. Finally I interrupted their conversation, "Dr. Anderson, this isn't possible."

He looked me straight in the eyes, trying to reach me. "We do medical research here. If we throw twelve cats in the chamber, bend them all, and then decompress each according to a specific table, one in the group will get decompression sickness. We don't know why. It just happens that way." I remained quiet and withdrawn and left the meeting with little hope of a future.

The next weekend I went over to the dive locker to pick up my gear and do a quick boat driver job for the boys. I was happy to be with my friends again, even if I wasn't diving.

It wasn't any surprise to me when I heard the chorus of well-intentioned divers comment on my spearfishing future. I was at the helm piloting *It's Time* through the marina while the boys prepared their gear for a quick assault on Split Rock. It would be a quick in-and-out affair as there was a birthday party for one of Hughsan's sons that we were attending late in the afternoon.

The boys were busy ribbing each other in anticipation of the dive ahead. Then the conversation shifted to me and a barrage of advice came from Hughsan. He came at me with a half serious smile to stir and comfort my emotions, "So the doctors told you that you couldn't dive. Let's face it Brynos, what could they say? They had to tell you not to dive. It's their job. They're doctors, that's what they have to say!" Craw shook his head in approval. Hughsan became more encouraged with Craig's support.

I questioned Hughsan, "They had to say that? It had nothing to do with me?" Then I waited for his next pearl of wisdom.

"It was for the medical records, they had to tell you no diving. It's for their protection, for the malpractice insurance. It's their insurance company's requirement!" He continued on, "They tell everybody not to dive again. Imagine if they said you're approved for diving, and a year later you get hit again and are crippled for life. You get an attorney and sue them all. How could they ever defend themselves? What's the doctor going to say, 'Yeah, I told him he could dive? I didn't know he would get bent again.' There goes a multi-million dollar settlement, reputations tarnished, insurance premiums skyrocket. No, he's got to tell you no diving, no matter what."

Craw added his two cents. "Yeah, Brynos, they stacked all the cards against you, for their own protection. Do what you want to do... dive!" I shook my head, not knowing what to make of my buddies' philosophy.

Then Craw took over and started with his own brand of dive logic. "Brynos, what age do you think the average person lives to?" He waited, but seeing that I wasn't inclined to respond, he answered the question himself. "What do you say? Maybe eighty if a guy's lucky?"

"Yeah, okay," I reluctantly responded.

"Let's say that you make it to eighty. I've got a question for you: do you need a hundred percent of your bones at age eighty?" He paused again for a moment. "I mean, do your bones have to be perfect when you die? This is an important question." I was puzzled with his reasoning and waited for him to continue. "If they do an autopsy and found your bones were only seventy percent whole, what's the difference? You're dead! You're not going to need them where you're going. So live your life. You go ahead and dive. So you die at seventy or eighty and you've got most of your bones left, good enough! You don't need them to be a hundred percent."

Craw was quite pleased with himself and the arguments he put to me and the dive mates. He moved back to his cylinder and continued tanking his regulator, beaming with the iron-clad argument so eloquently professed for my continued diving. I just smiled.

Sometime later, like a forgotten fragment of conversation, Craw questioned me from across the boat, "What do you think?" I shrugged my shoulders in an, "I give up with you guys" gesture and continued driving the boat in silence. Both of my buddies were pleased with their courtroom-like arguments. We continued under the bridge and out the channel to sea as I pondered this twisted logic and its faint glimmer of hope.

CHAPTER SIX

AFTER DIVING

Giving up diving "cold turkey" was tough. Sadness haunted me as if I had lost some part of my inner self. Diving was my hobby, exercise routine, and the base for my social connections. But more importantly, it was my unique connection with nature, a place of interaction with a higher power, my means of accepting this finite life, and a way of making things right within me.

My parents found their spiritual purpose through the Catholic Church. My mom was active in the Altar Rosary Society and my dad the Holy Name Society. They were both truly enriched by their religious connections. As a child, I was encouraged to participate in church activities and even served as an altar boy. There was a time that I could feel the power of God through the church, but the Almighty had other plans and sent me to the ocean instead. I would find my relationship with the water a conduit to the Godly forces in me and in nature.

As I grew up with the ocean, a deeper understanding of life was formed in me through my relationship with the sea. My initial childhood fear of the water was a dread of the ocean's vast hidden unknowns. It was an eight-year-old's fear to venture beyond the protective reef. But as I got older and traveled farther out into the ocean, I became more confident about myself and my relationship with the sea. Slowly, each experience in the water led me to appreciate God's grand design and meticulous handiwork. He gave me a gift to help me feel welcomed and loved in his home. I grew to feel that all living creatures originally came from the sea and would eventually return to the sea. I would be no different.

The ocean steadily became a very natural place for me. Whether riding its waves of pure energy or submerging myself in its watery mass, I felt most comfortable here in the sea. I would come to spend most days after school and weekends at the beach. It calmed me and helped me handle the stress of growing up.

My parents were supportive of my need to be in the water. When an aunt or uncle would ask my mom where I was, her response was something like, "You know Bryan, he's at the beach." Later when it became my lifestyle, she'd say, "He's at the Church of the Sea."

With the paranoia of further demolishing my bones and diving no longer feasible, I revisited my old surfing haunts. Surfing became unattractive to me years ago because of rude lineup crowds and the dangers of my nearsightedness. However, bodysurfing was still an option. Sandy Beach and Makapuu were world-class surf breaks only minutes away from the house.

I got to know both surf breaks intimately during my high school and college lifeguard years. Sandy Beach was my number one break. It pumped out a fast shore break with quick clean swells, hollow tubes, and shifting lineups that favored an experienced surfer.

Bodysurfing Sandy Beach was wonderful. There was no better break a surfer could ask for, except maybe a little more water to fall into where the wave broke on shore. Sandy's break was notorious for a shallow impact zone and freefalls right into water depths of 1 or 2 feet. It could be hazardous to the unskilled and skilled alike.

When I tried to surf Sandy's now, I came away with mixed feelings. The thrill of dropping into a large building swell, the challenge of cutting across the face of raw ocean, the excitement of getting locked in the tube for a second of glory, and the satisfaction of exiting the tube with a perfectly timed cut out all provided excitement and exhilaration. But somehow surfing felt different this time around.

The surf lineup was filled with young faces, and I was feeling like an old man amongst high school surfers. With my graying hair and mature features, I was visibly older. It was weird competing with teenagers for waves. I saw it in their eyes; they knew I wasn't one of them. I was a "wanna be," an adult whose time had come and gone. They looked at me like I could have been their dad, or worse yet, a senior citizen. I was a marked man of age, and I didn't like it.

I remembered my own thoughts in the surf during high school. These kids must be thinking the same things now that I thought then. The mental speak went something like: "This is our beach. Our waves. We rule the shore break. You're an old guy. What are you doing here? Don't get in my way!" For me, the only thing different was that I was the old guy, not the surfer on the biggest waves.

In my youth, I was a pack leader chasing shifting wave pockets and making the most daring takeoffs. Extreme takeoffs, 360s, and all the other crazy stuff was my stock in trade. Now, I was working hard to stay in the pack with everybody else. My once perfect cut-outs, under-wave escapes, and charge back to the lineups weren't as good as they used to be. I was far from being top-notch. Going over the falls more times than I would admit suggested that I had lost my competitive advantage. First-rate bodysurfing was an intense sport, and sadly, I was no longer first-rate.

I soon came to realize that at this time in my life, surfing was not the cure for the absence of diving. With diving, I didn't see the younger faces, only the ageless face of nature. Surfing put me in competition with others, and it was intimidating not being the strong surfer that I once was. I didn't need to have that constant reminder slapping me in the face while out in the water. After a few dozen attempts to find my new relationship with the ocean through bodysurfing, I realized that it could never replace diving.

Snorkeling turned out to be a passable substitute for scuba diving. Similar to scuba but more limiting, snorkeling leaves you totally dependent on the air in your lungs for depth. I could float on the surface all day long and only dive when something of interest offered itself to me. I loved snorkeling, but it wasn't diving. As a kid I snorkeled all through Moanalua Bay, and later as a young adult I free-dove island beaches after work as a lifeguard.

In my early years, mask, fins, and snorkel were always in my beat-up Volkswagen van, as was my surfboard that was chained to the inside ceiling. My dive gear was in a hidden compartment under the homemade bed outfitted in the back. It was a terrific life working the beaches and then diving or surfing after work.

Free-diving the shoreline was an easy passion. Pull up to any beach, park the van, do a beach entry, and dive to your heart's content. When you're done, exit the water, change clothes, and head back home. The best beaches had interesting underwater topography or abundant reefs close in to shore. Long, sandy beaches popular for sunbathing usually offered very little reef or undersea terrain to captivate my interest.

While I tried to reinvigorate my surfing and snorkeling interests, scuba diving and spearfishing kept nagging at me. My loss was always on my mind, especially the notion of not being able to shoot big fish again. I knew my personal limitations of sticking to a course of action that I had not fully embraced. The "no diving" order was one of those difficult orders that I was reluctant to accept.

There were options for diving with the boys, but none of them was completely satisfying. I also knew the dive group could be persuasive, especially when they believed my continued diving was harmless. Craw and Hughsan had even questioned how many of my bones I needed to take to the grave. I certainly knew my dear friends and how well they would tempt me into diving again. My strong resolve and self control remained a question for me.

The attraction to tank dive again would be too great to continue on exclusively with the gang. Sadly, I relinquished my part owner interest in *It's Time* and used the proceeds to order a new boat for shallow-diving the outer reefs. A few months later I took possession of a brand new, 19-foot Glaspros with twin 70-horsepower Johnsons. Outfitted with all the standard safety equipment and bottom painted for the backyard dock, it would stand ready for me to work the reef or cocktail cruise with the friends at a moment's notice. Christened *Bones*, it would serve as both a reminder and warning of my condition.

While *Bones* afforded me more options with the ocean, I still spent lots of time with the *It's Time* gang of divers. I drove the boat for the deep divers and they drove for my shallow water dives. Somehow it got started, and it soon stuck: the boys renamed me "Bones." I accepted it in stride, preferring it to my old nicknames of "Rocky" and "Brynos."

Life was good again. Captain Bones drove *Bones* all over the east end of Oahu and did a number of Molokai trips with and without the *It's Time* divers. I was doing well with my new life for awhile, but life being what it is, it sometimes takes you where it will. Often, one thing leads to another, and another, without any concern for your well-intentioned plans. It wasn't very long before I was full-on scuba diving with the group again.

It was an innocent enough dive profile, 20 to 30 feet along the reef. How could it hurt me? I reasoned. Then I started to stretch my profile to the 40 foot range. The boys were quite willing to accept my limitations and accommodate my shallow-water diving. Craw knew my concerns and soon talked me into using a pony bottle of pure oxygen to clean my bones before surfacing. He rigged up the whole system. I'd hook up a pony cylinder to my super eighty tank, fill it with pure oxygen, and use a separate oxygen cleaned regulator. I could dive, shallow or deep, and with ten minutes of pure ox at 10 feet, I'd actually be repairing my bones. I liked that concept. Maybe it was the kind of therapy the doctors couldn't recommend because of liability reasons, but it would be home therapy just the same.

Craw set me up with a large welding oxygen bottle for filling, special stainless steel whips and pony bottles for the special backpack rig he fashioned. The ox rig was a fabulous system, a main tank of regular air, a pony bottle strapped to its side with pure oxygen. Oxygen would only be used above 10 feet for dispelling nitrogen; using it at greater depths could be dangerous or even lethal because of pressurized oxygen toxicity problems. In no time at all, I was set for ocean ox therapy and some diving to boot.

Even though it seemed perfect, I still had a few reservations about storing oxygen in my garage. When we were installing the new system I asked the Craw about oxygen being in the storage area with paints and solvents. "Are you sure this thing isn't going to explode or burn down the house?" I asked.

"Bones, it's perfectly safe. You couldn't burn this thing if you put a match to it. It's only dangerous when you flood combustibles with oxygen. It's harmless otherwise."

"I don't mean to question you, but are you really sure?"

"Here, let me show you." With that, he took a striker from

his pocket and opened the valve discharging a steady stream of oxygen. "Click, click, click," the striker sparked steady as he kept it to the valve.

"Craw! What the hell are you doing?" I grabbed his hand and took the striker away from the green bottle. "I'm going to have a heart attack!"

He ignored me. "See, no problem. Not even an explosion!" he boasted proudly.

I started to relax, "Okay, okay I believe you. Now, what about me sucking on oxygen from a welder's bottle? Shouldn't I be using medical oxygen?"

"Oxygen is oxygen!" I'll tell you what Junior Boy at Gasco Welding Supply told me when I asked him the same question years ago. He looked me straight in the eye, then pointed up at the ceiling, "See that pipe coming from the back room? See where it splits off in a T? One side is welder's oxygen, the other side is medical oxygen. They both come from the same storage tank. If you want all the pretty equipment, you can pay more, but you have to have a prescription."

It seemed reassuring. I figured if it was good enough for Craw, it should be good enough for me.

Soon I was back scuba diving with the boys all the time. This time around, aware of my propensity for nitrogen absorption, I limited my depth to under 100 feet and became more cautious about my dive profiles. I was so cautious that I'd dial back two measures of safety on my dive computer to keep me clean of nitrogen. I didn't mind getting less bottom time; I'd much rather dive safely. Thanks to the Craw I had oxygen therapy after my dives, so I was extra safe for a lifetime of diving.

Some months later my diving would become an issue for me again. It was a Saturday morning and *It's Time* was short on divers. Hughsan called early with a proposal I had to accept, "If you drive for V and me, we'll pick you up at your dock, take you wherever you want to dive, and drop you back at the house again. We'll take care of all the clean up."

How could any respectable diver refuse an offer like that? Tank, dive gear, and spear guns were waiting on my boat dock when Hughsan pulled up. I ran out of the house, jumped on the boat, and we were off to Moanalua Bay. Weather conditions were perfect. We chatted and caught up with the news on the way out to our dive spots. Hugh and V decided to do the Shark's Cave, leaving me with Chris and Jamie's traps. I would have been delighted to do either spot, as both were on my list of favorites.

Hugh and V prepared for diving like an old married couple. Hughsan would get the gear out and organize while V attended to her personal needs: ponytail, sunscreen, and the like. Then she worked on Hugh with the sunscreen and other kindly touches. He'd tanked her vest and helped her with all that she required. V was quite capable of doing it all herself, but she allowed Hughsan to wait on her just the same. Underwater, the tables were turned; she waited on him. V carried the catch bag and an extra three-prong spear, assisting wherever required. She even told him when to come up if he pushed the limits for too much bottom time. It was a hand-and-glove deal. Hughsan was lucky to have a woman that could do all this diving and still doll up like a supermodel.

Soon we circled the drop zone. Hugh shouted a few last-minute adjustments and then both were in the water heading down for a run at Shark's Cave. There would be 45 minutes to kill before they'd surface, so the motors were turned off to let the wind push me on a slow drift toward Diamond Head. I used the time to prepare my gear and keep a casual lookout for them in case they came up early or had an emergency.

A short time later a red flag at the tip of a three-prong popped up some 300 yards away from the boat back toward Koko Head. Almost instantaneously a series of short bursts from Hugh's high-pitched rescue whistle pierced the ocean calm. I went to the helm, started the boat, and motored over to pick them up. V gave me the "okay" sign with her arm on the top of her head. I did the same with my fingers, acknowledging that I understood. When they were both onboard, Hughsan took the helm and started the short drive to Chris and Jamie's Traps.

I prepared for the dive with my full-body wetsuit and weight belt with dangling catch pin and bag. Hugh came back to help me with my tank while V took the helm. Slipping into my fins, I grabbed my long-gun and three-prong and waited for the final call. Hughsan went back to the helm, "Ready, Bones?" With the regulator in my mouth, I responded with an affirmative grunt.

He shouted depth readings as he watched the depth finder and rechecked the lineup, "Just a minute, Bones." He waited as we drifted down to his chosen target. "Now! You're over it, just outside of the reef, slightly Koko Head side."

"Splash!" I fell over backward on the upwind side of the boat. The water was cool but comfortable on my face. The entry bubbles cleared, I adjusted my gear, and turned down to swim for the bottom. The reef was there in front of me... on target. The clarity was exquisite. The sun's piercing rays lit up the bottom like a sugar white beach.

A slow, sweeping current moved from the Koko Head to the Diamond Head expanse of the reef. This spot was small enough to cover on one dive with the right strategy but too large to take down without planning and good currents. I calculated my dive plan for the favorable drift and quickly swam to the bottom at an angle toward the Koko Head end of the reef. Once at the bottom where the current was weaker, I swam against the current for a short distance to arrive at the very top of the reef. Then, I'd start my hunt of Chris and Jamie's traps. I'd use my "bread and butter" hunting routine to maximize my seafood return. I wasn't interested in waiting for trophy fish; I wanted as many edible fish as I could spear.

At the upper edge of the long reef complex was a 3 foot ledge rising from the sand to form a shelf-like plateau. This mini-ridge defined the outer position of the reef which separated it from the desert of sand that traveled out to sea. The reef moved 100 yards or so gradually back to shore to an inside reef area that vanished into rubble, jagged lava outcroppings, and small cutbacks. The whole area was in the 70 foot range. I was confident that my new-found caution and oxygen therapy would work just fine for these shallow diving profiles.

Once I arrived at the trap located at the start of the ledge line, I found it sparsely populated with non-edible angelfish and tropicals. A quick u-turn got me moving down the reef ridge with the current. Swimming 4 feet above the lava line, I dipped down a couple of times to investigate possible signs of game. It turned out that these stops were a result of wishful thinking... no spinies, parrots, squid, or other fish in hiding. I scanned the outer sandbanks for free-swimming fish and studied the rubble reef at the sand line to check for feeding parrots, inquisitive uku, or one of Hughsan's favorites, the grey reef snapper.

I was making good progress down the reef when another of Jamie's traps showed itself in the forked ledge slot. This was a section where the ledge split with one structure angling out to deeper water, while the other continued on before sweeping toward shore in a wide arc around the reef. My vision focused, and there she was–the icebox! Full of goodies! I mused. Ahead of me was a trap loaded with fish. I prepared myself for a haul of fish and swam over to take a position at the entrance of the trap. I put my long-gun on the top of the cage and looked for parrots or other edible fish. Plenty of fish scrambled about, but only one lone blue retired to the back of the trap. It was an emotional letdown, staring at a trap full of fish with only one good fish to work with. I made the best of it and told myself that I would be happy with whatever the sea provided.

A quick shooting opportunity arose when the clouds of smaller fish moved to reveal a bashful parrot hiding in the corner. I stretched my pole spear rubber and let loose the shaft with three stainless steel prongs. "Slam!" The spear stopped with a thud as the parrot was pushed into the chicken wire at the back of the cage. The noble fish fought to get away, but its scrap was only halfhearted.

The parrot was solid on the spear, so I pulled it to the front entrance and reached in to stabilize it for removal. This wasn't a normal, healthy, big blue parrot. Whoa, this fish is pretty beat up; it's starving, I thought. The parrot languished at the end of my spear. Patches of missing scales, a few shallow cuts, and a battered head told me that this poor fish was near starvation and repeatedly tried to break free of the trap for days if not weeks. Parrots eat corals, and while there were all kinds of reef fish to eat, he could not ingest any of them. It was a sad sight.

I put the fish out of its misery by killing it with my thumb and index finger in the eye sockets and placed it in the bag. The fish would be treated to nourishing a diver and his family, a far more fitting end to its life than dying of starvation and being cannibalized by the other fish.

I finished up at the trap and swam to hunt the inside fork of the ledge, looking for lobsters and parrots. There were sea urchins, tropicals, and a pair of cowries, but nothing that caught my interest. Soon I was at the end of the ledge where it intersected with a pull back into the main reef. I planned to work this bigger ledge for a while and then swim over the sand patch to a cluster of three lava tables the size of small houses. The lava structures stood on their own plots of sand some yards away like beacons in the distance. The sand patch and surrounding area between the ridge and lava tables provided a good shooting area for free swimmers. The last of Jamie's traps was kept in front of the lava table farthest away from the ledge.

I arrived at the ledge and slid down the 6 foot rock face to the undercut in the sand. It was so relaxing floating in slightly negative buoyancy; I sank effortlessly with my long-gun drawn ahead in hopes of shooting a nice ulua in hiding. It would be a rare shot, but it was still in the realm of possibility. A couple of omilu were more realistic, but even that would be a generous gift.

My relaxed body slid down to the sand poised for shooting. Surprise! Holy smoke! There I was, my head under the ledge, staring face to face with a white-tipped reef shark nearly 5 feet long. Beneath him was another white tip lying in the sand. They didn't move a muscle. The dark slant in their white eyes stared me down. They warned me boldly, leave us alone, or you'll regret it! Immediately, I arched my body back like a parachute to slow my descent. I skidded to a stop and slowly reversed direction with minimum body movement.

There I was with my bleeding parrot ringing the dinner bell, floating behind me like an appetizer spreading its enticing smells to invite the creatures into the 225 pound main course... me! I might have been an entree item on a fancy dinner menu for them, "Fine white Portuguese meat, served raw, wrapped in a black wetsuit garnish. A treat for discriminating tastes." This situation could get very serious.

I didn't resort to panicky behavior, instead calmly started my withdrawal. My mind raced. If he does this, I'll have to do that! There was lots of air in my tank, I had two guns to work with, and a previous shark-repelling experience that said I could fend them off. They held their positions calmly. Then, I remembered my buddy the Craw. I replayed all his nagging comments on how you have to threaten their lives.

"They're cowards. They're just looking for an easy lunch. Sharks look for the weak, the sick, the lonely, and then they purge them from the food chain like wild dogs," Craw constantly ranted.

His advice was seared into my brain. "You tell 'em, 'I'm going to eat you and your whole family ...cousins, uncles, and aunties.'" I slowed my retreat. My courage exploded. I stopped mid-water about 6 feet away from the sharks. My teeth clenched down on the regulator mouth piece in defiance, my facial muscles hardened into a scowl, my neck tightened, and my head pushed forward.

"Punks! You don't scare me! I'll kick your freaking ass! I'll eat you! I'm the man, Mafatu! Not the boy from the stream!" I felt empowered. I waited there strong and brave, having slapped their faces with a gentleman's white glove in an honorable challenge. I floated there in defiance, bloody fish and all, waiting to pounce on them, ready to eat them alive.

The sharks continued to lay there as I first found them. They didn't move or show the slightest interest. I floated with my chest erect, standing my ground. My breathing slowed as my body bulged forward. I waited for a reaction, but none came. I wondered if this was a standoff. Have I shown them that I'm not going to be their lunch? Are they afraid that I'll tear them apart? Or, are they just not interested in me? I couldn't figure on an answer at the moment. I looked at them more intently with my evil eye, studying their features and individual differences. They continued at rest. I played my threatening "I'll eat you" persona floating in contempt.

I told the sharks how it would be. "This is my line in the water. You'll not pass it without consequence." My new attitude and bold offense was pleasing to me. It was so different than the absolute terror of death I experienced in the Marshalls. The brainwashing Craw and the boys gave me must have taken hold. My next trip to the Marshall Islands would be a quest for personal revenge at Maloelap, and this was the best practice ever.

A doubt cracked my stainless steel armor. Am I crazy? Suddenly more realistic thinking surfaced. Why am I here with a chip on my shoulder daring these sharks to knock it off? I'm taunting these lounging teeth into a confrontation they aren't interested in. Wouldn't it be smarter for me to move on? I had made my point and stood my ground, but now it was time to get the hell out of here.

With more seasoned rationality, I turned away and swam on to the three lava plateaus. It was not a withdrawal from danger but a continuance of my hunting. The fact that these hunting grounds were down-current of the lounging dangers didn't threaten my manhood either.

A quick finning got me close to the center of the lava tables. The far inside table looked devoid of game, so I traveled to the two structures on the outside of the grouping. There ahead of me was the rock structure with Jamie's trap. From a distance it looked full, but I wouldn't know what was in it until I could get a closer view. I swam over to the trap; it was full of tropicals and reef fish of no consequence. Just to be sure, I hovered over the cage for a moment. No, no fish for me today.

At the last lava mound I readied myself for a full search for anything that I might take for the dinner table. I scoured the lava flow, indentations, cracks, and crevices. Nothing edible was to be found, and soon I ran out of hunting territory. Since I had enough air for a bit more action, I decided to make a long journey over the sand desert before reaching the artificial tire reef far down current.

I arched my swimming angle upward and traveled with the current over the long sandy valley. It was gorgeous, with clear water, bleached white sand, and lots of shell tracks visible where critters had come out at night to search for food. Rising to the 20-foot depth level to save air, I swam hard to make the long crossing. Soon the black tire cement foot encasements lay ahead. I started my descent and kept a good distance from the bottom until I found something of interest.

After some time, with no real hunting action and low on air, I surfaced to find the boat ready for my pickup. Although I was shy on fish, it was a terrific dive that tested my courage and changed my shark behavior. While the real life-and-death test would come on our upcoming trip to Maloelap, I felt like I was on my way to becoming shark-proof.

We drove back to the marina happy after another fine day of diving. I told Hughsan and V that I saw two white tips under the ledge who weren't the least bit interested in me. They didn't have to know it was the first test of a shark killer in the making.

It's Time slipped into the boat dock at the house. I tied her off with just one line to give me some time to unload my gear. The wife came out to say hello and visit while I finished tending to the equipment. It wasn't very long before *It's Time* pulled out and headed back to the Esplanade. Both my wife and I were at the patio window waving goodbye when she indignantly asked, "You're not going to be diving all the time with them, are you?"

With that stinging question, all the great joy of the day evaporated. An overwhelming gloom overtook my emotions. I could not help but retaliate, "That's it, I've had enough, I'm done. We're getting a divorce," I stammered. Blurting out this unmentionable thought in rage, the logic of parting ways soon became a calming, tangible solution to my marital unhappiness.

In the days to come, I weighed and reweighed my decision very carefully. I did not take this course of action lightly. Our marriage had been difficult for many years but this incident was just the last unhappiness that broke my strained marital life. Some of the dive boys vented their marital problems on the boat to the confidence of their buddies, but that was not me. My problems were my own and stayed my own all these years. Both my wife and I knew our marriage had been in trouble for a long time.

We were both good people, but just not good enough to be what the other person needed in life. From the beginning there were ups and downs and certain issues that we never learned to overcome. I knew now that our lives would be best served by parting ways. Our thorny marital problems got worse after the bends and my return to spearfishing and diving. Eventually our relationship became intolerable.

During the next year or two all the details of closing an old life and starting a new one evolved. It seems that when God closed one door he opened another for me to continue my journey of personal growth and self-discovery. Both of us went our ways to build strong new lives. That was how it was as I moved forward to enjoy life as a single person.

It took me some time to learn the difficulties of combining an active single life with a passionate diving life. Maybe I was slow to learn or didn't want to learn, but staying out to all hours of the morning at Waikiki nightclubs and diving hard all day was a recipe for exhaustion. I certainly didn't want clubbing to inter-fere with my diving, but on the other hand, the excitement of the club scene was a real attractant.

It became a battle to maintain both lifestyles, but I knew that one would have to give way to the other for me to survive. After a night out on the town it was common for me to show up at the boat lethargic, having spent all my energy dancing the night away. The boys were patient, but I still had to pull my weight on the boat and shoot my fair share of fish. They weren't about to baby me just because I didn't get enough sleep. Eventually the partying slowed and the diving became the focus of my social activities.

I brought a few girls around to meet the divers over the months that followed. On occasion, I would bring someone to our fish dinners or to a social occasion for one of the divers' families. For the most part, the boys were warm and friendly, but there was one girl I was fond of that the boys gave me a hard time about.

Their consensus was that we weren't well-matched and they took it upon themselves to let me know. While they didn't ever call her "the black widow," they started making jokes about how men could fall prey to the kiss of a black widow. I tried to ignore much of their teasing as I knew it was all in fun, but with Craw as the ringleader, they could drive me to the end of my patience with their ribbing. After one dive in particular, I was about to lose my composure with Craig.

Dusk crept in as Craw and I blasted back through the Hawaii Kai Channel after a late afternoon dive. We'd hoped to make it back to the house for a hot tub and beers before it got too late in the evening. As soon as we crossed under the bridge, I throttled back *Bones* to a slow, 5 knot, no-wake speed.

Craw drove for my Smitty's Reef dive and I worked the boat for him at Mount Terrace. Craw loved this spot since it produced good-sized ulua and was so close to our home base. Many of his other favorites were quite some distance past Koko Head or out to sea at the Penguin Banks.

I managed to get one scraggily parrot fish while the Ninja got a small ulua. The ocean conditions were good, the water perfect, and we were so relaxed after our dives. As we sometimes do, we were talking about beautiful women when the Craw started in on me. "So, Bonesman, tell me about this young female you have been seeing?"

Craig knew the story well, but I sensed that he was in the mood for some mischief. This young lady and I were becoming quite fond of each other. She met the divers and their wives and had even been to a few of the group functions. I ignored the Craw and continued to look ahead but he jumped in again, "Bones, I've noticed you seem to be exclusive with this one woman. Am I right?"

"Yeah, things are good."

"Good, good in the biblical sense?" he inquired.

"I'm not telling you." I laughed and chuckled aloud.

"Bones, you can tell me. I am your confidant, your advisor."

"Not for that stuff."

"So, would you say you are in love?" he continued.

"Knock it off. Let's talk about you and Susie."

"Bones, I am married to the best woman, but you, you are still searching, looking, and hoping for love."

"And your point is?" I asked

"I can help guide you with the wisdom of my years."

"Oh, I'm relieved." I sarcastically pushed him away with a smile.

He continued on, "I think this one has set the hook. I think you are in love. Are you not aware that love is like the sakura (cherry blossom?) The euphoria of its birth... the passion of its fleeting existence... and its sudden death. You must be careful."

"And you, what about you? Is that how it is?

"Oh, no, Susie and I are different. That's forever. This is for you, my words of wisdom."

"I'm privileged then?"

"Yes, you are my student. You must expect that it will not last. She will tire of you, turn on you, or turn into someone else. It is the nature of most blossoms."

"Ah, oh wise one. Thank you... you're so full of baloney!"

In a contrived voice of sincerity, Craw spoke again. "Bones, I think she has set the hook. Do you feel the hook? Sometimes it happens, the hook is so smooth, the lure so colorful, you swallow it, not knowing its danger. You have to be very careful."

"Alright, knock it off," I said, trying to be stern. That was a mistake; it only encouraged him to try another angle.

"Bones, she may be a black widow. You know what black widows do? They mate with the male. After they love them, they kill them. They fish with the lure of their web, but when you take the hook and swallow, the barb buries deep in your gut, and you are done for! The widow lulls you into a narcotic trance with her charm. You're on a high, intoxicated with the aroma of the scent. It's the natural drug they inject that makes you immune to the pain."

I protested, "You're so full of crap! Where do you get this?"

He went on anyway, "It's her lips that bring you into the web, her den of love. She looks at you with those innocent eyes. You're held in a hypnotic gaze, anesthetized. The widow lures you in with the kiss. Those moist tender lips… smooth… soft, they invite you in for a kiss. You are powerless."

Craw was hanging on me, pawing at my shoulders and getting in my face. He gestured with his hands and moved his lips.

Then he changed his approach to a serious tone, "Bones, you must be strong. Fight off the intoxication. Before it's too late, you must find out, is she the black widow? You must see behind the lips, does she have fangs? They may look like teeth, but the fangs are longer and have a hollow canal from the widow gland for their venom. When you kiss her lips, the fangs sink in like hypodermic needles. You are helpless. The embrace hides the inoculation with the venom. You are a victim. You are gone from the dive life. You follow her every command."

"You're on a roll," I said.

Then Craw added the final touch to his picture: "You'll spend the rest of your days carrying her bags at the shopping mall like a land zombie, neither dead or alive."

I couldn't get *Bones* back to the dock fast enough. I needed a break from his harassment. We unloaded and washed the gear, hot tubbed, drank a few beers, and let the dive gear air dry for tomorrow's round of dives.

He continued on with the black widow talk off and on for awhile. Each statement pushed the analogy further and elaborated on the horrid details of black widowism. The more he drank, the more elaborate the descriptions became. Actually, it was quite a break for me when he finally went home to his wife. Maybe tomorrow he'll forget about this widow business, I hoped.

Some months later, the young lady that the boys gave me such a hard time about found greener pastures elsewhere and moved on with her life, but that wouldn't stop the boys from harassing me about any date I brought around. It was always open season for teasing.

I did not know at the time, but several other experiences would prepare me for the woman of my dreams who was about to make her entrance. In the meantime, Hughsan spread the word that he was making final preparations for our next trip to the Marshalls. This time it looked like a great group: Hugh, V, Craw, his wife Susie, another dive couple and me.

Months before the trip, the boys started on the shark revenge scenario that I should dish out on our return to Maloelap lagoon. It started out casually, every now and then on the boat, and over a few beers here and there, but soon it built to a feverish pitch the closer our departure date approached.

As a result of the constant harassment, I was hyped up and ready to execute this punk shark that had the audacity to charge me in Maloelap. I developed a clear vision of going back to the sunken freighter to hunt this shark down in a gangland-style killing. As my mind entertained the concept of becoming an executioner, I grew more confident that this creature would die by my hand.

I tossed aside any beneficial attributes of this marine animal and criminalized its very existence. All the good that sharks do for the ocean environment were overlooked and purposely forgotten. So what if they evolved over millions of years to take their place as the ocean's top predator? So what if they removed the lame, sick, and dying fish from the ocean? So what if they served as the equalizers of various fish populations? I wasn't the least bit concerned. That punk would die.

All of my family and friends knew of the shark attack and my developing plan for revenge. Unfortunately, this strategy was met with some resistance from some of my family. My mom and Auntie Vickie became more vocal about their opposition to me looking for this shark and killing it. Of course, I dismissed their concern as just the kind of worrying that moms and aunties were tasked with.

Over coffee one morning my mom made her case. "Son, why are you going there looking for trouble with this shark?"

"I'm on a mission to set the score right," I responded with all the daring of being pumped up.

"It's not a good idea. You were spared once. Why do you want to test God's will again? I'm worried for you. Let the shark be, leave him alone. Don't go looking for trouble," she reasoned with her imploring green eyes.

"Yeah ma, it's alright. I'll be fine, don't worry." I tried to appease her.

We continued on with family talk but soon Mom came back to the issue. "Bryan, we don't eat sharks, so why kill them?"

"Ma, that's not the point!" I was a little frustrated. "He tried to kill me, so I'm going to kill him," I responded.

"That's not how it should be; you should only take fish for food. You're not going to eat it, so let him go." My Auntie Vickie sat there at the dining table with her hands wrapped around her coffee cup nodding her approval with Mom's point of view.

Then she jumped into the discussion. "You know sharks are protected. The Hawaiians believe they're the amakua of their ancestors' spirits. It's not good to kill them. It's going to be trouble for you."

"Yes, I know, Auntie Vickie, but these sharks live in the Marshall Islands, not Hawaii. They gotta be different." Both Mom and Auntie Vickie laughed, knowing I was trying to be humorous to relieve the building tension. Our visit continued, but the conversation moved on to other matters. I knew when I left the condominium that family support for this endeavor was out of the question.

My new girlfriend, Sandy Sands, was also fearful of the looming dive trip to the Marshalls. Our relationship showed great promise, but I did not realize at the time she would be my lifelong partner. We were just getting to know each other. Sandy expressed her foreboding thoughts about the trip in general and specifically my plan for revenge. As the time drew closer, she became more disturbed about the adventure and asked that I consider canceling the trip.

She had been having nightmares about the strangest things

and woke with weighty feelings of sadness and danger about me in the ocean. There was a constant theme of shadowy figures that appeared and then disappeared back into the darkness. The figures never became distinguishable, but as soon as they were close to doing harm, the images would disappear.

The three females in my life lobbied hard for terminating the trip, or at the very least, the complete avoidance of the shark at Maloelap Atoll. I was steadfast: I would dive to my heart's content and dispatch this creature to his death.

Finally the day of the trip arrived; dive gear and personal bags were packed and checked in at the airport. We finished ticketing into the Aloha Airlines flight at the Honolulu International Airport to Majuro, the capital of the Marshall Islands. The divers gathered at the lobby bar for a farewell toast before departure. After a three-hour delay, an announcement came that the flight was canceled due to mechanical problems. All passengers were to report back tomorrow for a reschedule.

Our luggage was left on the plane and we returned home to our families. The next day we checked in again and gathered for our lounge toasts. Again we waited, one hour, two, then three, and finally four hours. The plane had not been fixed and the flight was rescheduled again for the next day. Again, we went home to our families.

The next day we arrived for the third attempt but dispensed the lounge ritual, going straight to the gate instead. Again we waited, and three hours later we were informed that the plane was still not fixed. We were told to report back tomorrow for another attempt.

Upon returning home each evening I touched base with Sandy, Mom, and Auntie Vickie. It was an eerie feeling they conveyed that the postponement was some sort of an omen. Each of them were deathly fearful for my life. It was as if they had worked out a plan together to sabotage my trip. My mom spoke of the Hawaiian spirits wanting to protect the shark, Sandy spoke of her haunting dreams, and Auntie Vickie talked of the unusual circumstances of the plane breaking down three days in a row.

Each evening it wore on me that these coincidental occurrences were so unusual. I started to question the righteousness of my revenge. That last night I did not sleep well. I had visions of traveling into the ever-growing darkness of a hidden valley and fading away to lose myself into the elements. In and out of a troubled sleep, I finally awoke to a decision that I would abort the dive trip.

The group was informed of my decision. They were disappointed and talked about all the fun I would miss. I weathered their encouragement to continue on with my decision and checked my bags off the plane. It was not easy, but I had to make the call as I was now convinced that something wasn't right. Dark thoughts invaded my consciousnesses and warned of danger. It was finished; they left, I stayed back.

The next two weeks moved slowly as I wondered how the trip was unfolding for my buddies. I phoned Hughsan for a dive report the day after they returned. He gave me all the details, reiterating that I missed some great spearfishing. Then he asked, "Did you hear about Craw?"

"No, heard about what?" I asked.

"You should have been there. Whoa, it was close. We were diving an outside lagoon pass, beautiful water, full of action. We dove this same area the day before and did well. Well, Craw shot a tuna and was fighting it when he got charged by a big shark. It was a very close call."

"No, you're kidding!" I was stunned.

"Bones, I wouldn't kid you about this. We were all in the water at the end of the dive doing a shallow safety stop. Craw saw a tuna swim by and shot it. Great shot, solid hit, the tuna went down to the bottom for cover. In came a large thick grey that starts to eat Craw's fish. The tuna is fighting to get away but he can't. The shark kept biting and chomping on it. Craig and the shark start fighting over the fish! He's pulling at it, the sharks biting down harder and holding his ground."

"So what happened?" I asked.

"Craw pulled the tuna from the bottom away from the snapping teeth. They squared off at each other, eyeball to eyeball, and then the shark bolted up from the bottom to take a bite out of Craig. It was so close; Craw's very lucky."

"Wow! God, he was lucky," I said.

Hughsan cut my call short as another call tried to break in on his line. This was just too coincidental an attack for me to let it go. I had to get to the bottom of it, so I called the Craw. After a brief greeting and a general overview of the trip, I got straight to the point with a little teasing. "Crawman, I heard you had a shark problem."

As flippant as he could be, he responded, "Bones, you should have been there. We could have done some real damage to the shark population."

Before he could continue I interrupted, "I heard the story from Hughsan. So tell me all the gruesome details."

Craw was only too happy to oblige, "I was pressed into service to teach these sharks some respect. He insulted the ninja so I took it as my solemn duty to defend the bushido code."

Craw continued on, but I wanted the real scoop, so I interrupted him again. "How did it really go down?"

"Well, the shark was pissed off with me from the day before. We were shooting fish in the pass and I had hit this one on the snout with the tip of my gun when he got too close to my catch."

"Oh, so you started this?" I asked.

"Me? Of course not! The pass was really productive, a great spot with everything coming in and out of the lagoon going through the channel. There were a couple of sharks that just hung around, but they kept their distance. So, I shot a decent size fish, and this shark comes in for dinner. I whack him on the head. The next day we dove the same pass. I shot this premium grade tuna that swam by while we're decompressing. This same quarrelsome punk came in and goes for my fish. Then, he starts to fight me for... my fish. The nerve of this junkyard scavenger. He should have known that his insult would not go unchallenged. It was a matter of honor and teaching him some respect!"

"What happened next?"

"The shark started hacking on the beautiful tuna and tearing up my meat. I'm pissed. I see our evening's sashimi being torn to shreds and going to hell. I tug on the leader line and try to break it free from his greedy jaws. The tuna is stuck at the end of my spear shaft, thrashing on the bottom, looking for cover next to a coral head. I'm trying to pull him up to get him out of the crevice and away from the shark's teeth. The shark has his teeth locked on the tuna and isn't letting go. It's a dog fight. One of us has got to give in. This bum looks me right in the eyes staring up from the bottom. I'm staring him down. Both of us are in a stink eye stare down. The shark stops, lets the tuna go, and bolts straight up for me."

"Holy gees, Craig. What did you do?"

"The damn thing opened his mouth, peeled back his lips wider than his head, and then snapped it shut with a sound of clacking jawbone hitting jawbone. At just the right instant I pulled my legs into a ball toward my stomach, the second before the shark's jaws snapped shut. I ended up in a fetal position with my hands in a defensive push-off stance. Then the loser turned away and took off into the depths like a coward. Well, that's about it."

"What a miracle! You're here, and you survived! Thank God!" I was overwhelmed with the story. But, in typical Craw confidence, he continued.

"Bones, I brought much disgrace to the ninjas. This one had the audacity to attack then leave the scene alive and unpunished. So much disgrace. This one lives to brag of his assault. There'll be others who will think they can attack freely."

I laughed a bit and played into this conversation to give him a hard time about letting the creature go. It all made sense to me now. Call me foolish, superstitious, silly, or whatever you'd like. If this attack had happened to me, I would have lost both legs and bled to death in the water. I wasn't near as quick as the Crawman and I didn't have the killer confidence that he had with these creatures. The punk in gray would have had me for a meal even though Craw did the damage to his nose. I'd be guilty by association and be the easier target of the two. I came away from the conversation with the belief that sometimes one must listen to the voices within, even though the voices may originate from someone else.

CHAPTER SEVEN

DIVE MATE

From the moment I first met Sandy Sands, I knew this bubbly strawberry blond from Texas would be the love of my life. Sandy served as a real estate executive in charge of several highrise buildings in Honolulu; I was the board president of a building. We were introduced at the annual owners' meeting. Later, she arranged a business lunch at the Landing Restaurant in the American Factors Building where her company was located.

Sandy was particularly gorgeous that day. I was distracted by her looks and wanted to move things away from business and on to more personal issues. Trying to contain my romantic interest, it became difficult to maintain a proper business attitude with her. But when she leaned over the café table, moved her hand towards mine, and whispered, "I think you're cute," I lost all sense of restraint and immediately pounced on her for a date. My dating strategies were no different than my lobster diving tactics, when a spiny came out of its nest into the open, I immediately pinned it down.

Everything buzzed through my mind. How about dinner tonight? No, that won't do. What about breakfast tomorrow morning? No, that would sound too imposing. What do you think about taking the day off and going to the beach? No, that's too aggressive. So I spoke with a reassuring calm and just a hint of excitement, "You're so pretty. You probably already know that by the way I followed you around at the annual meeting." She smiled and lowered her face in a shy acknowledgment. Then I made my move. "How about we get together this weekend for dinner?"

"Yes, that would be fine," she responded.

I went back to the office elated with the possibilities. We chatted on the phone several times during the week. During one of our chats, I solicited her approval for a boat ride on the marina with a stop for dinner at a waterfront restaurant in Hawaii Kai. Through the course of our conversations, she told me she was a certified diver. I died in ecstasy and went straight to heaven! What a miraculous find, a female diver. I was stoked. For years, I had dreamed of a beautiful diving companion to share the grandeur of the oceans.

Sandy was gorgeous, smart, and a scuba diver! She would make the perfect mate and dive buddy. I wondered if life could get any better. It would be life's ultimate, a dive buddy for adventure and wonderful romance! But the "pièce de résistance" was that she'd be a girlfriend with a good job who could pay for her own gear and air card. It didn't matter to me that I might be getting ahead of myself; I was living in a dream.

I felt excited but quite nervous about this unique first date. We started early so I could treat Sandy to a marina cruise on *Bones*. Wine, pupus and the glorious sunset over Diamond Head set the stage for the evening. I hoped that might melt her heart. Then I parked the boat at the marina-mall dock where we dined at the Chinese restaurant above the dive shop. The divers had a similar setup with the restaurant's owner where we brought our fish and they'd prepare it to our particular requests. We dined on parrot fish I had speared earlier that day. Complemented by the house special noodles and sweet and sour pork, it was more than we could finish.

I believe that knocked her off her feet; I was sure of it. Then we boated back to my bachelor house and hot tubbed. That sent her over the top. I was certain that she'd be overwhelmed and fall hopelessly in love with me. I was amazed with my ingenuity for creating and executing such a crafty plan. It was indeed a fabulous evening.

This Casanova's strategy was the most clever I had to offer. I would not wine and dine her in fancy Waikiki restaurants and clubs. No, how could I compete with the others who tried to spend their way into her heart? No, I did not fish for her with fancy Tiffany lures; I'd fish with my own best tackle. Only the most colorful, best skirted, shiniest, fast running, jet headed lures did I spread before her.

This was the best I had to offer; it was all me. I felt confident that if she saw the bait and took the hook, it would be the real me that she wanted. Then, she would be the fish I'd land fair and square. Setting my own hook, my own way, is the only strategy I would use with this striking blond.

The evening was perfect in every way. She was wonderful. By the time all was said and done, my magic had worked its charm. I believed I would have a dive buddy to share my life with. But little did I know, we had both set hooks and landed our own fish, each of the other. I had been fished, too!

In the coming weeks and months we got on well together. It was a season for courting, filled with discovery, laughter, and good times. I got to know her and her family of Texans. Sandy was welcomed by my family and friends. Everyone loved and accepted her into our local ohana, or family. All the dive guys and their wives took a great liking to her. It was natural that our love grew and soon we were quite serious about each other.

We didn't dive together early on; I had steady plans for spearfishing on the weekends with the boys. Somehow, killing fish didn't have a real appeal for Sandy, but she was perfectly happy as long as I brought fresh fish and lobster home for dinner. Our informal arrangement worked just fine. I loved diving with my buddies and she enjoyed the free time with her friends. As a matter of truth, most of the divers' wives had better things to do than bounce around all weekend on a boat. So, for the most part, my dive plans continued on with the guys. It wasn't until many months later that Sandy and I had a serious first chance to dive together.

Our dive day weather conditions were perfect for the ocean, with warm and light trade winds, moderate wave height, small lines of surf, and clear calm water. It was the perfect invitation to take Sandy diving in Moanalua Bay, so I dumped my dive buddies for the pleasure of diving with her.

I prepared *Bones* for an adventure. My 19-foot Glaspros stood ready at the dock. It was outfitted with a custom fiberglass hardtop that elevated this stock boat to a class-act fishing and diving machine. The innovative addition would keep everyone in the cabin dry while the waves crashed over the bow when managing big seas. This was especially important to me when crossing the 28 mile Molokai Channel.

The look of the new cabin might not be traditional to some boaters, but the utility of the craft was much improved with the sleek dog house design. Some of my friends, especially "Billie Budd" (Mark Olsen,) called it the "manapua wagon." He was quite mistaken but I was not offended. His pilot house label was a reference to the Chinese food seller's self-propelled carriages used in the old days of Honolulu. These rolling carts were used by the Asian vendors to sell dim-sum, pipiau, and manapua cakes door-to-door through the neighborhoods. It's the kind of food cart you'd find in a third-world country. I didn't care what anyone called my boat; I loved my hard-top cabin enclosure. It was my ticket to safe passages to Molokai.

Everything on *Bones* was designed for diving. It had twin Evinrude 90's for horsepower and a large fuel tank under the deck. Four divers, ten tanks and all the dive gear were transported with ease using this power setup. It also used two blue storage drums for extra fuel on long trips. Special gas line rigs to connect and disconnect directly to the motors were installed on the spare tanks. With these rigs we didn't have to move the heavy fuel drums once they were lashed on deck. When the gas was spent, the empty drums were tied onto the cabin top for more space. I could see how *Bones* might look like a manapua wagon with the gas drums tied on the roof, but who cared, it was very functional.

I wanted to show Sandy a really great time for our first dive together. *Bones* waited at the dock, washed down and loaded with diving and fishing gear. Everything was well-organized and in its rightful place. There's nothing worse than a captain who'll let his boat fall into disorganization and ill-repair. How would he know where everything was in a split-second emergency? Lost moments could mean disaster at sea.

The twin motors warmed while I waited. They ran well and kept running, but still no Sandy. To kill some time, I double checked our stuff to see that we had everything: tanks, regulators, vests, weight belts, masks, fins, snorkels, knife, spear gun, and power head. I waited awhile longer, and then did my check off list yet again. Finally, she appeared at the back door and gave me a hand signal to help her with her bags. I responded and dutifully assisted her in the load-up.

We were both on the boat now. She checked her bags and talked under her breath as I cast us off and headed down the marina. She continued intently, "Let's see, makeup, hair conditioner, sunscreen, clothes tote. Yep, it's all here!" She also stuffed a bag of frozen peas in a pink fish feeding bag.

I didn't say a word but couldn't help but ask myself, what's all this junk for? Later in life, as a husband and father of a daughter, I would learn but as a bachelor I wondered about the usefulness of all this nonsense. Looking at this litter, the boat a mess, overcrowded and disorganized I silently told myself, we're just going for a dive. It's only 25 minutes away from the house, how many things could she possibly need?

I was frustrated with the delays, but at least we were on our way. We drove out through the channel and past the tourist dive boats anchored along Turtle Cove. I chose a spot a little deeper, between Diamond Head and Koko Head. As we sped by the dive boats, Sandy looked puzzled and asked, "Why don't we dive there with the tourists?"

I told her, "We don't want to dive here with everybody. We're going to a special spot, Shark's Cave. It's about 65 to 75 feet deep and if they're home, we'll see two small white tip sharks in their den. It'll be very exciting. When I dive with the boys, I see them every once in a while. They're so tame they won't bother us."

Sandy couldn't hide her feelings. It was obvious she wasn't happy. This is not what she expected on a romantic dive together. She looked back towards the dive boats we passed. I heard her quietly mumbling, "no, no, no... no sharks." I ignored this slight change in mood and continued on. Our conversation fell flat for awhile, but soon I slowed the boat down and circled our dive site.

We lined up with several landmarks onshore for position. Then, peering over the side, I saw the underwater cliff line and the outcropping of a lava tube jutting into a valley of sand. This was it. I set the anchor with a long scope for safety. The waves were a little rougher than I liked, but the water was perfectly clear. We would have a great time.

I helped Sandy suit up, taking all the extra time needed to make sure she was comfortable and had everything that she could possibly want. I looked her over in admiration. How could I ever find any better? She didn't even get seasick like some divers I knew. What a jewel. I'll work on the luggage thing later, I thought.

Soon we were done gearing up and sitting on the side rails. I led the way as we both leaned backward to splash over the side and into the water. Floating immediately upright at the surface next to the side of the boat, I noticed Sandy surfaced but moved awkwardly. Her hands were all over her head searching for her dive mask.

She had no idea, but it was upside down hanging on her ponytail. The waves pushed her against the boat and the scuba tank started to bang into the fiberglass hull. It got into a tight pattern where each wave crest pushed her into the boat and each trough released her back from the boat. I quickly moved to help her and used my hand for her support while moving the thumping tank away from my polished hull.

With her added weight, I had to inflate my vest for more buoyancy. I moved closer to reassure her. Now we were both intertwined. Our legs clashed together in a most awkward manner, with her fins finding the sensitive spots on my shins.

There would be no luck getting her mask on; clumps of hair fell from her head and onto her face every time we tried to position her mask. I didn't know how to help. Her finning and kicking intensified, and my shins and knees took a beating.

I power inflated her vest for more floatation. This would keep her afloat while she got situated. Then, I backed off a little to give my legs a needed rest. Grabbing the mask again, I positioned it close to the top of her head and handed it to her. She pulled the strap over the top of her brow and moved it back and forth.

These movements unraveled parts of her ponytail. More strands of hair dangled in her face. I tried to keep the hair off of her forehead and brows. Saltwater splashed in her eyes, causing her hair to move back and forth on her forehead. As soon as I brushed one strand aside, another clump appeared. It got extremely frustrating. I knew that if we didn't get all of the hair off her face, the mask would leak. Then, we'd be dealing with another problem 65 feet down.

There we were bobbing at the side of the boat with four-foot waves hitting us from the quarter angle. I hit the power inflator on her buoyancy vest again. It blew up like a balloon. She no longer swallowed water; she bobbed like a cork. For a moment I felt some relief. Then the situation turned on her again. She started gasping for air, Sandy couldn't breathe! The vest was so tight that there was no room for her chest to expand for a breath. I saw the panic in her eyes.

Her face turned a shade of light blue. I hit the exhaust button to release air, but nothing happened! The air was still crushing her chest. I saw her pleading eyes, and heard her faint whisper, "Can't... Breathe..." I hit the exhaust button again, wrong button, more crushing air! I immediately moved to the next button and jabbed it down. Nothing! The exhaust valve was stuck. The rubber must have sealed itself, or melted shut from lack of use.

I worked madly to release the vest's chest and waist straps. The damned things were so tight against her frame there was hardly any room to grab them. I struggled and watched her face turn darker shades of blue. Finally, the buoyancy vest strap released. Sandy turned out of the vest and air rushed back into her spent lungs. She floated free and swam to the ladder to catch her breath while I doted on her every move. It took some time to get her strength back, but she did–just enough to limp up into the boat.

With our change of circumstances I had the distinct feeling that an enchanting couple's dive to look at the pretty sharks might be out of the question. I wanted to do a quick dive alone while she waited on the boat, but my sensibilities suggested we call it a day. Sandy was relieved when we headed back to the house.

Call it love or hope springs eternal, but I made allowances for Sandy's incident. That could happen to anyone, I told myself. I've had bad days, ear-squeezes, sinus headaches, and mask problems. I've jumped in the water without fins, missing a weight belt, with eyeglasses on but no facemask, a tank of left-over air, a tank with the air off, and a host of other stupid stunts. It's all part of diving. Sometimes you'll have a bad day. In Sandy's case, I was understanding and protective, especially after she told me of her ill-fated boating date with another man before me. It's a wonder that she would even step foot on a boat after that incident.

When I met Sandy she was settled and living in the heart of Waikiki. Years before, after she first moved from Texas to live in Hawaii, she persuaded her best friend "Deby" (Deborah Kincaid) from Tyler, Texas to join her in paradise. Deby had only been in town for a week when Sandy set up an offshore boat trip with a male friend and his buddy. Neither of the girls had been boating in Hawaii yet. All of their previous experiences were with small boats on inland lakes.

That Saturday morning, Daniel and Joe picked up the girls and headed toward Kaneohe Bay on the windward side of Oahu. They would launch their craft from the public boat ramp. The bay is particularly beautiful, fishing in it and the distant ocean is terrific most times of the year. Before leaving Daniel's house, his father came over to meet the girls and send the foursome on their way. With words that should have been a warning, Daniel's dad parted saying, "You know not to leave the bay. The ocean's going to be choppy." The unstable ocean conditions were due in large part to the offshore remnants of a hurricane that had drifted by the islands a few days earlier.

From all weather indications, it looked like it would be an overcast and dreary day. The two couples, Daniel's golden retriever, and an ice chest full of bait consumed what little deck space there was on the tiny boat. There was no room to move with the dog lying in the aisle between the old style bench seats.

Sandy and Deby weren't concerned that the boat they boarded was a 14-foot ski boat. It looked sound enough to the occasional lake boaters from Texas. Both girls were unaware that there were no life jackets, flares, emergency equipment, radio, or safety devices of any kind. Sandy admits that it never crossed their minds to ask about the safety equipment.

The girls weren't the least bit concerned that the overloaded craft was undersized for ocean swells. They had no idea of what treachery might be played by the ocean in a melancholy mood. With a freeboard of only 12 inches, any small wake or disturbance would cause water to spill over the bow and into the boat. Any real boater would wonder if these joy riders were thinking properly. It was a ski boat, not a fishing boat. Somehow this fact was lost on both the men and their guests.

As they left the launch, two fishing lures were set and the

poles put into makeshift rod holders. They trolled through the channel and went straight out to sea.

The seas were very rough, still disturbed with a constant swell from the east of 6 feet or more. Once out of the bay, they traveled straight out for hours. It was a silent boat except for the sound of the motor and the waves crashing into the hull.

Deby got seasick early on and spent the trip with her head in a towel crouched over on the side rail. She was soaked. It drizzled off and on during the morning and the waves splashed relentlessly on her and her towel.

Sandy hung in there but was getting hungry and tired of the beating at sea. She shouted to ask Daniel if he would stop the boat so they could attend to Deby. He yelled back between the hammering waves and the flying spray, "We can't stop the boat; it'll swamp." Daniel determined that they needed to keep the speed up to cut through the waves. Otherwise, they ran the risk of stalling dead in the water and sinking.

It's not known if bilge pumps were installed or functioning, but the girls were put to bailing water from the floor boards as their boat duty. As the day wore on the girls' misery took its toll on them. Near midday, the boaters lost sight of Oahu. A speck of the offshore island, Chinaman's Hat (Mokolii Island,) was all that was visible of land. The "Hat" is a famous landmark along the reefs in the Kaneohe district.

Finally, there was a fish strike on the reel. Daniel was at the helm, so Joe rushed to his feet and turned back to get the screaming line. The rod peeled out monofilament with the familiar hissing of its gears racing in reverse. The thrill of fish was in the air. In the excitement, Joe lost his balance and tripped over the open tackle box next to the dog. A large trolling lure lay open floating in a couple inches of water in the bilge. Joe fell and his knee found the 9-0 skirted hook. It punctured the flesh and the barb sank deep into the meat of his knee. Joe rolled over on the floor screaming.

Daniel stopped the boat immediately and turned to help his buddy. He grabbed the pliers out of the box and went to the back of the boat to pull the hook out.

All were distracted by the emergency at hand. As the boat was dead in the water, the first nasty wave gushed over the bow and nearly filled the little boat. Gear started to float. Some of the loose stuff drifted out of the back of the craft. Stunned, everyone scrambled to hold on to something in the unstable and sinking boat. The second wave came over the bow and piled more water into the boat. It was hopeless.

Daniel instantly ordered everyone out of the boat and into the water. His solution was to keep the boat afloat by temporarily reducing its weight. Then, he would stay in the swamped boat and bail. Then, horror of all horrors, the back of the boat started down. The bow lifted slightly into the air for a moment and then shifted downward. The third wave crashed on the sinking boat, pushing it backward under the waves. In the course of a few seconds the boat was gone. The four of them were in the water, each feeling alone with floating debris about them.

Sandy grabbed the ice chest full of bait and wrapped her arm around its white nylon handle. Deby swam toward Sandy with the aid of a floating boat chair. Daniel frantically tried to gather his stuff but soon realized that it was useless. He gave up and treaded water with a look of hopelessness. Joe drifted awkwardly, sculling to keep afloat, moaning and bleeding in pain.

All the wreckage was pushed away by the waves and soon there was nothing in sight except the four boaters drifting in the water. The bait cooler and the boat chair would have to keep them all afloat. It was a grave picture.

Sandy began to think about not seeing any other boats on the way out. She knew it wasn't a good sign. Each person came to terms with the critical situation in their own way. For Sandy, she acknowledged the situation was bad but wouldn't accept that this would be deadly. Perhaps it was good that Sandy was new to the islands and had not read newspaper accounts of people who were lost at sea, never to be heard of again.

Deby began to show signs of life. She had been sea sick for so long but now she was making a comeback in the water. It was so out of place. Deby got close to Sandy and told her, "At least I'm feeling better." Deby began to think that this situation might somehow be a consolation for her previous suffering. She would soon realize that it was a sick delusion. Each of them treaded water, overtaken by their own fears and prayers.

Sandy made out Chinaman's Hat vaguely back in the distance.

She shouted to Daniel, "Why don't we swim towards the island?"

He cut her short. "It's too far. We'll never make it! Besides, the island is surrounded by reefs. We'll get cut to shreds." Sandy was frustrated and continued to hang on to the cooler for her very life.

Quite some time went by and then Joe erupted, violently thrashing in the water next to them. "Something's stinging me! Stinging me!" He was in horrifying pain as a Portuguese man of war attacked him without mercy. Joe flailed wildly, trying to get it off his back, neck, and arms. No one could do anything for Joe; he was on his own.

The agitated splashing was a frightful sight. "Stop splashing, you'll attract..." yelled Daniel, leaving his sentence unfinished. None of them would allow themselves to say that fearful word ...sharks. Kaneohe Bay was known to be a breeding ground for hammerhead sharks. Joe eventually wore himself out and calmed down to suffer in silence. They treaded water in quiet fear.

The beating of the waves and churning of the ocean sucked their energy and resolve. It would only be a matter of time before exhaustion would render them too weak to swim or too feeble to stay afloat. At nightfall there would be an even greater danger, the tiger sharks that come out to feed. Still, not one of them panicked as they concentrated on staying calm and afloat.

All were resigned to their fate. Deby moved over to Sandy again and whispered, "Joe's bad luck, he's bleeding. We need to move away from him." Sandy looked at Joe and acknowledged her concern.

Sandy thought about the dog for a moment. He was gone, probably drowned. In any case, no one would talk of the dog. They all knew that only a miracle would save them as dusk prepared to overwhelm the sorrowful scene.

After what seemed like an endless drift, and when all hope started to fade, they heard the faint sound of diesel motors running at high speed. It must be a boat way off in the distance. Some hoped. Some prayed. Would they be spotted? Would this be their rescue or a cruel hoax? Within less than 20 minutes, the heavenly sight of a commercial dive boat appeared.

It was a miracle! Three local diver-fishermen pulled alongside and plucked each of them from the water. There, collapsed on the deck, was Daniel's golden retriever, breathing but passed out from exhaustion. As the divers explained on the ride in, they found the dog swimming in the middle of the ocean. Instinctively they knew that there must be someone out here that had a dog, so they came searching for people.

It took Sandy and Deby several days of bed rest to recuperate from the ordeal. Both were black and blue from being pushed and punched by their life-saving floats. Both regretted that they never got to really thank the divers who rescued them.

They did not see Daniel and Joe again. Sandy and Deby realize that the boys were well-meaning guys who wanted to show them a good time. They didn't blame them for the trouble, but they wanted to get as far away from that experience as humanly possible. Their trip could have turned out differently if they were on a bigger boat or if they weren't in hurricane ocean swells. It's not like the girls could blame themselves either, because they didn't know enough to know of the dangers. They were fresh from the mainland. What did they know about the ocean? Small lakes and rivers were all that they had been exposed to, and that isn't anything like the ocean.

I knew I had to be patient with Sandy because of all that she had been though on the ocean. I still wanted her as my dive buddy and ocean mate. When the right time presented itself we would dive together again. Several months later such an opportunity surfaced. It was a slow weekend for social commitments, and the marine weather forecasts suggested a near-perfect ocean. So, with the passing of time and the forgotten pains of our first experience, I planned a wonderful dive in a unique and secluded spot. It would be a show-stopper for Sandy, a little lover's nook where we could dive, relax, and picnic on the boat.

I was so eager about this dive, I forgot all about our previous drama at sea. This site would be great... no tourists and no sharks. The plan was to motor around the east tip of Oahu and anchor on the inside reefs of Rabbit Island. Looking out from Makapuu Beach and Sea Life Park, only a small speck of *Bones* would be visible from shore. There in plain sight, but too distant to be noticed, we would have our afternoon dive in privacy.

Sandy prepared snacks and brought her entourage of stuff essential for a boat trip. I must say to her credit, the travel bags were fewer and a little lighter. I was having an influence on her. We departed and drove through the marina without incident.

In no time at all, *Bones* sped past channel marker one and out to open ocean. We turned left to round the horn of Koko Head, blowing past the jagged mountain coast. Deep blue seas greeted us as I hugged close to the Koko coastline working the swells for comfort and avoiding the whitewash of the volcanic cliffs. I knew this coast well, and while I would take no chances with Sandy, I wanted to give her the thrill of being very close to the cliff line. This sight was always so impressive to me... black rock mountains rising from the ocean depths below, just floating there anchored in the sea.

When going to the Rabbit with my buddies, we'd normally take the fastest route, straight from Koko Head to Makapuu Point, then round the horn to the Rabbit. However, this day was special. I would take all the time I needed to show my sweetheart the sights. This was the grand, round-the-coast scenic tour. As we motored, the stark cliffs blew by and we soon moved across the entrance of Hanauma Bay.

This thrilling coastline of crashing, open-ocean waves and rugged lava wall backstops ran from the edge of Moanalua Bay to Sandy Beach. Quite often, the violent ocean from the Kaiwi Channel makes this cliff line difficult to traverse, but on a calm ocean day, it's testament to the wondrous work of God's magic.

Bones drove on, weaving in and out close to the rock outcroppings and surrounding reefs jutting out under the sea surface. These were most impressive sights as gorgeous, greenish-brown reefs flowered outward into the blue then halted abruptly, falling into the oblivion of the mysterious deep. It was breathtaking. We came upon Eternity Cove, the Blow Hole, and Sandy Beach. I pointed out the lifeguard station that I was assigned to in college, but I prudently did not offer any stories of the beach parties or other activities of my youth.

After some time, we moved along the Makapuu Cliffs. When we came to the submerged sea-rocks midway to the Point, I purposefully gave it a wide berth. For some reason I was never comfortable with this area. To this very day, I don't know why, but it gave me a sense of sadness. I had no cause to feel this way about these rocks, but with the breakers crashing on its hidden top, it felt like a great ancient danger and a scene of much sadness. The place exudes a sensation of many Hawaiian lives lost and great sorrow. It could be my imagination, but somehow I knew wandering native spirits haunt this place.

Soon we rounded the imposing Makapuu Point and there before us lay Rabbit Island (Manana) and the smaller Flat Island (Kaohikaipu.) Sandy was overwhelmed. The salty sea air, sounds of waves, echoes from the cliffs, giant volcanic views, and the rich hued ocean all were beyond imagination to a girl from Texas. I was pleased; Mother Nature conspired with me in this romance.

I made one large loop outside and around the Rabbit before heading in towards its shore. We passed a small reef line and surf break that was a favorite for adventurous locals. There were no waves today; the water lay in peace. There was only inconsequential chop lapping against the black lava ledge that skirted the island.

We motored down and made a slow cruise inside to find an anchorage. A small patch of sand and coral just off the inside coast showed itself to be the perfect site for us. We were close to the left side of the island, just 75 yards offshore. By the lack of drift, calm winds, and slackened current, this would be the perfect anchorage and dive site. We'd be very safe in 20 feet of water. The abundance of corals and tropical fish were splendid. Looking over the side of the boat, I showed Sandy a small parrot fish feeding on corals and schools of fish moving about with no cares.

The motors were silenced and *Bones* cuddled up into the watery lap of the Rabbit's towering sea cliffs. It was awesome. The sounds of the waves gently purring against the hull were mildly hypnotic, but the overhead choir of sea birds kept us from giving in to the slumber of the waves. It was in perfect balance. This would be our ocean nest for the day.

The outside Rabbit was one of our dive crew's popular hunting areas. Hughsan and the boys had thoroughly explored and charted most of the seascape between Makapuu Point and the far end of the Rabbit. The undersea terrain was extensive and diverse, with shallow spots for lobsters in close and around the islands, beautiful underwater cliff lines a little deeper out, and lava ledges with big game at deeper levels. When the weather was good, we'd trek out there to hunt and gather. On many occasions we'd motor into these protected shallows inside the Rabbit for lunch and uptime before a second dive.

Sandy and I got our dive bags out on deck and readied ourselves for a dive. I was on my best behavior while helping her with her dive gear: I strapped the tank to her vest, secured the regulator, turned on the air, checked the gauge, and even tested her air. I helped her with her suit and cleaned her mask. Then I quickly put on my own gear and went over the side to wait in the water for her to drop in.

I was a bit worried when she splashed in, but she popped to the surface with her mask and all systems intact. We descended slowly hand-in-hand to the bottom. She was just fine, showed no signs of ear or sinus problems, and finned with a very relaxed attitude. It was wonderful; she was seeing what I saw, teeming schools of fish and a wonderfully diverse corals.

Sandy brought her frozen peas and fed the fish as we swam the reef. Reef fish became more abundant as all colors, shapes, and sizes moved in and out of the corals to get a better position for the hand-delivered meal. Sandy was having the time of her life; it made me so happy. I brought my speargun and had it in hand, just in case game fish came my way. Sandy swam at my side, arm in arm. Every now and then she tugged at me to watch her feed a trigger fish.

This was all fine and good, but not really the dive I envisioned. I wondered how much of this feeding the fish routine I could take before I lost my patience. We roamed the area in neutral buoyancy and had the most wonderful experience together. After a while, I started to get a little impatient. I had seen these beautiful fish all my life. Yeah, they were pretty, but I wanted to spear something. It seemed that every time a decent shooting fish came into view, she would tug at me with a smile to show me a beautiful angelfish or some other delicate creature. After I watched my second parrot swim by, I gave up and resigned myself to watching the small pretty fish. It's alright, it's her day, I told myself.

I was handling it pretty well when we stumbled upon a good-sized fish trap. It was a common thing to find fish traps while scuba diving. The catcher was full of tropicals and assorted reef fish, but the real prize was one large parrot amongst three smaller ones. It looked like the trap may be unattended or abandoned, so I got excited. That big parrot will make the perfect dinner, I reasoned. I worked it all out in my mind; it was a simple plan. One fish, that's all. I'd be in through the front, one three-prong, no collateral damage, and one great fish dinner. I swam forward and put my long-gun down at the side of the trap and moved into position with my three-prong.

I was getting my head and shoulder into the trap's entrance when Sandy grabbed me at the back of the neck of my wetsuit. I stopped in the front of the cage. She looked at me with indignation and shook her head from side to side in a motion of, "no, no, no, don't shoot the fish."

I was bewildered. What could she mean? Don't shoot the fish? I was blown away and almost motionless. I gave her a signal, "What do you mean?" questioning her with my hands.

Then she gave me a "holier than thou" look through her face-mask and stoutly took the position of a moral conscience that she would not be witness to this bloodthirsty behavior. I looked at her again, thinking to myself, I shoot fish. This is what I do. You know this is what I do, you eat the fish! What's the problem?

She gave me another even sterner look and started pointing to the surface. I was thinking wildly, what the heck's going on? I see a wonderful fish dinner, and she's giving me static! I picked up my gun and started to surface with her. As we rose, the more I thought about it, the more disturbed I became. Who does she think I am? I'm a spearfisherman. I kill fish so that we can eat! I kept telling myself, getting more wound up by the second.

We got to the surface. Sandy took off her mask and got into my face, "Bryan, we have to go back to the boat and get pliers to let the fish out."

I'm in total disbelief. "What?" I'm yelling.

Again she gave me the stern, serious face. "We have to let the fish go!" she insisted.

Not only does she not want me to shoot dinner, she wants me to save all the fish. That's it—she's out of her mind, I silently ranted. There we were, floating in the perfect waters of the Rabbit and she's demanding we have to let the fish out. I can't believe it; she's crazy! "Sandy, it's a fish trap, it traps fish. The fish are there to eat."

"No!" she said, "We have to let them out!"

"No way!" I protested.

She turned her back away from me and swam to the boat. I was madder than hell! I yelled at her over the chop, "No way am I going to let those fish out. People need to eat!" I swam after her. When I caught up with her at the boat ladder, Sandy wouldn't talk, so I wouldn't talk. I helped her out of her gear, then stowed it by myself while she sat on the bow looking into the distance, seemingly above it all. It was awfully quiet. There would be no laughter and romance now. I pulled anchor, cranked the motors up and sped home. The silence continued until we got back to the dock.

"Thank you for the dive," she said politely. Then she went off into the house with an air of disgust. I was left to clean the boat, dive gear and fishing equipment alone. It was a sore spot with us for a couple of weeks.

Eventually we settled our differences with a peaceful understanding. She can feed and release all the fish she wants, anytime. I can shoot all the fish I want, anytime. We just won't do it together in the same ocean. But she'll eat all the fish and lobster I bring home. Why is it so hard to figure women out?

Chapter Eight

FAREWELL AT SEA

We did not dive that Saturday morning. A great sadness overwhelmed us all. This day would be one of remembrance, celebration, and goodbyes. We rose to a tragic, most solemn occasion. Our community of divers, friends, and family gathered in the Esplanade Park to honor the lives of Craig and Susie Craw. A horrific and most public accident had taken the lives of our dive mates the previous Tuesday off Waikiki Beach.

I walked through the lobby of the Esplanade and back to the crowd of mourners already gathered in the park. I was nervous and unsure of how this day would play out. Hughsan took the lead in organizing the funeral service. There was only one small part that I would play, and yet I worried that somehow I might be unworthy, or even worse, I'd fail to deliver an exceptionally moving farewell to Craig and Susie. I was uneasy that my buddy and his wife would not be honored as they deserved.

The Esplanade Park was the perfect setting for our community's farewell. The boat dock served as our base of dive operations and was frequented by our divers and their families. Hughsan and Lungs both lived in the condominiums. Mom, Dad, and Auntie Vickie also lived there and were regular beneficiaries of the divers' excess catches.

The Esplanade apartment compound was quite unique for the neighborhood, with two white stucco waterfront residential towers. The Marina Building was nestled on the waterway with a floating boat dock and numerous boat slips spanning its frontage. Throughout the marina façade, there were spacious bulkhead landings and large boat lockers located in the basement of the building. Hughsan's boat locker housed many a diver's gear through the years. The second structure, the Park Building, fronted an attractive grassy area with tropical trees that ran the length of the marina front. This was where the memorial service would take place.

I passed the lobby at the end of the park building and traveled the walkway to the grassy area where crowds of people had already assembled. In the shade of two palm trees, and with the help of a few divers, Hughsan set out a staging area for the service. The other divers and their families gathered in close. Throngs of people continued to pour in from the side of the building and vacant lot. The lawn space filled quickly.

The Craws' death was a very public spectacle, with sensational local newspaper and television coverage. A mass of people was strewn about with folding beach chairs, beverage coolers, umbrellas, hats and sunglasses, and children's strollers, all dressed in a sea of colorful aloha shirts, muumuus, jeans and polos. The scene was reminiscent of a 1960's love gathering, but the mood was too grave and subdued to call it such. The people's faces showed cordiality that disguised their underlying grief.

I ambled down the path, and there it hit me. As profound as any altar in a ceremony of honor, as solemn as any funeral carriage of state, there ahead where the salt-wilted grass met the tranquil marina waters, the yellow *Katana*, Craig's faithful dive boat floated, at rest, waiting for its master and mistress.

All alone and with no captain, Craw's 21-footer lingered, moored in silence. While the funeral guests went about their sadness, there at the water's edge, the long sword of the fallen bushido diver stood ready to serve. It swayed to the slow rhythm of the surface currents in uncertainty, a sad vision of a warrior's mount left idle. Where the *Katana*'s cutty-cab bulkhead meets the aft diving deck, two mysterious symbols of local custom, tea leaf bushes, attached to port and starboard bulkheads. My skin chilled.

The *Katana* was Craig's great joy. Custom-built, it served as transport and home away from home for his frequent interisland channel crossings to his favorite dive spots on the north coast of Molokai and the offshore Penguin Banks. It was a sturdy craft, built with an extra layer of glass cloth to take a heavy interisland pounding. As only the Craw would require, it was outfitted with the best stainless or aluminum hardware. Craig was fond of saying, "Rust never sleeps." The *Katana* was designed for long-distance trips with a 90-gallon fuel tank, twin Evinrude 110-horsepower motors, state-of-the-art electronics, and a host of other goodies that negotiated the pounding of the treacherous 28 mile channel crossing to Molokai.

Three other features made the *Katana* the envy of everyone. The first was the heavy-duty stainless steel yard arm hoist fabricated for the *Katana*. What an eye-catcher, and so practical for the ship's captain. The hoist was bolted to the aft corner rail combing and deck. It stood upright to swing its arm out for lifting heavy tanks and equipment in and out of the water in rough seas. Not only was it purposeful and unique, it portrayed an image of serious diving.

The second moniker of Craw's design ingenuity was the stainless steel grappling hook anchor that lay in the anchor block with a strand of stainless steel chain. The heavy-duty, four-pronged hook, with its long shaft, led the boat's charge forward into open seas. It was a striking sight. One could imagine an anchor resembling a shooting star pulling the yellow *Katana* into fish battles.

The last notable item was the unique radio directional finder antenna mounted atop an extension pole at the amidships starboard side. With this special equipment, the Craw could find divers far out at sea by honing into the direction of their transmissions from the compact VHF radios they carried on their weight belts. It also served as a directional finder for navigational purposes if needed. Just by looking at the boat's set up at sea, anyone would know that the *Katana* was a serious diving machine.

The *Katana* looked so lonely floating there waiting for its master. She must have known that her captain would not board her again; it was too sad a picture to be otherwise. Disciplined and patient, *Katana* slowly rocked to the rhythm of the marina, waiting. The sadness of this image could have overwhelmed me, but I caught myself and concentrated on the task at hand. I quickly moved my mind back to the ceremony.

The Craws' lives came to an abrupt end while on their return trip from a day's snorkeling on Lanai Island. By all accounts, it was another wonderful day in Hawaii with sunny skies, gentle trade winds, and lush palms crowning white sandy beaches.

Three hundred yards offshore of Sans Sousi Beach in Waikiki, Craig flew their tiny Robinson R-22 helicopter low to admire the south shore reefs on their way back to the Honolulu Airport.

He was cleared to land with his flight path approved by Honolulu Tower. The chopper had been a recent purchase, and this would be the couple's first romantic getaway on the craft. They were scheduled to leave for another Marshall Islands spearfishing trip with Hughsan and the dive group the next morning.

Just off the beach without warning, a loud blast screamed from the rotor. Like lead, the copter plunged from the sky into the ocean. The helicopter crashed with the rotor blades folding over on themselves and slamming into the cockpit, killing both Craig and Susie instantly. Beachgoers on the Waikiki shoreline were horrified.

Onlookers witnessed the copter moving 200 feet above the water. Then, in a surreal instant, the copter fell and crashed on its side. Before anyone could react, the craft sank and disappeared beneath the surface chop just past the waves.

Honolulu Fire Department's "Rescue One" search and rescue team was dispatched. In a matter of seconds, Captain Manny Neves and his crew of specialists sped off to launch the 21-foot Rescue Boat at the Ala Wai Harbor and raced to the scene next to the War Memorial Natatorium on the beach.

The rescue boat arrived offshore to a chaotic scene with hundreds of onlookers pointing to different sites from various angles. Firefighters on shore relayed directions from eyewitnesses. The squad started their search immediately. Two scout divers went over the side with dive gear to be towed on port and starboard sides of the boat to scan the bottom for the crash site. The visibility was clear all the way to the bottom.

The rescue boat slowly maneuvered in search patterns as the divers surveyed the submerged reefs. Then, there ahead and further out to sea, a slick sheen of fuel glistened in the late day sun. The rescue boat motored to the suspected site. A loud hand slap on the side of the boat signaled that the scout divers had located the helicopter.

Captain Neves levered the boat into neutral. The scouts let go of the tow rope and descended to the chopper. It was demolished. Personal gear and broken parts of the craft were scattered everywhere in a tight circle. The crash's impact with the water shoved the aluminum shell of the lower chassis up into the cabin space; the clear, bubble-shaped canopy was torn away from the craft and dotted the ocean floor. Craig and Susie lay strapped into their seats. Both had sustained massive injuries.

The divers unbuckled the Craws one by one, bringing them up to the surface where the firefighters encased their bodies in a protective covering. Rescue One ran up to the beach and discharged the bodies to the EMS personal at the San Souse shoreline.

Some delay in the process of transferring the bodies from one agency to another caused the Craws to lay there on the sand for nearly two hours before being taken from the scene. A small somber crowd gathered round the covered bodies. There was no laugher or joy on the beach. Early evening crept in with an aura of uncertainty. The crowd of onlookers surrounded the bodies as if in a religious observance. It could not have been more eerie with a circle of strangers, silent in mediation on the gravity of the lives taken that lay before them.

The beachfront hotel's tiki torches were lit and soon brought a glow to the beach set against the backdrop of late sunset skies off Waikiki. Restaurant music filled the beach and surrounding area as soothing Hawaiian melodies floated down to water's edge. The hotel restaurant played Kui Lee's song, "I'll Remember You." The poignant melody drifted down the beach in a twisted annotation of their lives.

Newspapers, radio and TV stations reported the dreadful occurrence that evening and in the days to come. The images of the Rescue One boat and the red and white striped Coast Guard cutter so close to shore, canoes, personal watercraft, and the crowd of onlookers made this so public a spectacle, so final a life-ending event! It was a horrible shock to family, friends, and all who lived in the community. Everyone prayed for their eight-year-old son and only child, Travis.

Overwhelming grief traveled fast through our network of divers. Travis was kept isolated and radios and televisions were kept silent for fear of releasing the information to Travis too soon and in such a way that would cause further grief or damage. Emergency arrangements were made for help in dealing with

Travis about the loss of his parents. Susie's mom (Joy Anderson) and brother (Bruce Stanbery) flew into town immediately.

A near-capacity crowd filled the park for the Craws' funeral service. It would be a dignified memorial to honor Craig and Susie while giving everyone an opportunity to show respect and express their grief. The Senior Pastor of Calvary by the Sea Lutheran Church officiated the non-traditional open air ceremony celebrating their lives.

Dan Briner, one of Craig's best friends from sixth grade at Iolani School, gave the primary eulogy. Dan and the Craw started diving together at the age of 14 and continued on through college. Despite the seriousness of the moment, Dan brought some relief with laughter as he told stories of Craig's youth and the mischief that they stirred up at school.

After Dan's eulogy, "Kaiko" (Arthur Okimoto,) another classmate and long-time dive buddy of Craig, introduced the congregation to Craig and Susie as the divers he knew and loved. There were many people at the ceremony who didn't have the great pleasure of knowing them as we did. There were business associates of Craig's, educator friends of Susie's, Travis' classmates' parents, neighbors, friends, and many from the community who came to say "Aloha."

So many people were touched by the lives of Craig and Susie. While it was selfish to think that our divers knew the Craws better than any of their other friends, that's how we felt. Most of us considered ourselves their private water family while they were away from their biological families.

Among our loose-knit group of regular drift divers was a select core of deep divers who were near exclusive to themselves in their extreme trophy diving. We referred to them as the Banks Divers, the Deep Divers, or the Ninjas. Many of us had little interest in pushing the limits to the lengths that they did but respected their chosen diving profiles just the same. The Craw, Kaiko, "Aukai" (James Carson,) Gernot Spallek, and Peter Warwick were part of a band of ninjas.

Kaiko spoke eloquently as he told the gathering about the dive ninjas and the Mount Everest of dive spots where Craig and Susie dove 18 miles out to sea at the Penguin Banks. He moved the crowd's emotions with the vivid descriptions of the Superbowl and the Coliseum dive sites, the Craws' favorites. Kaiko announced that later in the week a group of his dive buddies would take Craig and Susie's ashes out to sea and dive the Superbowl to put their ashes to rest. That is what the Craws wanted.

Then Hughsan came to the speaker's position and offered his condolences to all family and friends. Hugh invited anyone in the crowd who wished to say something about the Craws to come forward. Several of Susie's friends filed before the crowd to share their stories. One dear friend came up to speak of her with great love and affection, praising Susie for being the talented educator she was. She spoke of Susie's devotion to the education of her students and to Hanahau'oli School. A group of women who called themselves Susie's Spirit Sisters lead the congregation in a stirring melody of "Amazing Grace." There was not a dry eye in the crowd. All of these women pained a very tender feminine side of Susie our diver buddies had not fully appreciated.

It was my turn to honor the Craws. I don't know how it was decided, but I agreed to do the toast. My task was a mere gesture of aloha, but for me it was the most serious bon voyage toast that anyone could ever be asked to carry out. I walked up to the front of the congregation. This toast would be my formal endeavor of sending their sprits to what lay beyond. I could think of nothing else since assigned this task several days ago. This banzai had to be done properly; it would mean so much to the Craws.

Although Craig's traditions lay solid in the Western world, being born and raised in Hawaii, he respected the local practices of many cultures. He was part Hawaiian from his maternal grandmother. Susie also embraced the varied cultures representative of Hawaii. Although she moved here from Texas, she was quick to learn and adopt most of our local customs. She loved Hawaii and everything about it. A big part of the Hawaiian style was embracing the best of all peoples. We were a melting pot of races, colors, and creeds. We teased each other's nationalities… haoles, protégées, kanakas, and the like, but we embraced our differences, intermarried and encouraged multi-ethnicities.

Early in his years, Craig developed a great love for the Japanese culture, especially the traditions of the ancient samurai. Craig fancied himself a samurai warrior, a fish hunter-killer. Within his interpretation of the bushido warrior class, the bushido code was his rule of conduct and sake his preferred celebratory beverage. For the Samurai in feudal Japan, Bushido was the code of honor, as chivalry was to the medieval European knights. I knew this was part of the idealist kid in him, but he was quite serious about it.

Craig was supported and encouraged in this respect for the samurai and its traditions by his deep diver group, the ocean ninjas. Sometimes joking, but oftentimes serious, the ninja code meant a lot to these aggressive divers. I knew that this final banzai toast would be important to Craw and the ninjas, but I questioned what the toast would mean to this varied group of people. We were not in Japan. What would three whaling banzais mean to Susie's mom and brother from Texas? It concerned me that this act of respect might be misunderstood and rejected.

As far as the toast itself was concerned, I had witnessed a number of banzai toasts and even done a few of my own. However, most often these toasts were held at birthdays, weddings, and other celebrations. Banzai is a toast for long life and happiness. Only once before did I participate in a banzai toast at a Shinto funeral. It was very solemn and respectful, but the congregation was primarily Japanese, not Caucasian.

One of the issues that kept nagging at me was whether the meaning of banzai would change from a wedding to a funeral. I believed it could be used in the here and now for a long physical life or for the hereafter for a long and happy afterlife, but I was still uncertain of exact meanings and subtle implications. Would some of the mainland guests mistake the banzai for the kamikaze charges in our war with Japan? I worried.

I looked over the crowd and saw their son Travis. Surrounded by the love of his grandmother, uncle, and a host of calabash family, he looked the picture of confused innocence. His muted smile painted over the uncertainty of this mystifying occasion, his tender eyes stared forward in attention.

Everything became a blur as I turned to the crowd and started my speech. "I'm a friend of Craig and Susie Craw, and I'm honored to lead the banzai toast." My voice was steady, but my body jittered as I gave the congregation instructions. "The banzai toast should come from your heart. With your hands resting at your side, let them fly up to the heavens as you shout, 'Banzai!' I will lead with a 'Banzai,' and then you will repeat with a 'Banzai.'

Please stand."

To keep my concentration steady, I looked over the mass of souls to the white concrete apartments towering behind the gathering. Each condominium stacked together, up and down, and side to side to form an unending stack of living spaces. It looked like a bank of living crypts, like the dead coral colonies in the ocean. I raised my eyes, letting the sun over Koko Head beckon them into a temporary glaze.

With a commanding voice I shouted, "May Craig and Susie's spirits fly to the heavens! Banzai!" I yelled with my hands flailing into the air above my head.

The crowd followed with a "Banzai" as hands flew up here and there like the waves in a choppy sea.

I paused, and then bellowed out a second charge, this time with more confidence and bravado in my voice, "May Craig and Susie's spirits fly to the heavens! Banzai!"

The crowd roared, "Banzai!"

I shouted aloud with more vigor and zest, "May Craig and Susie's spirits fly to the heavens! BANZAI!" My hands reached high to touch the rays cresting over Koko Head. The crowd roared "BANZAI" in a final, mob-like catharsis.

After this final charge, I felt assured that Craig and Susie would have a long spiritual life together. I retreated to my spot on the grass. With my eyes down, looking at the tiny blades of torn grass, I said to myself, Crawman, it's done, the best I could do.

Kaiko's teenage daughter was called before the crowd to perform a hula interpretation of Kui Lee's "I'll Remember You." It was as if this would be a theme for the Craws. All eyes followed as she made her way to the small clearing of grass. With all the sadness, recounted memories, and personal regrets of losing our friends, this beautiful young woman came forth with an offering of a fresh breath of love.

Her long, black hair fell past her shoulders, resting on a fitted pearl white holoku muumuu with an abbreviated train. Her petite size and tender demeanor gave all the feeling of grace and innocence. She was elegant. At such a time, in such a place, she brought the beauty of youth to a crowd so mournful.

"I'll Remember You" is a melody sung to the lament of promised remembrances of love. The music started. The young lady posed at a position of rest looking out into the crowd. The haunting voice of Kui Lee crooned through the tape player, "I'll remember you..." She started her hula, and with an inspired movement of her body, her elegant hips swayed and girly torso glided to model the tune in a traditional hula style. Lovely arms and hands danced ever so slowly to paint the love promise before our eyes. The crowd watched in awe, as thoughts of the Craws and the sadness of our loss surfaced.

"I'll remember you...

Long after this endless summer is gone..."

It would have been so easy for any of us to fall to our calls of sorrow, but it was the innocence of her eyes, moving, searching, and looking, that beckoned us to calm and peace. She kept us all serene; it was an inspiring performance.

Then Hughsan announced that there would be a flower-laying ceremony over our Split Rock diving location just outside Moanalua Bay. Space permitting on the boats, everyone was invited to attend.

The crowd took some time to disperse. People shared stories and caught up with each other's lives. Sometime later, after the crowd departed, some of the divers, family, and friends gathered at the boat dock to board the handful of boats for a flower-laying send-off. Our usual excitement of going to sea was absent, replaced by the weighty feeling of moral obligation and melancholy.

Katana led *It's Time* and a small flotilla through the marina in processional from our makeshift open-air church in the park. The journey to sea would be a symbolic farewell to where Craig and Susie would reside, deep in the heart of Maui Nui. For those mourners who were not familiar with the Craws' final resting place at sea, it would be a chance to experience the beauty of the Craws' ocean and its watery fields of blue.

Palm fronds, ferns, tea leaves, and other Hawaiian vegetation decorated the boats and gave signal to all who would observe the seriousness of our procession. The motorcade would have navigational right of way to all boats underway. In addition to our processional, the seriousness of our expressions gave public notice of the funeral rite.

We moved through the marina at a dirge's pace. As we passed the waterfront homes, people at weekend play calmed their activities and gave an air of respect as we passed. The boats motored up to the highway bridge; all boats inbound cleared the channel for our exit. Pleasure boaters idled their motors and remained silent as we passed out to sea. Beachgoers at the side of the channel stood and took notice of the unusual activity.

In less than 15 minutes we arrived at our dive site to moderate seas of navy blue. *It's Time* continued to circle atop the spot as the other boats followed to form a loose oval of moving craft. When we were all in position, motors were cut and boats silenced. In an orderly fashion, family, friends, and guests took turns moving to the back of their boats. Each picked a spot in the sea and threw flowers into the air to blow downwind and land atop the water. A floating circle of love began to form from the accumulating flowers. White and yellow plumeria leis, red carnations, ornate white tuberoses, blue and purple orchids, and butterfly crowns, and tea leaf leis bobbed together before us. Several large wreaths were also deposited. Soon the area was covered with a collage of colors and a sea of green vegetation.

The boats floated loosely for a time, caressed by the sea and intermingling with our ceremonial altar of flowers. Each person was silent with his or her own memories of Craig and Susie. When all had sufficient time to say their goodbyes, *It's Time*'s motors cranked up and commenced the processional back to shore. Later next week, the final interment of the Craws' cremated ashes would be attempted by the ninjas.

The Craws' Mariners Ridge residence sat on the foothills of the Koolau Mountain Range just behind and above the Hawaii Kai Marina. It was the perfect spot for a guy like the Crawman. From this commanding position on the mountain's crest, his was the ideal overview of the Esplanade Marina, the dive boats, Moanalua Bay and the Molokai Channel. The divers relied on Craig to give us a last-minute update on ocean conditions before diving. He was high enough on the mountain to see between Koko Crater and Koko Head out into the ocean toward Molokai and had the skill to judge sea conditions for our channel crossings. Although we primarily relied on the marine radio weather forecasts, it wasn't always right. Craw's weather calls were always on the money, as he saw it all live from his mountain-top nest.

Susie's mom and brother took up residence on the ridge during these times of sorrow. In spite of their unimaginable grief, their principal concern was the care and comfort of Travis. Friends of the Craws focused on the family's need for privacy but stood ready to help.

Early Wednesday morning, a week after the accident, the cremated remains of Craig and Susie would be put to rest. In compliance with their wishes, their wet suits and weight belts would be entombed in their beloved Penguin Banks undersea cave and their ashes scattered at depth in the Superbowl Crater. Only then would they be free to roam the moving currents of the Banks in peace.

These funeral arrangements would be an impossible task were it not for the ninjas who dove the site regularly. In the middle of the ocean, the pinnacle of all dive challenges, the Superbowl would care for Crawman and Susie for the rest of time.

To understand the significance of this dive spot, often referred to as the Banks or the Penguin Banks, you have to have a feel for the geologic development of the Islands. Over four hundred thousand years ago, just a blink of the eye in geologic time, the islands of Maui, Kahoolawe, Molokai, Lanai, and all the smaller offshore islands in between were all one island, Maui Nui. The largest island in the Hawaiian chain, Maui Nui, was even bigger than the Big Island of Hawaii.

Through the passing of time, the island sank and the smaller volcanoes separated from each other to form the islands we know today. The seabed between the islands is really the one island, eroded and washed away by the waves over the years. The Penguin Banks are the submerged part of southwestern Maui Nui.

The Island of Molokai's sunken Penguin Banks extend way out to sea toward Oahu, but much of it underwater in the 150 to 300 foot depth. Looking at a nautical chart, it becomes obvious that the submerged island forms a massive undersea current-swept plateau that runs for many miles. The reputation of the Banks as a fertile fishing ground and its close proximity to Oahu made the undersea mountain range a natural curiosity to the Craw and his watermen friends.

Years ago, in search of adventure and the ultimate diving

spot, Craig, Kaiko and their mates found the ledges with an airplane spotter looking for wave and color changes from above, and Craig and the boys using a depth finder and loran coordinates from his boat below. In constant communication with each other, they fine tuned-the ledge line and marked it with triangulated coordinates. It wasn't long before they discovered the most extraordinary dive spots at the crest of the plateau's edge, the Superbowl.

It was early morning on Mariners Ridge the day of our final farewell. The ninja divers launched the *Katana* to meet with *It's Time* at the Esplanade boat docks. Susie's brother Bruce joined the divers and brought the Craws' urns with him. While Travis slept, Susie's mother Joy sat in the living room rocker staring out the plate glass window looking down at the marina and the boat docks in the distance. She watched the boats prepare for departure. It was an ideal view; she sat alone and would follow the boats' progress out to sea until they vanished into the horizon.

This would be the first trip out to the Banks for the *Katana* without its master at the helm. It's always a sad occasion for a mariner when a boat and its captain part ways, but this occasion would be a parting most final. The sword of the master would take its captain's remains to his ocean grave to unite with nature. All that would remain would be loving memories and the temporary headstones of dive suits and weight belts where few would dare dive.

The crew of *Katana* and *It's Time* completed important last-minute preparations before heading out to sea. The *Katana* would carry Kaiko, Aukai, Patrick, Keith Turner, and Bruce. Kaiko and Aukai were long-time dive partners from Craw's younger days when the ninjas discovered the Maui Nui spots. I could think of no better pallbearers. Patrick and Keith were part of the current deep-diving group. Patrick would serve as the boat driver and Keith as the cameraman for the service. *It's Time* transported Hughsan, V, Dan Briner, and three long time friends of the Craws. Everyone on the boats would bear witness to the passing of the Craws into the sea.

The divers headed out to the Penguin Banks in fair weather. Kaiko knew well that this service is what Craig wanted and held on tight to a comforting feeling that he would fulfill his buddy's request. He played back the mental images of their conversation on the way back from the Banks shortly after the passing of their buddy and regular Banks diver, Dr. Gernot Spallek.

Gernot was a successful medical practitioner who operated a clinic in Waikiki. A committed family man and avid deep diver, he and the ninjas were dear friends and frequent dive buddies. Because of the rigors of Gernot's schedule, he dove whenever time allowed, not necessarily when someone was available. Occasionally on the calmest of days, he might dive a site alone. A master diver and man of extraordinary talent, he was comfortable with everything at sea. He kept his dive boat at the Kuapa Marina and would often be seen traveling in an out the channel to the ocean.

It was a tragic day for his family, friends, and patients when the Banks took Gernot. It was nearing the end of whale-watching season when he went for a dive before the mammals migrated back to colder waters. Gernot did not return. Late that afternoon when his return was long overdue, his wife called his buddy Grant for help. Grant alerted the divers to the situation. Craw gave the Coast Guard the dive site coordinates, and the divers launched the boat. Gernot's wife joined the divers and motored out to assist in the Coast Guard search and rescue operations.

Just before dark the Coast Guard radioed that the boat was anchored on site but there were no signs of Gernot. The divers continued their search out to sea with only the stars to light their way. They drove through the night doing search patterns to account for wind and wave. The sounds of whales were everywhere, but none of the frantic searchers would enjoy them this dreadful evening.

Early the next morning the Coast Guard radioed that they found Gernot floating lifeless some 28 miles offshore. He was at peace and unharmed by any sea creature or predator. It was a tragic time for the Spallek family; his 10 and 12 year old boys would grow up without their loving father.

Days later a flotilla of boats made its way out to the Superbowl to scatter Gernot's ashes above his final home. As the boats gathered calmly above the Superbowl, Gernot's family tearfully let free his ashes as Hawaiian leis were gifted to the sea in his honor. A cloud of puffy remains filled and expanded into the sea to the sounds of whale songs. The humpbacks were everywhere. Just under the funeral party of boats, a slow shower of steady whale air rose from the sea floor to bubble up throughout the floating enclave.

With permission from their mom, Gernot's sons jumped into the deep to bathe with their father and the whales. Soon, one by one, dive buddies, guests and other family members joined in the immersion and sent Gernot to the sea.

The untimely death of such a champion diver and dear friend shook our dive community to the core. Gernot's death served as a constant reminder of our own mortality. With this frightful memory fresh in his mind, Craw told Kaiko and the other divers how he would like to be remembered with a last send-off at sea.

Kaiko carried these burning images of Craw's last request to this present moment. Now, here he was on the *Katana* taking Craig and Susie out to sea. These were unsettling thoughts, but Kaiko struggled to put them on hold as he rehearsed the dive plan for a smooth, successful service.

The *Katana* and *It's Time* sliced through calm swells at a quarter beam angle toward their final destination. The crew busied themselves in preparation of the one-shot-only burial dive. Kaiko tried to concentrate on the dive plan, but his mind raced from one thought to another. He remembered Susie and her close brush with death at the Superbowl five years earlier. It was widely known that she cheated the sea with her life once before.

Craig and Susie went out for a day of diving at the Superbowl on the Banks. While surfacing from their dive, the currents turned brawny and swept Susie away from the anchor line 60 feet under. Susie struggled and spent all her energies trying to swim back to the safety of the boat and its auxiliary air tanks. There was nothing she could do; the currents were too strong. She was swept away and surfaced when her air supply fell to empty. She knew she was in trouble; while underwater she felt her legs go limp and physical sensations cease. Susie was seriously bent. She surfaced with no boat in sight and did all she could to remain calm and plan for survival at sea.

There was nothing Craw could do either. Susie surfaced before Craig and disappeared into a vast blue wilderness. Craig could not go after her without decompression time, or he, too, would end up with the bends. Craig agonized over his situation but could do nothing until he was cleared to surface and look for Susie. He reassured himself that Susie was very skilled and would float at the surface until he found her. All she had to do was float, breathe, and stay alive long enough for him to find her. Craig had no way of knowing she was struck with decompression sickness.

When Craig's diving computer cleared, he surfaced to climb aboard *Katana* and search for Susie. Nervously he scanned the ocean in every direction to the horror of finding an empty sea. He remained calm and called the Coast Guard for help. The officer on duty launched a broadcast bulletin on the radio and initiated an immediate search for a missing diver out on the Banks.

Susie floated in pain semiconscious, paralyzed from her waist down. Her inflated diving vest kept her floating upright as she drifted away. Craig started search patterns down current of their position, trying as best he could to account for wind, wave, and tidal movements. Controlled and disciplined, he focused his energies on the search and dispelled any negative thoughts of the gravity of the situation. Several hours passed; an empty ocean loomed everywhere. There were occasional sea birds overhead and startled flying fish fleeing the *Katana*'s path, but other than that, nothing of Susie. Several additional agonizing hours dragged by with still no sign of her.

Four hours later the Coast Guard radioed she had been found and picked up by a fishing boat. Susie was in transit, the boat speeding back to the harbor. Her condition serious and symptoms severe, she was rushed to the decompression chamber for emergency treatment. It was doubtful if she would walk again, her nerves overcome with the nitrogen from the bends. After two months of treatments in the recompression chamber and extensive therapy for over a year to put her back on her feet, she was rehabilitated to walk with a slight limp.

The ninja divers' thoughts wandered to the many wonderful dives they shared with Craw. To the man, each diver tried to control his feelings and mentally rehearse the specific tasks that he had to perform to keep the service proper.

For the average recreational diver, the Maui Nui dive spots

at the Penguin Banks were world-class challenges. Along the miles of underwater plateau that spanned the distance from west Molokai to south Oahu, the Superbowl and its smaller twin, the Coliseum, stood out as unusual geologic wonders. At this particularly elusive place, two dormant volcanic craters dimple the edge of the towering ocean plateau. The top of the plains lay some 180 feet undersea. Then the cliff line drops off to 250 feet before sharply sloping down into oblivion. Right at the very edge, the 100 yards round caldera of the Superbowl lay stamped into the terrain with its outer, upper-wall formation remaining intact like a ring of stone. The underside of the outer edge line eroded, forming a large arch at the cliff line into the crater.

As schools of predator fish come up from the depths, it provides the perfect grand entrance into the volcanic undersea stadium. The inside floor of the fish dome is filled with sand and weathered rocks of all shapes and sizes to form an expansive carpet for the fish habitat. The walls jut up from the sunken caldera bottom at 235 feet to the top of the plateau in typical volcanic cliff-like formation.

Away from the arch and deep into the right side of the crater wall is a small cave. It has no particular name, but it is there where the markers of Craig and Susie's lives would be placed. At this depth, it's too deep for seaweed, tropical fish, or other life that one might see at a reef. This was a dark, cold place where giant fish congregate, a kingdom left to large schools of ulua, uku, and sharks. It's a trophy spearfisherman's paradise. Only a handful of masters would dare to operate in this environment, much less take the lives of these monster predators in hand-to-fin combat.

Just 75 yards south of the Superbowl lies the Coliseum crater. It's a slightly smaller replica of the Superbowl but has fared more poorly over time. At the front of the crater, where the edge meets the ledge line, the thin rock structure has completely eroded away. The part that is washed out is evidenced by the rubble that's strewn about its opening. A sizable part of the caldera wall is missing, exposing the crater to the open currents of the deep. It was given the name of the Coliseum because its aging façade resembles its namesake monument in Rome.

Connecting these marvels together is an industrial cable lying on the bottom running from one crater to the other. The long steel was placed there by Craw, Kaiko, and their buddies years ago to make maneuvering between the shooting galleries easier in times of whipping currents. A hand-over-hand on the cable is easier than trying to swim straight into the current. Imagine being "narked" at 230 feet, dragging a fighting fish between spots. Nitrogen narcosis, the excessive buildup of nitrogen in the brain, becomes a problem for most divers past 100 feet. It makes a person feel invincible like a drunk and debilitates the diver with mental confusion. In a raging current, the risk of being confused and swept off the plateau into the depths is real.

Sometime close to midday the boats found their way to the Banks undersea cliffs. It's no easy task finding a precise spot 200 plus feet down 18 miles out at sea with only a distant island reference, depth finder, and a Loran Radio Direction Finder (a forerunner to the GPS system.) Miles and miles of cliff line run underwater, so finding the right spot is part luck and part skill. Both boats worked and reworked the area attempting the perfect line up for the divers' entry.

Accounting for wind, waves, currents, and boat position is critical to landing a diver on the exact spot, particularly at the Banks. Kaiko knew the Maui Nui dive spots well. He and Craw discovered the sites and dove them for years. It was only natural that Hughsan contacted him to take the lead on the Banks funeral service. Although Kaiko was not a part of our group, Craig often talked of him and made a Banks dive with him every now and then. It seems Kaiko's life with the Fire Department and the time constraints of raising a family made him less accessible for his passion of deep diving, but we all knew that Kaiko could be relied on to find the Superbowl without difficulty. There could be no mistakes today; the divers had to find the Superbowl on their first dive.

Each of the three divers would use his unique ninja diving rig while Patrick kept a safety watch topside. In addition to their standard personal gear, the pallbearer team used Genesis steel 120s capable of carrying 3,500 pounds of air, and a high-performance Scubapro regulator with a backup octopus. Attached to the 120 was an aluminum 19 pony tank with a separate high-performance regulator cleaned for oxygen. The mini tank was filled with pure oxygen for the last 10 to 20 feet of scrubbing the nitrogen from their bodies. No spear guns would be used today.

After fine-tuning the boat for an exact position with land-based triangulation and depth-finder readings, Kaiko gave the signal that they were above the spot. The new GPS onboard confirmed his decision. After some preparation, the divers were ready and splashed over the side for the ceremony. Losing each other during a dive of this magnitude had no place in their preplanned profile, so they dove in tight formation. Kaiko carried the package containing Craig and Susie's weighted wetsuits and laminated photos with little Travis. Aukai swam down with two containers housing the ashes of the Craws, and Keith followed the burial procession filming the ritual for Travis. It would be a documented memento of his parents' final resting place which would be given to him when he was older. The team hurriedly finned its way toward the bottom before the currents had the opportunity to blow them off course.

Kaiko lead the way down, lost in his rehearsal of the task at hand. There was no place for his grief now; this was a serious endeavor of the utmost consequence. Any slipup could be dangerous and potentially life-threatening. Everything had to be carried out precisely for the divers' safety and the importance of the occasion.

It was a lonely trio of silent aquanauts, one following the other, each seeking the bottom of the near-endless blue that would reveal the edge of the vast Maui Nui plateau. Kaiko did not pay much attention to the cool water against his face or the small organisms floating on the gentle currents. His mind raced with anticipation, hoping to see a particular black seabed rising up from the deep void.

Would we land in the right spot on the cliff line or would we be off the mark? The question repeated in Kaiko's mind over and over again as he scanned for signs of the Superbowl. Slowly a shadowy darkness rose–it was the cliff line. Two craters were vaguely visible ahead. They were upstream of the Superbowl, so the divers adjusted their descent to angle directly to their destination. This gave the divers the bearings they needed.

At 200 feet the divers landed on the top of the Superbowl's

inside upper wall. Soon they were floating over its edge. It was majestic. A school of oversized ulua hovered around the bowl and open arch leading through the cliff. The fish moved quite peacefully, allowing the divers a path into their domain. Ulua drifted in and around the arch to give the divers more space to conduct their service. Perhaps it was coincidental, but a feeling of welcome was present.

The divers effortlessly dropped down another 30 feet to the center of the caldera and made their way to the cave at the other end of the inner ridge. With ghostly breathing sounds from their regulators, these three mourners made their way to the lava vault. It was dark and eerily blue. Kaiko and Aukai waited for their eyes to adjust to the darkness to find the right niche to leave the symbols of their friends. This would become a grave marker that few would know and none would see.

There ahead, on the right, was the perfect place. Both wet suits and the laminated family picture were lodged deep into the fissure. There was a moment of pause before Aukai backed up and led the way out to the center of the bowl. At just the right spot, he hovered upright and the simple service began.

Aukai handed Craw's urn to Kaiko first. Kaiko pried it open. The water rushed in to create an initial ash cloud, a round puff of greeting, as Craig and the ocean took on each other's substance.

At the edge of Kaiko's arms the dark, indigo blue water exploded into eruptions of fine white powder. Methodically it grew in size. The three ninjas were in a fantastic dream as Craw's ashes seemed to call to the ocean, "I am here, I return to you from where I came." Slowly the ashes moved through the water in a cascade created by a massive, ever-expanding cloud bank. Vapors of cream moved outward, surrendering Craig's transformed flesh into the elements.

Cloud after cloud of ashes puffed opened, growing to fill the area, invited by the soft undercurrents and moving tides. As the increasing mist grew even larger, the vibrant white grew fainter. Soon the fading clouds of Craig's former life filtered toward the arch. The once billowy clouds turned lighter and lighter until they became transparent threads.

A serenity moved through the divers.

After a respectful pause, Kaiko opened Susie's container. The ocean rushed in to greet her with excitement as the currents came forth to take her as they did her husband. Now it was both the sea and her waiting partner that came to welcome her. The faint wisps of Craig's ashes bloomed forth again with the bright ashes of Susie. For a moment it seemed as if Susie's ashes gave new life to Craig, but soon Susie, too, was overcome by the spirit of the ocean as she coupled with her husband.

The Craws' fading ashes, now intertwined, swirled out through the caldera arch. The crowded school of ulua serenely witnessed the internment. The farther the Craws drifted, the less they remained. Muted shards of surface light reaching the particulates reflected the ashes in the most magical hues and tones. Sparkled dust moved toward a lone, majestic black coral tree that stood sentinel to the outer entrance to the lava arch.

The coral plant rose from the lava with an eerie likeness to a weeping willow the size of several large men. A slender, hardened, brownish-black trunk expanded to smaller branches and tiny threads. The skeletal bush was covered with thin agile fibers of breathing coral colonies living off the nutrients that drifted through its web.

As if drawn to its living filters, the fading remnants of the Craws sparkled in a last faint farewell before final surrender. It was as if a tree of life had taken the old physical remains and filtered the past into a new spirit reborn. Kaiko, Aukai and Keith watched the miracle, inspired with a new reverence of their own lives being a mere expression of nature's elements. It was obvious to each of them that this is where we all shall return, either by soil or sea—back to the cells of nature.

It was over all too fast, this changing of the departed remains into the endless spirit of the ocean. The divers started their slow ascent to the surface. Each took the journey in melancholy reflection of their friendship with the Craws. There was more than enough time in unrushed decompression to review their life connections with their dive buddies. Silently to the sounds of their regulators, all were lost in their private reflections, each reliving personal incidents with Craig and Susie. As was the standard practice of the Maui Nui divers, pure oxygen was used to purge their systems of any excessive nitrogen during their decompression stop. To their pride and self-satisfaction, the ceremony was executed exactly as planned.

The divers surfaced at the boat where Patrick helped them out of the water. When they were safely aboard with their gear stowed, Kaiko opened his premium sake bottle imported from Japan and prepared for a deep divers' sake toast. Aukai, Patrick, and Keith gathered with Kaiko, who dispensed a generous portion of the rice wine into their glasses for the Kanpai Toast. Once served, Kaiko raised his glass and signaled the others to raise their glasses. This classic toast was eagerly adopted by the ninjas as a commemorative toast of good times.

In a way that only Kaiko could present with his humble disposition and silent, stoic stature, he led the toast. Similar to the Banzai toasts, Kaiko waited for a repetition of each phrase before moving to the next. Smiling with a sense of relief that all had gone well, he shouted in a sumo wrestler's deep, guttural voice:

"KANPAI!" (CHEERS!)

Patrick, Aukai, and Keith responded, "KANPAI!"

Again Kaiko shouted, "KANPAI!"

All three divers followed suit, "KANPAI!"

Then the clincher. In the loudest of male bravados, Kaiko yelled in climax:

"KANPAI!"

At this point, the boys were in a frenzy and shouted in unison, "KANPAI!"

The boys sipped the ceremonial beverage, marking its unique flavor with their memory of the spiritual experience below. After a pause, conversations ensued, old stories shared, and new memories were stored.

Katana drifted with the currents. It was satisfied that the crew had put its captain to an admirable rest. *Katana* knew well all the guests onboard and served them as loyally as its master. Only now, after a farewell at sea, would Katana accept its sad fate of never seeing its master and mistress again in this world.

The ninjas felt content that they performed their duties in an honorable manner, in accordance to their code. Kaiko took the helm and cranked the *Katana's* motors up to start their long journey back to shore.

The seas were perfect for trolling, so *It's Time* and *Katana* set out the fishing lines and lures to see what gifts the ocean might provide. *Katana* sliced through the wind and waves as it dragged a modest lure spread of jet heads and feather jigs.

Immediately after the lines were in the water, "Slam," the fist rod went off. One quick aku (skipjack tuna) was brought aboard. "Slam," another, and then another. *It's Time* was having similar fishing success. Well before they neared landfall, six good-sized aku were aboard and in *Katana's* coolers and four aboard *It's Time*. The ninjas were thrilled to have scored this cache of fish. It was a gift of happiness for the divers jumping around and reeling in their catch. The excitement and good fortune helped to lighten their dark moods.

The ship's crew squawked back and forth on the radio to *It's Time* boasting of their catch as the ships competed for poundage of fish. Kaiko was just as excited about the aku swimming to the boat as the other ninjas, but he wasn't so sure that it was their good luck or great skill. He and Craw had made this same boat trip so many times before with nowhere near the success they were experiencing today. It was a welcomed curiosity. Kaiko began to feel that other forces may be at work but kept his thoughts to himself.

Long-time dive buddies build complex bonds of trust and loyalty between each other. They develop certain skills of reading each other's minds in the water. With one fish after another jumping into the boat, Kaiko felt a stirring of emotion within him and a feeling of some other presence.

As the crew fished, a gradual feeling of peace came over the divers. Kaiko replayed in his mind the white ash clouds of his buddy being welcomed into a loving sea and Craw entreating his wife to their new home. It was a natural miracle of a return to life as it started. These were visions implanted in Kaiko's mind for all of time. Then the idea occurred to him, could Craw be sending these fish up for us? Is it the spirit of our Craw, home at last, sending provisions to care for his companions? Kaiko moved back to the deck cooler, relaxed and looked aft to the trailing boat wake, mesmerized.

Through the years I've had numerous occasions to visit Craig and Susie at their ocean dwelling. It's usually been on our return from diving the outer islands that I would swing by to say "hello." It's never been a big thing; we didn't really plan to visit or anything like that. The thought would just occur to me while out at sea to stop by and say hello to Craig and Susie. I'd adjust my course and make several trolling runs over his spot or bottom fish for uku.

Sure enough, more often than not, I've felt Craig's spirit there with me as I fished the ledge for food. Of all the places I've trolled in the ocean, I've been most consistent at bringing something home from Craig's place. It just happens; fish come up from the bottom as if they were sent to me.

CHAPTER NINE

MAFATU THE BOAT

In the grand scheme of things, a woman like Sandy, born and raised in the vast dirt plains of Texas with a name like "Sandy" and "Sands" must have migrated to the oceans of Hawaii for a higher purpose. I believe she did, all to find a man of the sea, such as me.

After an appropriate courtship, in the dead of winter we flew to Dallas, Fort Worth for a small wedding before her immediate family. Then after the festivities, we returned to Hawaii for a reception at the house as *Bones* looked on to welcome its master and new mistress.

I was a practicing financial planner, so my everyday work week was quite different from my weekends of spearfishing. There were clear delineations to my life on land and sea. I didn't know that soon both would meet to improve my relationship with the ocean.

Sandy and I were newlyweds when we went to an annual insurance company's Easter conference at a world-famous resort on Maui. It was a couples' all-expenses-paid, four-day, wine-and-dine affair with high-powered insurance producers from all over the country. This annual event was a popular forum for socializing and sharing insurance ideas for high net-worth clients.

It was the last night's formal banquet, capped off with a gourmet dinner served in the grand ballroom to the tunes of a full orchestra. The evening would serve as the grand finale of the event. For a simple guy like me, it was an elegant affair.

On stage to the right of the formal orchestra was a brand-new white, fully-loaded, Lincoln Continental Town Car parked on display as the convention's grand prize. What a door prize for a convention! Later in the evening, the master of ceremonies made an announcement that it was time for the drawing. He asked everyone to take their seats, and when we all settled down, we were informed that there were ten keys hidden in the ballroom. Only one key would start the car.

"If your key starts the car, it's yours!" the master of ceremonies proclaimed. Then, he instructed everyone to reach under their seats, as the ten keys were taped to the bottom of the chairs randomly throughout the hall.

I was not very impressed with the odds of winning with nearly five hundred people in attendance. There were bursts of commotion as each person discovered a special key. A woman screamed out with a shrill of excitement, and one gentleman hollered out "yes!" as he did a victory dance at the table. There were other signs of public excitement, and soon the room was in turmoil.

I went through the motions and reached down, knowing that it was a waste of my time and continued my conversation with another broker from Honolulu when I felt an unusual protrusion of tape under my seat. "No way. Tape? Tape and a key?" I questioned myself in disbelief. I worked it free. There it was: a silver key, right before my eyes. I shouted loudly, "I got one!"

Cheers crescendoed from my table. Meanwhile, the orchestra played on as the announcer asked all key holders to come up on stage. There before everyone, ten of us anxiously formed a line at the Lincoln. One by one, with a drum roll, each person was seated in the car and when the orchestra paused, the announcer instructed the key holder to start the engine. If no sound came from the vehicle, the audience sighed in disappointment with a long exaggerated and somewhat downtrodden, "Ah!" Then the participant would leave the stage and it would start all over again for the next person in line.

I kept motioning each participant forward ahead of me in my best Hawaiian hospitality. Since I wasn't going to win the car anyway, I wanted to avoid the public display. Before I realized it, there were two of us left; and again I motioned to the gentleman ahead of me to go first. He got into the vehicle, again... no start! The crowd sighed, and then the room came to life and roared wildly.

I had the key! The announcer ushered me into the car. I

turned the key, and it fired up instantly. The crowd roared even louder! I was motioned out of the car and escorted to the side of the stage. I gave the announcer my card but kept the key. He said that someone would call early the next week to make arrangements to retrieve my prize. Yes, I won the dazzling Lincoln Continental Town Car!

Back at the table, I became a celebrity. Broker after broker came over to congratulate me as I held court for the next 45 minutes. Later, when the evening started to fade, Sandy and I went back to our room exhausted from the excitement. It was hard for me to calm down; I couldn't help but be excited.

It started as a curious thought. I wondered if somehow the company would exchange the car for cash. I already had a car, but a new larger interisland boat would really be grand. The benefits played in my mind like a music jingle that wouldn't leave. Molokai diving would be more accessible with a larger boat, so I'd be able to go more often. More divers and tanks could be safely transported to our dive spots, so we'd have more fun. Interisland overnight dive trips would be more comfortable and much safer, too. A larger boat would also make Sandy feel more comfortable going offshore. I wondered about all the angles and how I might persuade the company that I should have the cash.

After some time, it was finally settled in my mind. I'd sell the executives with a foolproof rational for my request, a car that big wouldn't fit into my small Hawaiian-style carport. The car was too big; I measured my structure and checked it with the stats in the glossy brochure I received at the convention. What was I to do? Sell the house? If they didn't buy into that, I would continue on with the extra expense and additional upkeep of a luxury car.

Come Monday morning I was on the phone with the promoters asking if they would substitute cash for the car. I explained my hardship with a small carport. I tried to sell them on the idea that I might better use a new boat to travel, sort of a transportation thing, kind of like the automobile. Wow, was I surprised–they didn't even care. The executives sent me a check for the promotional fleet price of what they were going to pay for the Lincoln.

I hit the jackpot and would get a new boat! Awesome. I sold my old boat, combined the proceeds with the car money and threw in some additional cash. Then I was off to the San Francisco and

Seattle Boat Shows to find the perfect interisland dream cruiser. Months of research went into narrowing down my choices before I left. Top on my list of manufactures were Radon, C-Dory, and SeaSport Boats, but I would keep all options open until I saw the boats at the shows.

This new cruiser would fulfill a lifetime of dreams for little Mafatu from the Niu River. With a boat of this caliber I could easily conquer the blue water beyond any reef. I'd be free to travel interisland and broaden my diving range. No longer would I be relegated to diving the outer islands in only the best of weather conditions. With the safety of a bigger boat I could conquer the remnants of my childhood fears.

I had a steep list of requirements for the boat, but first and foremost, it had to be safe, big enough for channel crossings, but small enough for me to handle alone. That meant a boat no larger than 28 feet; 25 feet would be ideal. I wanted a boat built with the best fiberglass construction techniques and components designed for rough water. An easy wash down aft deck with big water-purging scuppers was high on the list after Sandy's boat sinking episode. She was particularity concerned with the height of the boat's hull and its freeboard. Who would blame her for her caution? The manufacturer's number of years in business and solid reputation were also important for my long-range ownership plans.

The style of the craft was of particular interest to me. I wanted a deep V-hull to reduce the pounding through the open ocean. After years of crashing through harsh seas, it would be nice to have the comfort of slicing through waves like a sharp knife through warm butter. A large, open aft deck was also desirable to troll six fishing poles or handle four divers suiting up comfortably. A fully-enclosed forward cabin was an absolute must for crossing the Kaiwi channel, even if wind and wave spray engulfed the whole boat. I wanted to steer the new boat high and dry while talking to the boys as we headed to the outer islands. The cabin should sleep two or three and have a strong lockable door with decent room for storage. If we left the boat for shore leave, I'd like to have our gear protected from theft.

Finally, the boat had to be affordable to own and operate. To address this issue, I would keep the cost down by avoiding excessive creature comforts and stylish luxuries. My boat didn't need fancy colors, plush carpeting, over-stuffed furniture, extensive electronics, or other high-dollar additions. Just give me something austere that would stand up to fish blood and a strong fresh-water hosing inside and out. Yes, I wanted a real wash and dry with as little exposed wood as possible. Wood rots over time unless meticulously cared for and varnished. There was another thing about affordability: the cost of operation.

Many boaters forget that a dive boat runs on fuel. With the weight of all those bodies, tanks and equipment, pushing it through the water takes a good, strong motor or two. Because of the size and weight of the loads I would handle, the cost efficiency and safety of a diesel motor became an advantage to me. Although I was initially more comfortable with gas outboards, the cost savings and fuel safety issues got me over the concerns. A diesel motor it would be.

My cousin Larry, a fishing addict and long-time resident of the Northern California Bay Area, arranged his vacation so we could take in the San Francisco Boat Show for as long as it took to find my boat. He visited Hawaii a number of times over the years and each time we'd fish ourselves silly. Every time I think of him, I still see him sitting on the port side aft deck holding his big bull mahi mahi off the west end of Molokai. Larry and his trophy mahi were framed by the setting sun exploding in the background as we headed back to Oahu after a long day of fishing. What a memory.

Larry and I had a great time at the boat show. After four days, I narrowed it down to the Radon or the SeaSport. I was leaning toward the Radon because of the hull thickness, but then the SeaSport company owner told me, "It's not the thickness of the hull, it's the weight of the fiberglass cloth that gives the hull its strength." He went on to explain that their manufacturing process carefully controls the amount of resin used to impregnate the layers of cloth so as not to add additional weight, while making the hull stronger. He also boasted that SeaSport used a double-hull construction technique.

It seems that in the Pacific Northwest, where the boat was manufactured, the hull was designed to attempt to survive a direct collision with a floating log. In that part of the country, floating logs in the wilderness frequently wash out to sea. The first hull was the thickest: if a log hit and pierced it, that energy would travel through the half-inch balsa core spacer which would absorb a large part of the impact. The second, thinner inside hull could flex and pull away from the balsa to absorb the rest of the force and bend rather than break apart. I had not heard of this before but was suitably impressed. This feature was a definite attraction for Sandy.

The owner of the company invited me to see their plant and how the boat was built. I took him up on it, and two months later I traveled back to the mainland to visit their Seattle plant and the Seattle Boat Show. With one short tour of their operation, I was sold. The boat was ordered and built to my exact specifications, one of which was the addition of an extra layer of fiberglass cloth on the outside hull. Despite the owner's reassurances that this was not a needed upgrade, I was very particular, knowing that I wanted to be able to hit an interisland barge at night, survive it, and drive home.

My final order was drafted for a 25-footer with a fully-enclosed cabin and large aft deck. It's a deep V-hull with modest reverse chines and a swim step that spans the width of the hull. I went with the lighter motor, a Volvo 185-horse power diesel, duel prop with lots of torque.

The craft would be called "*Mafatu*" after the chief's son who found his courage at sea. It would also be called *Mafatu* after the boy from Niu Stream who aspired to become the boy of legend. It wasn't until many years later that I would learn the meaning of Mafatu. A visiting canoe team of Tahitians at the Molokai to Oahu Canoe Race translated Mafatu to mean "strong heart," or "stout heart." What more fitting a nickname could I have found for myself or my boat?

Six months after my order, the dream boat arrived by weekly cargo barge from Seattle at the Honolulu Harbor. It was shipped shrink-wrapped and loaded on a heavy-duty trailer ready to roll home. What an exciting time; at last my boat was here. However, *Mafatu* would teach me a hard lesson: the free money that allowed me to purchase her would not be free. I was to pay for my good fortune.

It was a bit unnerving driving the boat home during rush-hour traffic, but we arrived without incident at my marina home in less than an hour. I took all the time I needed to back her up into the longest part of the side driveway with Sandy cautiously guiding me back. Immediately and quite unexpectedly, we had a problem! At a distance of 6 inches from the front concrete parameter wall, we ran out of driveway. The trailer tongue stuck out more than a foot and a half into the sidewalk. The protruding tongue was an obstacle to walking on the sidewalk or children playing on the cul-de-sac.

I imagined a neighbor walking at night to stumble on the tongue and break a hip. Then I saw the children playing ball only to run into the trailer to suffer massive head injuries. I dreamt up all sorts of injuries and lawsuits. The liability awards mounted in my mind.

A contractor was called for an estimate to remodel the front of the house and attached wall to accommodate *Mafatu*. While I didn't want to do any renovations, I needed an extra 3 to 5 feet of driveway depth to get the trailer off the sidewalk. There was no other solution but a remodel. Construction options were discussed and a contract signed to remove the front wall and the patio overhang to accommodate the boat... Cha-Ching! That cost some serious money, but it did put a new look on the old house.

Then there was *Mafatu*'s inaugural launch. I drove a special-edition Jeep Cherokee for towing *Bones*, but the car was still fancy enough to use for work. Although it would have been better for boating to drive a powerful pickup truck, a boating fish-truck would not enhance my career. I was also too frugal to own two vehicles, one for work and one for play. The dual-use arrangement of the Jeep for boat towing and business driving worked quite well.

I prepared to launch *Mafatu* Friday evening after work to enjoy the boat over the weekend. When I pulled into Hancock landing there was no one there to rush me. I wanted to do this alone to develop a routine that made it easy for me to get the boat in and out of the water without any stress or wasted time.

I backed the Jeep up and made a slow reverse turn to angle *Mafatu* toward the middle of the ramp and ease her down into the water. The boat wasn't going very fast; the jeep was hardly moving. I applied the brakes as the grade of the ramp got steeper. The brakes locked, but the boat continued purpose-fully down the ramp. *Mafatu* was so much heavier than *Bones*. All four tires froze and ground into the gravel. The sound of screeching gravel and the offensive smell of smoking rub-ber announced that *Mafatu* would not stop. It was headed for the water without hesitation. As the angle steepened the trail-er picked up speed, dragging the Jeep down to the water. My heart stopped.

I was in a panic. Pumping the breaks repeatedly did nothing to arrest the downward motion. I put the car in drive and put some gas to it. That only caused the tires to spin out of control while *Mafatu* continued down to the water. I pulled the emer-gency break but still heard the sound of road pebbles slipping and the smell of rubber. I was doomed. I resigned myself to a total flooding of the Jeep as I watched the water rushed to greet me in the rear view mirror.

The boat smacked the water and floated up from the trailer. Boat, trailer, and Jeep stopped instantly. I got out to see the dam-age. None! Water was up to the lower portion of the rear fender and the tail pipe exhaust was bubbling, but no damage. For safety reasons, my light-weight Jeep was upgraded to a new Ford F-250 heavy-duty truck with a tow package. Cha Ching!

In a very short time it became evident that my new pickup truck didn't fit well in the downtown office underground park-ing garage. Added to that was the inconvenience of driving a large, gaudy truck to see investment clients. That wasn't very flat-tering for a respectable investment advisor. So, as a solution to that developing problem, Sandy gave up her tiny Miyata sports car and bought a new, bigger BMW. I would drive it for business Monday through Friday and she would drive it on the weekends while I drove my dive truck. It was the only compromise that I could come up with under the pressure of the situation. Sandy wasn't happy trading in her two-seater sports car for a big beefy truck, but she went along with the plan because she knew I was in a bind. Cha-Ching!

I'll admit that our dwelling on the water was an aging home. The black asphalt driveway was close to 30 years old. When not in the water, *Mafatu* sat proudly in its new parking spot at the side of the drive in front of the newly-remodeled entryway at the front of the house. After a few weeks, the asphalt started to sink and crack around the trailer.

I was aware that the entire driveway was cracking, but the size and length of the cracks resembled age lines, not serious rips or tears in the blacktop. It was obvious that the boat was too heavy for the driveway; it sagged and had to be repaired or replaced. I reasoned that if I had to replace the driveway, it should be with steel-reinforced concrete, not asphalt. The job went out for bid. The least expensive bid was given to me by a Tongan concrete crew that barely spoke English. Their bid was about half the other estimates. How hard could concrete work be? I questioned. I took a chance on them. Cha-Ching!

The Tongan crew was definitely not my wisest decision. The rusting, cast-iron sewer line was too old and brittle to withstand their digging. The sewer line collapsed, the main electric conduit line fractured, and other utility lines had to be rerouted in the process. All of these additional expenses were completely unwanted and totally unplanned, requiring contractors and more money for repairs. Cha-Ching!

This gushing of money was getting old, real fast. It seemed like *Mafatu* took on a life of its own and demanded we accommodate its needs, no matter how expensive they became. Sandy and I were being sucked down into a spiraling money pit. There was no reasonable way out, so we just kept writing checks. All the projects and all of the additional complications took weeks, which then dragged on to months. As one thing happened, that created the need to fix another thing.

When the Tongans showed up, I mean *if* they actually showed up for work, they brought their families with them. Wives, girlfriends and children spread their palm mats on the grass under the coconut trees and camped out for days at a time. Our home became a mini refugee village. Needless to say, the neighbors weren't very pleased.

What really sent me over the edge with the Tongans was running out of concrete on the final pour. The fact that they chose to pour the cement driveway on a Friday afternoon and ran out of cement at 4:30 p.m. was the last straw! I was beside myself with anger. There were no cement truck deliveries until Monday.

They said that they would try to match the color of the concrete but couldn't make any promises since they have to use a different company for a small finish load. My beautiful, new, elegant concrete driveway was ruined.

In hindsight and after spending a fortune getting *Mafatu* up and running, I realized that I could no longer afford to get lucky. "Free money is never really free."

After all was said and done, we started to enjoy *Mafatu*. Finally! Then as luck would have it, Sandy was informed that the stork would be blessing us with our first child. I would learn that I would be changing diapers more than I would be cleaning fish. Sandy's boss didn't make me feel any better when he said, "That boat's going to be a really expensive planter box sitting in the front drive."

Sandy and I were thrilled to know that we would be starting our family but I knew I'd have to get as much boating and spearfishing done before my new life of changing diapers and babysitting kicked into high gear.

It wasn't long before talk of a special interisland boat trip hit the divers coconut telegraph. Ideas were thrown around about diving Molokai, Kauai, and even Lanai. As the selected three-day weekend approached, heavy channel seas restricted our travels to Oahu. It was just too rough to make the interisland crossing with our boats. Discussions turned to hiding behind the wind block of the Koolau and Waianae mountain ranges. By necessity we decided on a dive trip to the northwestern tip of Oahu, the other end of the island, Kaena Point.

The water was gorgeous on the west coast. During the summer months, a blue, clear ocean and calm seas made diving there like stepping into a glassy lake. But during the winter months, it was another story, with north shore waves wrapping around Kaena Point to make it a big wave surfer's paradise and a boater's nightmare. I had surfed this coastline during my early years and life guarded a few of the beaches. Unhappily, I didn't know of any good offshore dive spots but fortunately the ocean warriors had a bunch of deep water sites on their "A" list. They dove these spots as back-ups for the bad weather conditions that sometimes restricted access to their preferred east coast sites.

Our trip was organized so that *Mafatu* and *It's Time* would take the adventure together. *Mafatu* would have Grant, Devon, Gman, and me onboard, while *It's Time* would have Hughsan, V, Gordon, and Lungs to fill its crew. For this inaugural adventure, *Mafatu* carried 120 gallons of fuel in the main tanks, 60 gallons of reserve in blue drum containers, full dive gear for four, 120 pounds of ice, food for an army, and a hodgepodge of 24 steel and aluminum tanks. We also carried a full array of trolling gear with outriggers. Needless to say, this was a heavy load for a 25-foot boat. Once at sea, *Mafatu* barely did 12 knots, nowhere near her usual cruising speed of 16 to 18 knots.

The voyage to Kaena Point would take a big part of the day, traveling from east Koko Head along the south shore past Diamond Head, Honolulu, Pearl Harbor, and the Ewa Plains. We'd round southwest past Barbers Point to travel along the west shores of Ko Olina Harbor, Nanakuli, Waianae, past Makaha to the northwest point of Kaena. This route would take us through splendid city landscapes of Honolulu proper and along the se-rene rural coastline of the west shore.

Without the speed, our trip became a slow fishing troll to the west coast. We arrived mid-afternoon in position off of Kaena Point to send the boys off the side and down to the Ulua Warehouse dive spot.

Grant, Devon, and Gman suited up and sat on the aft comb-ing waiting for *Mafatu*'s final lineup at a good position over the Warehouse. Ocean currents moved in a light Kaena Point drift, so once we were on the spot I goosed *Mafatu* up current to allow the divers time to get to their bottom target without drifting past it on the way down. The boys plunged over the side outfitted for fish war and hoped to bring up a big score of ulua.

Grant led the way down with Dev and Gman close wingmen on the assault. The Ulua Warehouse is a challenging dive spot 250 feet deep and far out to sea off the infamous Yokohama Bay (Keawaula Beach.) The large mountainous lava dome boasts a cliff overhang that's a natural collection point for deep ocean-dwelling fish. At the bluff facade is the grand entrance to an enormous recessed cave and numerous chambers. If a school of ulua happened to be there, this grand hall would become a shooter's dream, allowing each diver to choose any number of large finning targets.

It took the divers a while before the dark shadows of the cliff line came into view to assure them they were on course. Clear, comfortable water drew them deeper as they adjusted their descent into a hunting-pack strategy. No hand signals were used; each diver adjusted his position naturally to his partner's descent relative to the hunting ground. These expert shooters had been diving together for so long their actions were almost guided by an unknown sense. Each was an integral part of a pack of lethal predators come to harvest game.

Grant was a most unusual character. In his twenties, he started diving in Alaska with a dry suit in 4 degrees-below-0 weather and 30 mile-per-hour wind gusts in January. One of his coveted dive routines was hunting for King Crab that traveled in piles. If you find one, you'll find 50. The larger ones have a pretty dangerous bite, so getting more than a few to the surface could be a tricky feat. This winter diving just did not compute to us tropical divers.

A tough outdoorsman, Grant had been a fish-and-game man, wilderness logger, and skilled bush and airline pilot. Finally, he moved to Hawaii to warm up and hunt the real goodies, lobster and ulua. Getting a commercial pilot's job in Honolulu made it possible, and soon after he hooked up with the deep divers and Hughsan.

The three men descended, and Gman filmed as Devon and Grant hunted. Devon carried a JBL gun and Grant sported a Blue Water Rife shooter. They neared the top of the cliff when Devon peeled off formation and drilled down into the cave to pursue an ulua exiting through a side chamber. "Slam!" The crack of his gun going off resounded though the cavernous hollow of the lava chambers. It was a solid hit on a good-sized white ulua. Devon fought the animal and subdued him without incident.

Grant swam deeper into the cave, followed by Gman. To the left and ahead of them in an antechamber lay a school of large ulua near motionless, resting in comfort. Grant relaxed himself and angled toward the cache of fish. Slowly he moved, not stirring the sand bottom with his fins or causing alarm with his movements. He singled out one giant and swam in its direction just 30 feet away. Closer and closer he finned in plain view of his prey and the entourage behind it. The fish did not rouse, but from the side of the pack one lone striped ulua moved out and toward the intruders. Grant stopped, angled his gun out for a shot. The inquisitive ulua swam fearlessly within range, and at 9 feet he turned sideways to leave. "Bam!" Grant made a perfect broad side shot directly into the gill plate.

The ulua went ballistic and flew though the cave like a hurricane in a peaceful inlet. It was an awesome fight, and as the ulua attempted to exit a crack in the cave's ceiling, Grant was dragged upwards. Then a loud snapping sound pierced the water, the leader line went limp, and Grant was released. The fish lingered for a second near the roof of the cave in a daze. Grant's spear fell from above and landed upright in the sand a few yards away from Gman.

Grant moved in fast with his loaded three-prong. He hoped he'd get to the ulua and deliver a killing blow before he came to his senses and scooted out through the fissure. Grant lunged his three-prong forward and aimed for the spine just at the gill plate. "Swoosh!" The lance flew to its mark and secured its target with a grasping force. It was over. Grant got his ulua.

Compressed air goes fast at 250 feet, especially when a diver is landing a trophy fish. It was time to leave. Each of the divers began exiting the cave. With no time to waste, Grant retrieved his spear shaft and swam away as he worked his catch onto his fish stringer.

The divers started their ascent to a decompression stop of 30 feet. As they rose, a vast school of bait fish streamed above them silhouetted against the sunlit surface. It was a wonderful sight as clusters of thousands of fish moved to a common communal sense of safety and survival.

Mixed together in this swerving, recoiling, undulating curtain of fish were opelu (mackerel scad,) omilu, and kamanu (rainbow runners.) As the divers got closer, there in the sunlight mixed in and away from the school were seven Galapagos sharks. Moving in and out of the silvery black mass, they were feeding, gorging themselves with mouths open and teeth chomping. The horde of wolves drove the school to each other as they coordinated the attack, taking turns and working in unison to fill their jaws with all the morsels they desired.

The Galapagos has the shape of a grey reef shark, but it's bigger and more aggressive to humans. An ocean dweller that grows up to 12 feet, it thrives in reef environments around islands. As the eating machines made pass after pass at their prey, the sea of bait fish moved wildly here and there at the mercy of each shark. Like a flock of birds, the fish swooped and swooned in mass to avoid the slaughter of each attacker, giving up as few individuals as possible to protect the group. There would be little the school could do to stop the hemorrhage of fish until the sharks had their fill.

Once Gman, Devon and Grant arrived at their decompression stop near eye-level with the shark's feast, they tried to keep their distance but could not avoid the feeding frenzy completely. With bleeding fish on the stringer, the divers didn't want to become part of the food chain, so they created their own loose-knit sphere of predator humans a slight distance away from the bloodshed. Both shooters kept their guns at the ready and watched nature unfold.

It was a busy scene. The divers instinctively gathered together, each taking a different position looking away from each other, serving as guard to the others. The jittery bait moved in every direction. At times the divers became part of the ball of fish. Sharks slid through their protective circle, moving over and above them to eat their fill. One hungry beast moved repeatedly below Grant and nearly swam through his legs with open jaws scooping up his fish. The trio remained diligent, looking for any signs of attack behavior directed at them. The sharks did not get seriously interested in them, as there were just too many fish to consume.

After 25 minutes the divers surfaced to find *Mafatu* only a few hundred yards away from them. I sped over for pickup to find Grant and Gman raving about the sharks' feeding event like adrenaline junkies. Distracted from all else, they threw the trophy fish in the cooler without so much as a boastful tease. It didn't matter; we would have fresh ulua for dinner tonight.

I put *Mafatu* in gear and dead-reckoned toward Kaena Point. Since our knowledge of the area was restricted to the deeper dive spots, I decided to do an exploratory dive in the 60 to 80 foot range along the coast to create my own list of shallow sites. We motored to the Point to start my search.

Most visitors to Oahu don't know that the west and north shores of Oahu do not connect by highway or improved road, so each side of the island remains isolated from the other. Only a narrow skirt of eroded land lies windswept by the Kauai Channel where the Kuaokala Ridge of the Waianae Mountains intrudes into the sea. A four-wheel-drive trail gouged by potholes affords the foolhardy traveler a treacherous passage around the point. All the beach diving I did on the west coast ended where the paved road stops at Keawaula Beach. What lay past the bay would remain unexplored for me and most island residents.

This dive would be an opportunity to discover what lay hidden all those early years of beach-entry diving. I was eager. Grant took the helm as we cruised parallel to the shoreline in the 40 to 80 foot range looking for cliffs, drop offs, and ledges with the depth finder. In no time we were in some bumpy terrain. *Mafatu* slowed and I looked down into the water from the aft deck for color changes that might tell a story of the bottom. It confirmed that finger after finger of lava mounds ran from the shore toward the sea. Each of the spines would make its own mountain and valley habitat.

All geared up, I went off the side alone and straight to the bottom. For me, this dive fit right into my new profile of shallow-water diving no more than 90 feet in depth. This trip worked well for us; Grant would drive for me and I would take the helm for him, Devon, and Gman.

I landed on the top of a round lava mound and slowly dropped along its slope to the sand valley floor to look for fish. The scene was pretty and quite unique. Stark, long undersea volcanic formations ran offshore slightly higher than house height and nearly as wide. It was an intriguing sight. With terrain like this, I would expect the area to be teeming with life, but it was not so. There was very little marine life around the mountainous cracks and crevices. Nothing of interest stirred through the sand or the sweet spot where the sand meets the ledge. This is strange, I thought, as I moved up and over the next ridge to uncover another similar scene.

I was disappointed. By the time I left the third valley I settled on a reason to explain the barren landscape... overfishing! Here on the rural Makaha coast, many indigenous people lived a more traditional lifestyle. The local spearfisherman and divers were skilled watermen with generations of knowledge passed down through an ancestral way of life. These local divers probably cleaned out the near-shore dive spots long ago. Without tribal chiefs to "Kapu" or restrict the area for restocking, modern methods must have taken a toll on the fish population. I didn't think to disparage these divers; we were no better on the east side of the island as each year the prized fish grew fewer and fewer. Our divers were forced to dive deeper to score the large fish. Strict fish and game regulations would solve this problem, but none of us wanted that.

I came to terms with the terrain and accepted the fact that the whole coastline would be similarly barren, so I relaxed and checked out the sights without the anticipation of hunting or hoping for a big score. Accepting whatever the ocean would give, I enjoyed every bit of this world-class scenery.

I swam with the current through this delightful terrain like a long-distance hiker moving down through unusual river beds and up through mysterious channel bank mounds. I took greater interest in exploring the lava strata as it abruptly ended at the cliff face. Every inch of it was different and atypical. I could have continued on to darkness, but my air supply had a different plan. A quick glance at the pressure gauge warned that only 425 pounds remained. I kept moving to shallower water. I had a chance at another mound by stretching my air a little longer at 40 feet, but soon my regulator became hard to draw and I resorted to deep sucking to take what little air remained. Out of necessity I hit the surface with about 50 pounds and a tank that floated like a cork.

Back on *Mafatu*, the boys were attentive and trailed me by 100 yards. They anticipated I would surface soon as my bubbles became more pronounced in shallower water. Once at the surface, I raised my arm to a large okay sign on my head; Grant saw me and acknowledged with the same signal. The boys motored over to pick me up where I debriefed them about the scarcity of fish.

Done for the day, *Mafatu* traveled back to the rock shoreline past Keawaula Beach and dropped fore and aft anchors in anticipation of berthing for the night. It was a shallow anchorage that offered no protection from wind or swell but this would have to do, as this was all there was along the shoreline. Our crew busied itself cleaning up and transitioning the boat from dive platform to restaurant and bunkhouse. *It's Time* motored over and rafted up in anticipation for the evening's entertainment.

Lungs came over onto *Mafatu* while Grant and Gman went over to *It's Time* to talk with Hughsan and V. Divers and crew went from boat-to-boat in a sunset happy hour that dragged on as both boats prepared a potluck dinner. Hughsan set his two-burner cook stoves into service, one for the fish and one for a vegetable dish that V created to gourmet standards. I set up *Mafatu*'s makeshift galley on the dinette table, manned with two butane bottle stoves similar to Hughsan's, one for a large pot of rice, and one with a fry pan to sauté our fresh fish with magic galley spices.

Hughsan prepared ulua with a seared, blackened-fish-style crust while we cooked our ulua in a lemon butter concoction with white wine. When the cooking was done, all our food was passed over to *It's Time* for a grand fish buffet at sea. The chow hounds lined up patiently and dug in with all the hunger of empty stomachs adrift on the high seas. Heaps and heaps of food were piled on aluminum camp plates, with each diner finding a spot on the boat to savor the fruits of a day's labor.

The ulua was scrumptious. Hughsan unleashed *It's Time*'s fish magic with a bold searing of the fillets. A dark, blackened sesame oil with rub spice achieved the unique Asian style of crusted spicy outside and tender inside fish fillets. Each was a masterpiece of different cultures. It would be the most perfect floating cocktail-dinner party ever.

Our conversations ran the gamut from the retelling of the day's dives to discussions of our families and mutual friends. It shifted from group discussions held boat-to-boat to more individual conversations between divers.

I called for attention to propose a toast. Several divers were taken from us in past years. The German, Gernot Spallek, a wonderful husband, father, and pioneer deep diver was lost at sea off the Penguin Banks; a Brazilian, Peter Warwick, young husband and ninja diver, was killed in a motorcycle accident. Then there was our dearly missed Craig and Susie Craw, taken into the sea off Waikiki.

A moment of remembrance moved through the group at the thought of our departed friends. I spoke up, "For our friends, Gernot and Peter, Crawman and Susie, we salute you." I shouted and the boys answered the call:

"Banzai! BANZAI!
Banzai! BANZAI!
Banzai! BANZAI!"

After a long day at sea and with our bellies full, the divers were quickly running out of steam. Slowly conversations slackened, joking subsided, and crew members made their way back to their own boats to ready their bedrolls.

Hughsan's crew unlashed their rafting lines and drifted 75 yards away to drop their own hook for night anchorage. We watched them move about as they prepared under the illumination of their main cabin lights.

Mafatu floated calmly at anchor, swaying along the rugged cliffs bathed by heavenly stars in the shadow of the dark side of Oahu. Without the city lights, we were in an oiled ocean canopied by specks of distant sparkles. Other than a vague outline of the towering mountains in darkness, we had no point of reference. *Mafatu* became our cradle, the center of our world. With the blackness on the ocean and glimmering light from the sky, I felt at home. This was the life I loved at sea, but oddly enough, the one I had feared as a child.

Grant uncorked another bottle of wine and splashed some red into our waiting cups. There was a short salute, and then all fell silent as each man breathed in the spirit of nature's miracle... air, land, and sea. It was so calm and peaceful–the only sounds heard were ripples lapping against the boat's hull. I reflected on my life and the life I led in the city. It may not be life at all. It may be a mere existence, no miracle of being alive. Out here, away from civilization, the marvel of being alive was happening. Here, at sea, every moment burned with meaning. My thoughts challenged me on the conventions of the life I lived.

The boys continued to enjoy the evening when Grant spoke up. "Good wine?"

"Fabulous," Gman responded.

"Good stuff," Devon agreed.

I nodded, holding my glass up in a toasting gesture of approval. There would be spurts of conversation every now and then, but for the most part, we were into our own worlds. Grant, Devon, and Gman sat comfortably on the motor box and the side combing as they relaxed with their last glass of wine. I busied myself by cleaning the galley table.

Gman decided that he would take the roof of the cabin and was up there settling in next to the spear gun rack. I never liked the idea of sleeping on the cabin roof. If the ocean got bouncy, or if you rolled over in your sleep, it was a long way down to the water.

Devon would sleep on the deck. I would sleep in the starboard V-berth while Grant chose the port side bunk of the berth. I was already settled in when Grant stumbled in to find his spot. He puffed a few pillows, got his blanket arranged, and burrowed in for slumber.

I was very tired but couldn't find a good position to relax. I tossed and turned. It was a familiar problem. Falling asleep on the first night at sea was usually difficult for me. I was always so excited to be on the ocean that it was wasn't easy to calm down. It usually took another day offshore before I would adjust to the excitement.

Lying on my back and propping myself up with a pillow, I looked out through the center roof hatch to study the stars and try to tire myself. It wasn't a successful technique. Just as I was falling into a calm state, the boat would move with a wave and twist at anchor; my whole porthole of vision would change and I would snap out of it. It got to be a bit frustrating. Maybe I should have tried counting fish.

Grant was too quiet, too soon. How could he be asleep so fast? I wondered. "You awake?" I whispered.

There was no response. Maybe my voice was too quiet. "You awake?" Again I whispered a little louder. No response. I moved my hand close above his face, wiggled my fingers, and moved my hand in and out to block his vision. Still, there was not a movement or twitch. He was asleep. What luck he had. Here I lay bored, tired, and restless.

Sometime later Grant started into a low-growl snoring which promptly escalated to a full-throttle country freight train in a matter of a dozen breaths. At least he would have a good night's sleep, I mused. It might have been an hour or so later, out of nowhere, and quite suddenly, Grant tore his sheets lose, yelled an unintelligible command, reached for the ceiling hatch, and started pulling himself out for escape. He mumbled wildly as he tried to make his way up the hatch. Maybe Grant, the airline captain, was having a water-landing dream or something.

I grabbed at him, "Hey, Grant, what's going on?" "Grant!" He continued to mumble, showing signs of some mental confusion.

"You alright?" I asked. It took a moment, but he let go of the hatchway and flopped back down on the berth to take hold of his senses.

"Bad dream," he moaned.

"What's going on?" I asked.

"Oh man, I was in the boat. Sleeping. We broke anchor. The boat hit the rocks. We were going down. I was trapped in the cabin. Couldn't get out. Trying to breathe. Water rushing in. Choking. I'm okay now."

"The boat hasn't moved. We're safe. Go back to sleep," I said. He fell back to sleep before I had a chance to talk with him further.

So there I was fully awake, disturbed by the picture he painted of our watery fate on *Mafatu*'s maiden adventure. The rest of the night was spent listening and feeling. I lay there with coiled muscles, waiting for every twist on the anchor that would cause our fatal line break leading to shipwreck *Mafatu* on the nearby cliffs.

Months past as *Mafatu* and I got to know each other intimately at sea. We were well acquainted by the time Sandy's parents visited their new son-in-law and daughter in Hawaii. Aside from spending many hours at sea enjoying the boat, I had invested a good deal of time upgrading Mafatu for aggressive diving and spearfishing.

Finally, long overdue and eagerly awaited, Sandy's mom and dad flew in from Dallas/Fort Worth to spend the Christmas holidays with us. I looked upon the visit as my first real opportunity to get to know them and fish with her father. If I was to have any luck at all, they'd be like my family, one in which the men dumped the women to go boating and the woman entertained themselves at the mall. Everybody seemed to be happy that way; everyone got to do what they wanted.

Sandy's father was straight out of a western movie. He's kind of a cross between Gunsmoke's (the popular TV series of the 1970s) Sheriff Matt Dillon and the barely understandable Festus Haggen, his loyal deputy. Jim certainly spoke with a Texas drawl that got noticed. He was an educated man, professionally me-

ticulous and detailed. He spent much of his career writing training manuals for F-16 aircraft pilots. Middle age, medium framed,
very fair skinned, and with all the energy of a dynamo, he kept
his four daughters and son running with his nonstop activity. Jim
was one hundred percent Texan with a Texas can-do attitude. He
would prove to be a handful for me.

Dorothy, her mom, was a kindly woman with definite opinions
about her faith and the Catholic Church. An enduring believer,
she followed the church's teachings and tried to instill specific
church thinking into her children. She always felt that she hadn't
done her job as the children became very independent thinkers
in regard to the church; they probably got that gene from their
father's side of the family. Dorothy was slowing down as her dia-
betes kept her less mobile than she had been in previous years.
Still, if her daughters were going shopping, she'd tag along all
day without a complaint, only to return home exhausted to be
waited on by the entire household.

Of course I planned to behave like the perfect son-in-law. I
picked them up at the airport with colorful flower leis dressed
in my best aloha shirt to reassure them that I was worthy of their
daughter. We headed straight home to relax and get acquainted.
With the long flight and the difference in time zones we had a
simple early dinner and the folks soon settled into bed.

In the months before Jim and Dorothy's arrival, Jim told me
all about fishing in the Gulf of Mexico off the Texas coast. He
loved fishing and went out of Port Aransas on charter boats for
many years. Jim's fishing style was more that of a dead-bait, bottom fisherman. In the gulf, their fish stock involved red snapper and small Gulf sharks. Sandy said he was very excited about
spending some time on the water with me. I hoped we would hit
it off since we both loved the water and preferred it above all else.

Jim and I talked a lot about fishing since Sandy would check
in with her parents at least once a week. He'd tell me about the
excitement of shark fishing and how good the fillets tasted. Jim
had a special fish recipe for the grill with lemon pepper sauce
and spices. Whenever he brought shark fishing up, I tried not to
encourage him and kept my silence on the issue. He was pumped
up now that he was in Hawaii and hoped to hook a few sharks for
the grill.

I mentioned that not many people here eat shark because the Hawaiians believed some of their ancestors took the spirit of sharks in the afterlife. They then became their family's amakua. This fact didn't seem to bother him, not knowing any Hawaiians and feeling that his European ancestry would preclude eating any of his relatives. He was dying to hook a shark. I skillfully evaded the issue for the longest time but I felt my luck would soon end.

It was too difficult to say "no" to my eager father-in-law, so I compromised with my conscience. My plan was to motor out to sea late in the afternoon, set a shark line overnight past the Shark's Cave, and come back early the next morning when everyone was going to work to pick up our catch. Then we'd sneak it back to the dock. If we were lucky, we'd arrive in the early morning and fillet the shark out before anyone could notice.

Jim approved the plan and we were off to set lines. This being my first attempt at catching shark, I figured our rigs would have to be simple but very strong. There were enough materials in my locker for only two rigs.

A sizable surface buoy was attached to each anchor line down to a chain and small danforth anchor. With a strong anchorage, I knew that whatever took the hook wouldn't pull the rig very far from where we set our lines. The last thing I wanted to do was lose our hooked sharks to other fisherman, who just might happen to be Hawaiian. The anchor line had a scope three times the depth of the water. To these anchor rigs, I attached three industrial wire leader lines with shark hooks holding an aku head on each hook.

Jim and I dropped the lines at sea with a couple of beers late in the afternoon. We were back at the house in time for dinner and an early bedtime since we'd be up early to check our lines.

After breakfast we tore out through the channel and dead-reckoned straight to Diamond Head Crater. After 15 minutes or so I could see the first buoy bobbing high in the water. There was very little movement counter to the wind and waves which indicated that our plan may not have worked. We pulled up alongside and hoisted the buoy onboard. There was little weight or resistance. As the anchor rose from the bottom, the anchor line came up shredded and unbraided. Only one of the three strands of nylon line was intact. The first and second hooks were empty of bait, but on the last hook a sizable shark head was left dangling.

It was a sobering sight. A shark head larger than the size of a watermelon with chunks of severed flesh dangling from the crescent tooth mark incisions was staring at us, just floating on the hook. Where was the body? Was this shark eaten by a bigger shark? That's what must have happened to our predator. What a disappointment.

We pulled the rig from the bottom and surveyed the damage. It was obvious, the anchor line was shot; this rig would not fish again. We sped off to the next float 300 yards down current. The buoy rode low in the water. I cut the engine as we drifted in towards the rig.

It was mind-blowing. Thirty feet below in the translucent water was a dark menacing figure, a shark two to three times the length of a tall man and two times his girth. He hovered around the smaller figure of a man-sized shark hooked to the anchor line. It was a scary sight. Thank God Jim and I were safely in the boat. We stood looking over the side stunned by the length of this leviathan.

My thoughts connected things together in a flash. I realized that the first shark was taken by this beast, leaving behind just a head. But that did not satisfy him. Now he was after this shark, another captive meal.

We arrived just in time to interrupt the blood fest. I was upset because this catch was Jim's shark, not the animal's breakfast. I banged my fist on the side of the boat to sound an alarm that there was danger from above. That got the monster's attention! Jim and I grabbed the float and pulled the line in hand over hand. It was heavy. Not only were we pulling the anchor, but we were also dragging a reluctant shark up from the bottom. The giant circled in close but would not take a stand. "Scavenger! Coward!" I called the beast safely under my breath. I completely discounted the animal's position of king in the ocean's food chain.

The hard work was done, and our 6 foot shark thrashed at the surface. He was still very green, so I took my three-prong loaded with a 38 caliber power head and slammed it into the back of his head. "Bam!" the muted sound of a gun going off underwater pierced our ears. Clouds of blood disbursed. The shark was dead and we hoisted him on deck quickly before the king of sharks could cause a problem.

I examined the shark rig: the first hook was empty without bait, our shark was on the second hook, and on the third there was an additional casualty of this eating machine, another decapitated shark's head. This greedy monster shark swam under our boat and waited for the return of his next meal. Didn't he have enough to fill his gullet? Hadn't he done enough damage for one night?

To say that Jim and I were excited would be a grand understatement. We were overwhelmed and totally thrilled. I was particularly happy that we were successful enough to catch this shark without having to spend the night on the boat bottom fishing. Jim had his shark and would prepare him on the grill for Saturday night dinner.

We slipped in and back to our boat dock all jacked up on the sights we had just witnessed. The image of one very large shark consuming several man-sized sharks dumbfounded me. At least in the jungle, animals consume their large catches over a period of time, leaving some bones and skin behind. Not this creature: all of the carcass was consumed. All that flesh, consumed in one meal, it was beyond my comprehension. Now we had work to do.

We made our way though the marina with the shark tail hanging out over the boat rails. There was just no way we could have stuffed him in the boat and hidden the carcass. If anyone looked out to the marina through their living rooms, it would be hard to miss two guys and a shark. As we pulled into my canal, some of the neighbors came to their patios to witness our arrival. I was embarrassed and hoped we could keep a low profile.

One of the fishing guys across the way came out to ask with a signal of his outstretched arms, "How big is your catch?" Jim stood on the aft deck to lift the tail high into the air without moving the heavy side of the shark's body. He was beaming with pride; it was clear that this was no wimpy shark. So much for stealth and keeping a low profile, I thought.

Jim and I dragged the shark across the dock to the rock wall where he would be elevated for filleting. Sometimes butchering a large fish like a shark or marlin could take hours of backbreaking work. Bending over the fish on hands and knees was just too much to handle in the hot sun. The four-foot retaining wall was just perfect for me because I could stand up and save my back while I cleaned fish. Additionally, a tall row of airy areca palms ran along the waterfront wall providing ample shade to work the fish sheltered from the direct sun.

In about an hour and a half, three dull fillet knives, and a father-in-law cheering me on with Natural Light beer, it was done. We had a plethora of fish fillets. Jim gave a few portions to the new mainland neighbors next door. I sternly warned him not to go any farther in the cul-de-sac to the long-time local residents. Then, just before dark, we took the carcass out to the end of the channel entrance and fed it to the fish. Later that evening we called the family to let them know we'd be having a BBQ the next night.

We spent the next day sightseeing and came back early to prepare for the Saturday night grill-out. Teriyaki chicken and lemon pepper shark would be served, along with a variety of side dishes and a host of pupus. I manned the gas grill down on the lower patio, which was conveniently situated next to my boat locker and floating dock. It was a beautiful setting. What more could a man ask for? A fine home and good boat right at his fingertips.

Our party was underway. Most of the relatives were in the house prepping for dinner in and around the kitchen when my mom slipped out through the patio door to visit with me. We talked on the phone early that morning when I explained the situation about the shark. She expressed reservations about serving shark but would not make an issue of it for fear of creating a family incident.

"How are you, Son?" Her kindly smile always lifted my spirits.

"Fine, Mom. Everything's going well. Sandy's parents are having a good time."

"That's good. Be nice to them, Sandy is a good girl." Mom looked over the grill with an inquiring eye. "This the shark?"

"Yeah."

"Don't eat it," she said.

I was silent.

"You don't want a curse from the Hawaiian spirits."

"Yeah, I know, Ma."

She came closer to me, clasped my shoulder and moved her face closer to my ear, "Please, don't eat any of it." Not a moment too soon, Auntie Vickie came out to see what we were up to.

"Bryan, what's up with you?"

"Not much. How about you?"

"I'm good," she said in a party mood. Mom started back inside and Vickie stayed with me for awhile. Auntie Vickie was part permanent babysitter and Mom's enforcer. Even now, she took her guardian's position quite seriously.

"Shark?" Vickie asked with a smirk. "That's not so good." She moved her head from side to side in disapproval. "Not so good."

"I know, Auntie Vickie," I said as I continued on with my grilling duties.

We stood there making small talk for awhile. Then after a natural pause in our conversation she asked, "I'm going in to check on your mom. Need anything from the kitchen?"

"No, I've got everything. Thanks."

I finished the grilling. A platter of lemon pepper shark and a tray of teriyaki chicken, each kept separate and away from each other, were added to the buffet table.

Food preparations completed, Sandy instructed the family to start, and all slowly grazed through the buffet line. Each dinner plate that left the buffet did so with a generous portion of food. Most of the table seating was taken by the Texans, except for my Mom and Auntie. Other family members scattered throughout the living room and patio to enjoy the meal as there wasn't enough room to seat everyone of a group this size.

As the dinner party host, I would take my plate with me and walk from group to group making sure the food was to their liking and their drinks filled. It's a technique I learned from my "life of the party" dad who entertained often in our home when I was growing up. Anyway, I worked the house to make sure everyone was having a good time. I happened by the main table, where the Texans, Mom, and Auntie Vickie where discussing the food.

Both knife and fork were working as Jim took another morsel of shark from his plate and held it before his mouth, just finishing the chew of the previous fillet.

"Darn, this sure is mighty good shark," he slanged cowboy style. He saw me hovering close by and hollered, "Bryan, you sure grill up some good Hawaiian shark."

Mom and Vickie continued to eat with faces lowered, smiling and silent. I cringed but graciously responded to my father-in-law, "Thank you Jim, I'm glad you're enjoying it."

I continued on with my host duties through the night. It became apparent to me that while the Texans smacked their lips and filled their bellies, not one of the locals would go near the shark. In the good conscience of respecting Hawaiian traditions, I would not go near the shark flesh, either.

CHAPTER TEN

MAFATU'S GRAND ADVENTURE I: MOLOKAI & MAUI

There was no excuse for not going on a major adventure now–I was captain of the *Mafatu*. For years I dreamed of a significant ocean exploit, one of adventure and personal fulfillment. I felt like too ordinary a guy to put my life on hold, drop my career, and abandon my family and friends to do something really exceptional like sail around the world or go on a dive safari spanning several seas for months. Even if I were that kind of guy, I didn't have the financial resources to support such outlandish desires. That aggressive adventurer would not be me; I had too many responsibilities and not enough cash to allow myself the luxury of such wishes.

My dream for a diving adventure wasn't one of running away from a boring, humdrum, everyday life. I didn't want to run away from anybody or anything. No, I was happy with myself and where my life was headed. I only yearned to experience more of the ocean that I loved and become more of the water person that was hidden in me. I didn't need a world-class adventure; all I needed was my own interisland getaway for four or five days to bond with *Mafatu* and enjoy the sea.

My desires were about to be satisfied with a trip that I refer to as *Mafatu*'s Grand Adventure. We three captains–Bugs, Billie Budd, and Bones–were about to embark on the most audacious fish and dive trip ever. *Mafatu*, this 25-foot-long by 8-foot-wide fishing boat, would be our floating home and diving platform as we explored the islands of Molokai, Maui, and Lanai.

Bugs, an avid reef diver from grade school, was a master commercial diver of extraordinary talent with many channel crossings under his belt to Molokai's fertile west coast diving. While in high school, he and his best friend dove the coast extensively for fish and lobsters. The diving partners operated a lobster business and earned good money selling their catch to the neighbors in the marina. Later in life, Bugs did the Molokai trips when he visited me on leave from oil rig diving.

Bugs was on a trip home this summer to visit with family. It was a custom for us that when any of the relatives returned from the mainland, fishing and diving were an important part of their reunion tour. Their wives and children accepted this as the price of living away from Hawaii. Going home was about being in the ocean. Bugs was the captain of his own boat in Texas, the *Reel Lady*, a 21-foot Wellcraft with a 140 Johnson.

Billie Budd (Mark Olsen) sailed the Maui-Molokai-Lanai triangle at length in his earlier years as captain of his boat *Nomad* and later as crew on other yachts. The old *Nomad* was a 36-foot Cheoy Lee sloop that he berthed at Ala Wai Harbor. Budd was my best friend since high school. A constant buddy through the trials and tribulations of life, he spent his non-working life as a surfer, sailor, and fisherman. Budd's current boat, the new *Nomad* is a 28-foot Bertram rigged for trolling offshore. His wife was only too happy to see him go on our trip. Like all of our wives, she knew that when he returned from the ocean, he'd be a happier person for having been to sea.

I also had an early start at interisland boating, having sailed through the Maui Nui Islands on my boss' sailing ship the *Spenserian* during one high school summer. Overnights and two to three day trips on other sailboats would also be part of my education through the years, but when I hooked up with Hughsan and the diving ninjas, I learned a new interisland diving assault technique. It was a highly-refined, hit-and-run tactic for weekend warrior spearfishermen.

We three had discussed this trip for a long time, and now it was about to happen. The excitement of preparing for the trip and the exhilaration of our departure kept us bustling with emotions. For each of us, it was an adrenaline rush and an euphoric state of consciousness.

Beneath the excitement of this dream trip, childhood fears and doubts wormed into my enthusiasm. I put them aside, but they were there. The intimidation of the open ocean I felt as a child would always be with me, but it wasn't the fear of the ocean itself that troubled me; it was the fear of being unable to succeed and master its challenges, the fear of failure. While I would surely command this voyage, it would be the eight-year-old Mafatu of Niu Stream that would look over my shoulder.

"Bonezie, morning to ya mate," Budd hollered in his best English accent as he walked across the back lawn and down to the boat dock. "It's a fine morning for an ocean voyage, mate."

"Aye, Billie Budd, it 'tis," I replied in the best limey I could muster.

Budd always imagined himself an English seaman of the whaler days. It was sort of a fantasy of his, having read too many books about pirates and seafarers. I played along and sometimes got into the charade in a big way. We always felt like we were kids together so we amused ourselves playing these games. On many occasions Budd and I barked orders and made comments at sea in our best imaginary ocean English of the whaling fleet. We amused ourselves to see who would quit with the gibberish first. There were many times we fished and humored ourselves silly pretending to be English pirates in the thick of crossing the great seas. Sometimes I think we still act like kids playing together.

"Billie... Budd..." Bugs snapped out a British greeting. He had witnessed our foolishness before and politely played along.

"Aye, Bugs, mornin' to ya," Budd responded.

We paused from loading the boat to welcome Budd on deck as he hauled his personal gear onboard. As an afterthought, Budd asked, "I have a two-man Avon life raft in a stowaway case back in the car. Should I bring it along?"

I paused for a second then responded, "Nah, I think we'll be alright." I was concerned with the extra weight and the space it would take. We were already overloaded with extra fuel, a slew of dive tanks, and provisions for a long week.

A little later, Budd returned to the issue again, "Bones, what about the raft? It's really a good idea to take it. It won't take up much room. I'll tie it on to the top of the cab so it'll be out of our way."

"Nah, I think we will be okay," I repeated.

We continued on with the preparations, but sometime a little later Budd brought up the life raft again. "Bones, you sure about the raft? We could use it as a dingy to go ashore along the cliffs." He was insistent.

Maybe he had a point; it might come in handy. Besides, how would Bugs and Budd feel about their Captain if the boat sank and I had told Budd he couldn't bring the life raft? I gave in, "If you can tie it on top of the cab, go ahead and bring it along."

That being said, Budd brought the oversized lumpy roll aboard and lashed it down. From a distance, it looked awful. It had the appearance of a lashed down, rolled-up dead body on the roof for burial at sea.

We did a final check followed by a final re-check of the boat. All food, drinks, water, ice, dive gear, fishing gear, and creature comforts were accounted for. Mafatu cast off and headed down the marina towards the Hawaii Kai Bridge. Overloaded with stuff, we rode especially low in the water. While I was at the helm, Bugs and Budd busied themselves lashing and stowing for the channel crossing.

We departed at 7:45 a.m. from the southeastern point of Koko Head for the northwestern tip of Ilio Point of Molokai Island. No matter what the weather, crossing the Molokai Channel is always an adventure. The channel, also known as the Kaiwi Channel, is said to be the third roughest in the world. It's the wind that makes this waterway so treacherous.

In the geological scheme of things, it all makes perfect sense. Two major island masses, Oahu and Molokai, rise up from the ocean floor with only a small open space between them. The pre-vailing winds blow against the mountain chains, are blocked, and then funnel into and through a small, valley-like opening. The winds pick up speed and strength as they flush through the slot. As they do, the steady gusts whip up the ocean, creating large waves.

Adding to this, the undersea base of the islands rises up from the depths to restrict water flow through the islands, causing a strong upwelling of currents. The channel becomes a breeding ground for mountainous, blue-water seas and violent ocean tempests. Ocean conditions like these can be most perilous to a small craft caught unprepared.

Each channel crossing in a small boat must be executed based on up-to-the-minute marine conditions. Since our coveted diving grounds are on the north coast of Molokai, we needed to be north of the island. However, it's not always a simple matter of heading east from Koko Head to the northwest tip of Molokai. Our route would depend on the right conditions for a safe crossing based on current, wind, and wave circumstances. Any good boater knows that current conditions are subject to change at any time, as a weather system might appear out of nowhere.

On a perfectly calm day, racing across the channel directly to our destination was the best of all trips. A smooth 2 or 3 hour ride gets you to the dive spots fresh and relaxed. These were the crossings that we prayed for. However, these circumstances were more of a rarity than the norm. On a windy day, with seas of 3 to 6 feet, a direct approach into crashing waves isn't smart; it's always dangerous and ill-advised. Such conditions would warrant falling off course from the wind toward the southwest end of the island to take the swells at a quarter beam. This lessens the pounding and danger in transit.

It's not only dangerous for the boat when beating directly into the wind and waves; the men get grumpy when they arrive for a dive with aching backs and beat-up bodies. It makes for a less enjoyable day.

By falling off course, we'd be father away from the dive spots, but we could put the hammer down and speed through the protected lee waters of the west coast. It might add another 45 minutes to the crossing, but it was well worth preserving our bodies and having the chance to troll the west coast. On days when the channel was 6 to 9 feet, intelligence dictated that we turn back to port.

We rounded Koko Head and immediately found ourselves in thick seas of 3 to 4 feet with tight wave intervals. These swells would challenge the overloaded *Mafatu*, but I was confident *Mafatu* could take them. My decision was to take the most direct course allowing for our comfort. This would mean falling off the wind and crabbing up to save time as conditions allowed. All in all, it would be some work navigating, but a completely doable task.

"Capn' Bonz, goin' roun' the horn, are we?" Budd broke out in the excitement of passable seas.

"Aye, aye mate, roun' the horn it is! Batten the hatches and hold on to your privates," I replied, elated that we were finally in the channel.

Bugs, Budd and I got comfortable in the cabin for the three hour slug across the channel. Constant wind-driven spray from the waves against the bow flew across our windshield and over the cabin. It formed a curtain of mist flowing back beyond the boat's aft but we were comfortable, dry, and braced for the constant rocking of the boat against the sea.

Bugs and Budd caught up on old times and swapped stories of diving and fishing. There were occasional grunts and groans from the crew, questioning my skill at avoiding the watery potholes on the road forward. I was unaffected by their cheap shots, knowing that no matter how well I steered clear of bumpy troughs and rogue waves, there would always be complaints, unless that person was at the helm himself.

As we neared the Molokai shore, the size of the waves diminished in the shelter of the island. We took advantage of this and set the *Mafatu* to trolling. Bugs and Budd lowered the custom fiberglass outriggers and secured them in place at 45 degree angles, port and starboard.

Two Penn International 80 TW's were placed amidships closest to the outriggers to form our outside lure spread. Two 50 TW Penn's were placed at the aft rail with lines taking the second spot on the outriggers forming the inner spread. All the reels were threaded with 80 pound test lines and double crimped.

Bugs presented the lure spread with two additional jet head lure hand lines straight back past the whitewater. Then, Budd topped Bugs off with an added enticement of his personal giant marlin teaser lure with a 9-0 SS hook hidden in its skirt. He placed this bad guy right down the middle of the whole lure smorgasbord. We all agreed this would be an irresistible feast for any game fish.

With the fish lines set, all we had to do was wait and hope. We used this trolling time to recuperate from our slugfest crossing. Flat, calm water welcomed us as we moved even closer up to the northwest point. Budd and Bugs worked the deck and tweaked their lures for mahi and ono. These fishing grounds, just outside the Molokai Ranch Lands and the Sheraton Molokai Hotel, had been very productive for us in the past. Maybe the fish gods would smile on us today. I played back the many memories of overnight anchorages in front of the hotel as we drove along the coast. The trips with Hughsan and our overnight assaults to the north coast underwater ledges were particularly memorable. Good times, all of them.

Mafatu turned the corner and motored past Ilio Point to drive up along the north coast. Navigating over our dive spots at the tip of the island, I was surprised by the calm seas. It was much smoother than I expected. Perhaps the ocean swells flattened out against the lava cliffs and were no longer free to flare up as they did in the middle of the channel. Although there was more chop to the ocean, it was smaller and less directional. This was the type of ocean that *Mafatu*'s deep V hull was designed to eat up and spit out. It would be a comfortable troll along the coast. We were finally here at Molokai and I was exhilarated.

Bugs and Budd continued to work the lines as I scanned the water looking for the promise of fish. Water discolorations, currents, eddies, disturbances, small fish feeding, birds overhead, and other signs of life were telltale disclosures of possible fish activity below. We hoped for mahi or ono, but there were no signs of any action. Then, sometime past Ilio point, "Slam!" went the reel. A fish hit the hook on a blind strike.

"Fish on!" cried Bugs.

Budd hollered, "Oh, yeah!" at the top of his lungs.

Bugs was in no mood for playing the fish or angling sportsmanship; he wanted dinner in the box. He horse-reeled the fish alongside the boat and Budd gaffed. It all went so fast. It was tense; a miss of the gaff, a few scrapes of the skin, and the beautiful ono fought himself free to throw the hook. The fish was gone! Bugs and Budd uttered a flurry of cuss words, and then the excitement turned to disappointment. Finally, Bugs relieved the pressure. "It's alright, we'll get the next one. This was just practice." I could see Budd's face, relieved that he would not be held responsible for the lost fish.

A few minutes later, farther down the submerged ledge line,

"Bam!" Fish line screamed out of the 50 TW Penn mounted on a black-and-gold short tuna stick. The sweet sound of peeling line filled our ears with the hiss of a solid hookup. Budd and Bugs yelled directions to each other over the sound of the diesel motor. There was a machine gunning of words and demands as plans for the gaffing were negotiated on the fly.

Billie Budd came through. It was a solid gaff close to the head and next to the spine. What a score! There would be mahi for dinner tonight. Bugs and Budd perfected their coordinated reel-and-gaff technique. Enthusiasm and boldness filled the decks as the two anglers strutted about with confidence. It was a good start that helped create a harmonious mood.

We continued to motor on down the coast. Two-foot waves carved the beautiful, royal blue seas. With the protection of the cliffs suppressing the full potential of the swells, we played the coastline to our advantage and enjoyment. The sun beat down heavily on the crew as they worked the deck with the lines and lures. We passed the Mokio Point outcropping and continued to troll the rugged coastal cliffs.

The plan was to make our way to Kalaupapa. These few miles of lonely cliffs from Ilio Point to Mokio Point were my idea of a diving heaven on earth. For me, it was as close to feeling the beauty of God that anyone could experience. It was the ocean's ultimate heiau, or altar to the God of Creation. This undersea terrain was always spectacular, the game fish plentiful. We would troll through the area but wouldn't dive it today, as there was just too much to explore ahead.

We spent the better part of three hours working the 30 and 50 fathom underwater ledges. *Mafatu* passed Paualaia Point and we were well on our way to the peninsula. It was glorious: rich blue seas, stark black cliffs, and bright sunlight amidst scattered clouds, all making the perfect start to *Mafatu*'s grand island voyage. We traveled for some time without further fish activity. I could see Budd and Bugs hoping for more action as they patiently waited for more fish.

Soon we were upon the protruding Kalaupapa landmass, a peninsula fallen into the ocean from the lava cathedrals above. From way out at sea, that's what it looked like. It was the eye's explanation for this unusual landmass jutting out into the ocean from the mainland of Molokai. Most geologists believe that the peninsula was formed much later than the island as a small shield volcano spewed widespread lava to extend the landmass onto the jagged mountain range. In any case, Kalaupapa was a natural paradise and historic hellhole.

Before us lay the tropical peninsula and the infamous leper settlement of Kalaupapa. *Mafatu* was on course to navigate close to the inside shore. We would get near shore so we could turn back out to sea and sweep past the barge dock area in one continuous troll. This fishing strategy had worked well for us in the past, and we hoped it would score for us again. I needed Billie Budd to fetch some of his Kalaupapa Barge Harbor magic he had been known to conjure up on past trips. If anyone could get fish to bite, Budd could get ono to take our lures.

Several years back, Budd and I hit the jackpot on the *Bones* and brought in four mammoth ono trolling in large circles just outside of the wharf. I was counting on Budd to create that enchantment again as he and Bugs worked the trolling grounds. Anticipation was high, knowing that this pristine water could produce a wealth of fish.

All the waters that surround the Kalaupapa National Historic Park up to a quarter mile out are part of the national park established by the United States Congress. In old Hawaii, before the white man intruded, Kalaupapa was a thriving community of native peoples who prospered there for a thousand years in near isolation. These Hawaiians lived in the most isolated coastline of the Molokai Coast but flourished with their ancient ways of respect for the spirit of the land. They were completely self-sufficient by farming and fishing.

Kalaupapa was known for its rich, fertile land that brought forth prized produce. The natives used their highly-regarded sweet potatoes to trade with outsiders in the early days of the islands. Kalaupapa was a model village of peoples adapting to the mana, or spirit of the land.

The Kingdom of Hawaii removed the natives from the land in the mid-1800's. The royal advisors believed that the only way to stop the increasing spread of leprosy was total isolation and quarantine of all suspected lepers. Kalaupapa was the best natural landmass to meet the Department of Health requirements for a village jail. The monarchy decreed and then forcefully relocated all lepers in the Islands to the peninsula. This once native Shangri-La deteriorated into a world-class hell of disease and death. From 1865, when the leprosy isolation laws went into effect until 1969 when they were abolished, this tiny haven served as detention center and death camp for thousands of patients.

Currently, the settlement's lifeline of supplies flow from the outside world through a tiny wharf area where deliveries arrive once a month from April through October. At other times the ocean is too rough along the north coast for boat landings. There's also a tiny airstrip for landings of food and supplies. A small group of old-time residents still reside there, comfortable with their long life of segregation. Since it's a national park, tourists with special permits may visit the site on a daily basis in a program controlled by the park rangers.

After several unfruitful runs at the ono grounds near the harbor, we continued around Kahiu Point to the deserted east shore of the settlement. As we motored past the Molokai Lighthouse and rounded the corner, the most inspiring scenery grabbed my soul and made everything else appear insignificant.

Lying before us were the towering palis of Kalawao stretching past Pelekunu. These regal cliffs, draped down from the heavens, are set to a backdrop of baby blue skies laced with cloud banks tumbling down through the sky. The cliffs fall to a black boulder beach and lovely bay below. This ageless panorama of mountains is interrupted by a piercing sliver of a valley meeting the ocean in its center. No master artist's oil on canvas would do it justice. So unimposing is its delicate union of valley and cliff that one scarcely notices its hidden vale upon first sight.

This spiritual sea coast of Kalawao Bay is a place of wonder. Two offshore islands rise up from the sea to shelter the cove from the east, and the Kalaupapa Peninsula juts out to protect the bay from the west. And of course, the shoreline of cathedral cliffs shields the cove from the main island's weather systems. The scenery is incredibly awe-inspiring as ocean cliffs fall thousands of feet into the sea and jungle backdrops reach out to grab you. These scenic areas have been featured in numerous Hollywood movies, "Jurassic Park" being one of the more notable.

Mokapu, the larger of the two offshore islands to the east, is farther out to sea than the smaller Okala Island. It's only 360 feet tall, but from the deck of *Mafatu*, it looks like a towering giant. The whole island is steep. It's more than a 45 degree grade, making hiking perilous and illegal. Our only interest in the island was to admire its beauty.

The smaller Okala Island is also very unique. Slightly over 400 feet tall and as steep as its sister island, it harbors a secret that it stubbornly guards from the casual adventurer. If someone were to make a special effort to snorkel the shoreline round the island, a glowing light will appear from under the water where the rocky edge meets the sea. It would be easy to miss unless someone was searching for it. When diving a little deeper down with scuba tanks, the light of an underwater cavern as big as the island itself explodes forth.

The island is a gigantic lava bubble that formed offshore. What you see on the ocean is just the crust at the surface. Equipped with scuba tanks, a skilled diver could explore inside the island all the way down to the sand bottom. Crawman introduced the ninjas to this hidden paradise years ago–a natural geologic miracle.

We trolled a few rounds in and around the two islands. After some time running our best fish lures we came up empty. It was getting late in the day, and soon it would be time for grog. We headed to the overnight safety of an inside protected anchorage.

Mafatu nestled in the lee of a lava cliff that stands out to sea and forms a smaller natural cove at the east end of the bay. It was the perfect spot, and I had anchored at this very site on other dive trips with the boys. We three adventurers would be secure in this natural cocoon for the night. Except for a small patch of black sand beach at the base of the sea cliff, rock and stones carpeted the beach until the settlement encroached on shore and protruded into the sea a quarter mile down to the west. Ahead of us and 100 yards down the rocks, Waikolu Stream entered the bay with a parade of sparkling white water splashing through the dull, black-boulder beach. The rich, cobalt blue bay waters were calm, with hardly a ripple disturbing the tranquility of the scene. In 20 feet of water Bugs and Budd set the fore and aft hooks to anchor us.

We took a moment of pause as each man moved about to gather his sensory impressions of this Eden. No one could possibly come close to recreating the feeling of this setting. It is here, in the raw, where heaven meets earth, that the ocean caresses its union. It's where the yin and yang of life are mixed under the Almighty's guiding hand.

I was lost in my own feelings for the moment as these fortress cliffs overwhelmed my senses. Faint sounds of ocean energy filled my ears with thunderous silence: the silence of a vague white noise and the sound of thousands of gentle waves lapping against the cliffs and echoing back to sea. Each individual vibration cancels other vibrations to become a soft, muted sea sound. A silent hum of nature is the essence of this mysterious place.

The towering dark cliffs overpowered my eyes with their jagged jewels of color. Black lava pinnacles shot up from the cobalt sea, with sea brush randomly taking root in crack and crevice. Dark and light greens and all shades of salt-weathered vegetation lay against the lava formations. Scanning the vast pali cliffs, one loses perspective of splashy individual colors, but when a rock outcropping or protruding bush 900 feet above grabs your focus, its natural color explodes before your eyes.

The history of this remote place affects me like no other. As a child, I was deeply moved and inspired by the selfless work of Father Damien. Along with a cadre of other loving beings who came to help the unfortunates, Father Damien stands out above them all. After 12 years of devoted service, leprosy overcame the Belgian. The Catholic Church canonized the humanitarian a modern-day saint. Being here was always a profound experience for me... being so close to those anguished souls who perished and who some say now roam the settlement.

As we gazed about, there were occasional outbursts of "Wow," "Awesome," and "Unreal!" There were no other words to describe our disbelief and wonder.

Budd abruptly changed the mood and jarred us back to the here and now. "Let's go ashore and hike to Father Damien's Church. It's just over there on the bluff." Bugs and I perked up.

I spoke up as the voice of caution, "Now wait a minute. Isn't this place a reserve or something? Don't we need permission or a special permit to step ashore?" While I was not sure of any of this, I put the question to the crew hoping that one of them would know.

Budd stated as fact, "Ah, come on. This place isn't part of the

Colony. It's just a valley along the shore. The reserve starts at the bluff where Father Damien's Church sits. It's way over there! This is another deserted valley along the coast. The park's that way," Budd noted, pointing to the church.

"Let's snorkel to the cliffs and see if there're any opihi," Bugs suggested. Opihi, a prized Hawaiian delicacy, is a small shellfish that inhabits coastline rocks at the water's edge.

Budd chimed in, "Yeah, I'll launch the Avon and we can fool around on shore."

Well, so much for this captain's concern. We grabbed the snorkel gear, took a few spearguns, and were off to the cliff line snorkeling our way to the beach. A dazzling cliff face fell below the surface to reveal some interesting underwater terrain. Through the whole snorkel we saw only small tropical fish that didn't make for good spearing.

In a short time we were at a small spit of a black sand beach crowned by steep lava cliffs. I knew it was fruitless to argue with these two, so we went exploring. Budd stowed the raft up shore and we moved over the boulders toward the stream. Rock to rock, boulder to boulder, we crawled like crabs toward the freshwater stream that trickled gracefully into the bay.

Heaps of washed-up ocean debris stuffed between rocks and boulders covered the high-water mark. Plastic cups, jugs, wood floats, and driftwood lay scattered. Above the shoreline where the vegetation met the rocks and boulders, a trash band separated land and rock line with every manner of discarded material left as a sad marker of our modern society.

Budd and I continued on, eager to find Japanese glass floats and other washed-ashore treasures while Bugs led the charge of gathering opihi. It wasn't very long before all three of us were combing the rocks for opihi. Hawaiian opihi is a saltwater snail or limpet that inhabits the rough waters where rock and lava formations enter the sea. The snails possess a one-sided conical shell and move along the rocks above, near, or below the waterline. They stubbornly attach themselves to hard surfaces with a leg-like muscle and feed on the moist algae growing along the shore.

In Hawaii, opihis are considered a delicacy, selling for $100 or more a gallon. Best served raw, chilled, and garnished with seaweed, it is often too salty for visitors but a delight beyond comparison for local palates. As a food item, it might be considered something like poi. The locals go crazy for poi and opihi, but most mainlanders can do without it.

Stealth was the art required for an effective opihi harvest. We were not experts, but each of us knew how to sling an opihi knife pretty well. A metal knife or flattened spoon served as a tool for prying the crustaceans from the rock surface. If we approached the creature loudly, walked heavily on the rocks, or made sloppy advances with our knives, the muscle would clam up and bond to the rock. Then, even slick blade work would not pry it loose. Sometimes, I think, the creature could read minds, so it was best to approach the rock with disinterest, then pounce on it quickly with the sharp edge of the knife in one fast swoop. It would be an easy pry. In any case, we were doing very well filling our pockets with opihi.

Looking up the valley, we saw a lush, wild jungle gushing forward onto the beach. Green plants and wild ferns flourished everywhere. We headed up to the wild turf fronting one side of the brook. Stream water rushed toward the shoreline rocks and broke into splinters of frothy white atop crystal-clear, cool water moving through the boulders.

Ahead, nearly hidden in the brush, two shy wild goats waited to drink from the stream. They stared at us in confusion for a brief moment before withdrawing into the bush. Each of us, at our own pace, moved into the watercourse to cool our sun-baked bodies. We dipped in small pools of backflow. The sounds of miniature cascading rapids comforted our bodies and relaxed our minds. This was paradise. For the longest time I daydreamed: life would be ideal here. I could make a go of it, living off the land and sea. I knew these were crazy dreams, but I indulged my inner child for a moment.

We continued on and followed the stream 100 feet back to a larger pond. How odd, I reasoned. A man-made concrete levee restricted the stream to create a natural swimming hole. How out of place it seemed. I was disturbed to see something created by man in so natural a setting. Leading away from the hidden pool was a water pipe that ran all the way to the distant peninsula. My euphoria of being in a natural paradise waned and my excitement cooled.

Then I had a chilling thought: this pipeline would be the source of Kalaupapa's water. An inner sadness filled my spirit. Perhaps I felt an aura of the brutal history of suffering endured by the lepers. Whatever the cause, I felt uneasy, my spirits dampened.

Haunting images from old movies played in my head portraying the abused patients. In times past, a sentence to Molokai was a decree of death. I meditated for those who had suffered here, who had walked these stones, and bathed in these waters. I was humbled, my sense of importance reduced to no more than an inconsequential pebble on the shore.

Time passed, and it was getting late. Budd realized that the trek to Father Damien's Church would put us into an early-evening return to the boat. With no flashlights we'd have to traverse these rocks and boulders in the dark of night. It was obvious that it would be more dangerous, so he resigned himself to foregoing the trip. As dusk crept into the valley, we left the beach to return to the boat.

Standing on the rocks and looking offshore for the last time, we were treated to a wonderful picture of our floating home. *Mafatu* lay resting at anchor rocking in the lap of a caressing sea, the nurturing lullaby set to a splendid backdrop of two protective offshore islands. We rowed the Avon back with a feeling of great satisfaction of our exploration and discovery.

Once onboard, we got to our chores of tidying up, winding down for the day, and preparing for the evening. *Mafatu*, the fishing machine, went through a transformation as it became our floating residence at sea.

Unfortunately, some months later back in Honolulu I learned that the entire area is a Federal Reserve in preservation. Our adventure ashore was at the edge of but still within the park's boundaries. Had we known, none of us would have taken the chance of an illegal anchorage or landing.

Mafatu floated at peace in the shadows of the cliffs. Each of us took turns standing on the swim step with a short ration of freshwater to wash off the salt. Then, cleaned and freshened, we would enjoy the rest of the evening comfortable and warm. With no particular boater's pride, we pinned the towels and swim trunks on the outriggers for drying. From a distance we looked like a cheap, third-world, rural shack with our clothes hung in the open air. Sure it was a horrid sight, but what would it matter?

Only the wild goats would object to the eyesore.

Grog master Budd took charge of "watering the crew" before dinner. We used this cocktail time to catch up with each other and relive the day's events, much like campers use the fire pit to share in a song of "Kumbaya." Our evening meal became a group endeavor, with Bugs preparing the opihis (he could make something elegant out of anything,) Budd tossing the green salad (he was always concerned about scurvy at sea,) and me cooking the rice. The main course was mahi mahi prepared sashimi style. We used no dinner table and ate sitting on coolers, engine box, and the side combing of the cockpit. We had our fill of nourishment.

We lulled in the bay and enjoyed some of Mother Nature's after-dinner entertainment. A number of mountain goats came down from the top of the cliffs to observe our presence. After some time the goats went back into the hills, leaving us to float alone in the sea.

Sleep came early; we were exhausted from the day's excitement. Budd slept on deck, while Bugs and I slept in the cabin. As a safety procedure, I set the anchor alarm to beep at 9 feet if we pulled anchor and drifted into shore and 60 feet if we drifted out to sea. The GPS off-position alarm was also set to its lowest setting of a tenth of a mile. This would warn us if we broke anchor and moved from our position. With these technological features in play I knew we would sleep soundly, but I soon learned that sleeping in the cabin might have been a bad choice. Bugs' snoring was enough to wake the whales, and with the echoing effect of a fiberglass V berth, it was an orchestra of mighty thunder. I finally got to sleep as exhaustion overcame me.

We woke the next morning with *Mafatu* calm at anchor. Each man rose to his internal alarms and was left to fend for coffee, cereal, and milk. I gazed over the craggy coastline, the sharp towering cliffs, the green jungles, and the old settlement. All this ancient natural beauty provided an awesome backdrop to our modern day adventure. The deserted north coast of Molokai is nature at its wildest.

Between swigs of coffee and a light breakfast, Budd talked about abandoning our planned adventure and spending all our time here. "It's just too perfect to leave!" he would say several times. Budd felt a great connection with the place. It was a very tempting plan which we discussed at length. Bugs voted to travel on to Maui and see what the sea would bring us. I teetered back and forth; Kalawao Bay was my favorite place, but I knew that we could do another Molokai trip. Maui and Lanai required a greater commitment of time. It would be difficult to get away like this again anytime soon. We could always squeeze a few days off for Molokai, but taking a week off for interisland exploration was very difficult with our varied schedules. I threw my chips in with Bugs and we prepared to depart. Budd accepted our lead.

We pulled anchor and rounded Okala Island, traveling past Huelo Island heading east. I left Kalaupapa filled with wonder of what would become of us this day on the high seas. *Mafatu* had never been farther away from home than Kalaupapa, and now we were about to travel to Maui.

Bugs and Budd immediately set the deck for fishing and put the trolling lures in a modified full spread. We hugged the cliffs and dragged fish lines across the underwater ledges and sea bluffs. There was no rush to get anywhere, so we traveled at an easy troll of 7 to 10 knots. I was careful navigating the obstructions and slowed the boat down to 5 knots when we passed the jagged cliffs of Pahu Point.

We fished Wailua Valley and on past Papalaua Falls. It's a rare visual treat to behold the Hawaii that the natives saw of years past without the scars of Western development. We live in cities, concrete streets, custom homes, interconnected with wire and wireless communication lines. What do we know of the true nature of life? The ancient Hawaiians lived in villages with hued dirt trails, thatched homes, interconnected by wireless drums. What a bold contrast. Life and death played out at the end of a spear, a mysterious disease, or some cause of nature. Our lives play out with more regularity and predictability of work, retirement, sickness and old age.

Bugs roamed the deck, checking and rechecking the lines as he admired the cascading ocean waterfalls. The fishing action was slow, perhaps due to the course I took too close to the cliffs. I didn't care as I would have sacrificed any fish to follow the coastline intimately... the sights, sounds, and energy were too exceptional to let fishing lure us out to sea and pass on this experience. I wanted to see all the geologic evidence of how the lava flowed into the sea. I wanted to see it all up close: fallen tree stumps, driftwood tossed high on the cliffs from fierce storms, and green sea brush trying desperately to survive the relentless salt spray.

Budd soon joined Bugs in his impatience. They applied another two spinning reels with Rapala lures to their mix of fishing lines. They'd cast toward the cliffs and jig in back to the boat as we moved forward, hoping for small omilu traveling close to shore. Just before Halawa Bay, Budd's spinning line spooled out like a dragster out of the gate on fire. I immediately turned away from the cliffs and dashed to deeper water so the fish wouldn't run into a submerged rock or outcropping to cut the line.

The reel screamed, the pole bent over to a 45 degree angle, and the fight was on. With this lighter 20 pound test line it was a careful operation of give and take angling skill. The drag was set at mid-range but adjusted constantly for the run of the fish. Any excessive pressure on the line might snap it and our fish would be gone in an instant. Budd's talent soon brought him to the side of the boat.

"Whoa, it's an ulua!" Budd shouted. Bugs gaffed him on the first attempt. What a thrill. This was no small top-water fish; it was a good-sized predator from the deep. What a score! With the fish gaffed and in the box, we headed back to the cliffs to continue on.

Two minutes later, "Bang," the same action, the same drill. The line screamed, pole bent, and I headed away from the cliffs. Bugs played the challenge up to the boat. "Ulua!" he shouted. Again, the excitement followed. Budd and Bugs worked the fight out like a team of choreographed wrestling stars. With the second one gaffed and the pressure to catch fish satisfied, we headed forward to Halawa Valley. Wow, what luck, I thought. Success had come so early in the morning; we already had two big ones in the box.

Halawa Valley is a well-known fishing spot for the locals of Molokai. Widespread stories abound about its natural beauty, terrific terrain, and submerged reefs with abundant marine life.

We rounded the corner and motored in close to its entrance. It wasn't long before our spirits fell. The half-moon bay was nothing like we'd imagined. Coming into our view was a low-lying hill with sloping wilderness vegetation proceeding to the waterline. Packed in, where the ocean met the shore, were a multitude of tents, shanties, blue tarps and lean-tos which littered the area. It looked like a scene of squatters, activists, and other locals who might have gathered to reclaim their natural resources.

These were times of native Hawaiian activism. We might not fare well in this frontier environment. City folks driving in from Honolulu in a good looking boat to look at the natives, I didn't think we would be greeted as long-lost brothers.

I scanned the outer shoreline for interesting lava structures, tiny inlets, small peninsulas, or other topography of significance to divers. Was there any evidence of underwater ledges, reef lines, or other structural abnormalities? There were none that I could see with such a hurried view.

I put *Mafatu* in neutral as we hovered at the mouth of the bay. Bugs and I looked over the territory and imagined the possibilities. My eyes kept focused on the water. It wouldn't do for diving. It looked like river water, loaded with brown and greenish soil runoff. There was no evidence of clear water anywhere near shore. We wanted beautiful clear water with lots of structure. Not much discussion ensued; we knew by looking at each other that this was not it for diving. We had been spoiled yesterday at Eden's Garden. Halawa didn't capture our interest, so I put *Mafatu* in gear and we pressed on.

We reached the east end of Molokai, and to our amazement, the channel to Maui was calm. Budd was ecstatic. He had sailed the Pailolo Channel in his early days, so he was more familiar with this part of the island than we were. The channel between Molokai and Maui is only eight miles wide but always smoking rough with strong winds and giant ocean swells. According to Budd, it's the fourth roughest channel in the world.

Budd insisted that Bugs and I seize this unique opportunity to dive the offshore Moku Hooniki Island at the eastern tip of Molokai. He believed that this calm was a gift and we should accept this good fortune to dive the "Pinched Island." The offshore rock is located close to shore, a few miles south to southeast of Cape Halawa. During World War II it was used by the military for target practice, so the place is strewn with decaying munitions above and below the waterline. It's currently protected as a state seabird sanctuary.

Bugs and I suited up as Budd put us in position to work the island's windward side. A small, local bottom-fishing boat fished the waters nearby, but it was far enough away not to be of concern to us. Bugs prepped for diving on the port side, while I took the starboard. It was a quick and easy routine in smooth seas. At other times, when the water was rough, gearing up was quite difficult. Imagine getting dressed with heavy tanks and weights while being tossed around on deck like a pinball in a relentless arcade game. No matter if the seas were passive or violent, once we fell back in the water, there was calm no matter what the ocean was doing topside.

We flipped back off our respective sides of the boat and dropped into the water. Bugs went forward as I went sideways closer to the island. We drilled down to the coral-covered lava structure that lay before us. Soon all our concerns were dimmed by the sounds of our regulators.

The water clarity was fantastic, with visibility over 100 feet. It was the start to a great dive. Small tropical fish darted about, a few undersized parrots and bunches of inedible reef fish milled around, but for the most part, the place was shy of any game fish. We worked the area for 10 to 15 minutes hoping our long-guns would see some action. Nothing. Beautiful scenery, but where were the fish? Then it occurred to me: maybe this place was fished out.

Knowing that our supply of tanks was limited and wanting to conserve air for better fishing spots to come, Bugs gave me a look conveying, "What are we doing here? Let's move on." I gave him a thumbs-up signal and we were on our way to the surface. I wondered about the lack of fish and whether the ocean currents were normally too strong for fish to thrive here. No, that was not the answer, the tropicals lived here. Maybe the bottom fishermen cleaned the area out. No that couldn't be the answer either. There were all sorts of maybes but the only one that mattered was, maybe there'll be more fish on our next dive.

While we were in the depths, Budd hove to and maneuvered the *Mafatu* back toward calmer water to wait for our pickup. He whiled away his time reading from Jack London's classics but he didn't get much reading done on this dive. We were at the surface as quickly as we went to the bottom. Ever diligent, Budd was soon on the scene.

Boat driving for drift divers is neither an easy job nor one to be taken lightly. With divers down and a boat driver at the helm, lives depend on one man's responsibility and skill. Bugs and I knew we could rely on Budd to retrieve us safely from the ocean no matter what was happening topside. We knew that of all the possible boat drivers, we could entrust our lives to Budd without reservation.

After we secured our dive gear and rested briefly, Budd put the throttle down and aimed *Mafatu* for the closest part of Maui. We sprinted across the Pailolo Channel like we owned it.

A little after mid-day we came upon a pristine bay on the west shore of Maui. At first, we weren't sure exactly where we landed, never having been this far north on Maui's west coast. I figured we were somewhere between Kanounou Point and Hawea Point. That's a lot of coastline to navigate, so we cruised into the biggest indentation along the coast that was visible to us from far offshore. It never dawned on us to use the GPS map feature to figure out where we were. Maybe this is the same know-it-all mentality that leads men to get lost while thinking they know where they are.

We neared a bay and saw pleasure boats, chartered day sailors, motor yachts, and large tourist catamarans anchored along the cliffs and in an inner bay. It was quite a surprise and a very unusual sight. The waters were calm with no currents or waves. Clear water and good underwater formations were all around the area.

We cautiously motored through the gathering of boats, sun revelers, snorkelers, and families swimming in the water before us. I'm sure we looked like cocky fisherman too long at sea to the hoard of tourists. They stared at us strangely as we motored through. I was careful to watch for swimmers and posted Bugs as lookout at the bow. There were suntanned visitors everywhere in the water. We were driving through sort of a swimming pool party mob.

Mafatu kept its careful course as I scanned ahead for a place to drop the hook. We flew our full regiment of holstered outriggers, Penn international reels, and spear guns. As we parted the crowd, glaring looks kept coming at us. I thought that maybe the tourists were more than just surprised to see us. Maybe we were too close to a swimmer or had disturbed their snorkeling. I wasn't sure, but I was getting the sense that these hostile looks were specifically directed at us. Budd and Bugs didn't say anything, but I could see the look of confusion on their faces.

We found a nice spot, dropped the anchor, and proceeded to fit in with the tourists. We took off our shirts, put some lotion on, and swaggered around the deck like we were tourists ourselves, but the mean looks grew harder to ignore. What was going on? I wondered. We had some lunch, drank a few sodas, and snorkeled with the visitors; but still we didn't fit in. Being treated like outcasts started to wear on my nerves.

Finally I figured this must come to an end. I got on the radio to get to the bottom of our snubbing. I hailed on channel 16.

"*Mafatu*, calling for radio check, anybody read?"

The captain of the tourist catamaran next to us, a stocky guy who had been watching me, replied, "Read you loud and clear." Click.

"*Mafatu* calling, please switch to channel 68." I gave it a moment and hailed again, "*Mafatu* calling. This is the fishing vessel *Mafatu*. We came over from Hawaii Kai and aren't familiar with this place. What's with all the activity?"

"This is a state marine preserve. Protected waters. No fishing!" Click. The reply was terse.

The lights went on in my head. Now it all made sense. They must think we're here to fish like criminals. "Thank you Captain, we didn't know." There was no further response from the snob. I'm sure every boat in the bay monitoring channel 16 switched to 68 and got the scoop. As it turned out, we had stumbled into Honolua Bay, Maui, a world-famous surf area and state-designated Marine Life Conservation District. How were we supposed to know? Was I supposed to live tethered to the GPS? Was it criminal to have fishing gear?

In the old times, Honolua was a staging point for the Maui cattle ranchers shipping their beef to market in Honolulu. It's a calm bay with deep water where a ship could get close to shore. The Paniolos (Hawaiian cowboys) would swim the cattle out to meet the boats. It was a beautiful setting with a colorful past. Now it's a tourist Mecca similar to the Hanauma Bay Reserve on Oahu.

There were no further communications from anyone in the cove. The snubbing continued. We knew we weren't wanted, so we pulled anchor and went out to sea. The three of us decided to hunt the coast for game fish way away from the pretentious tourists and highbrow charter captains.

Trolling along the coast was wonderful but somewhat uneventful. When it got late in the day, we decided to take anchorage close by off the Kaanapali Coast. We found the perfect spot in 12 feet of sandy water offshore of the Sheraton Kaanapali Hotel where Bugs dropped the hook into the sand and played out the anchor line. It was a pleasant niche next to Kekaa Point (Black Rock) in front of the sunbathing tourists. In the old days of Hawaii, this site was a popular fishing village. Today, however, it's a plush resort where we had a ringside seat to observe the beautiful people working on their tans.

I had not noticed the signs of what was to come, but before I knew it, Bugs had seated himself on the port rail combing at the fish cleaning station. He immediately went to work cleaning the two ulua we caught earlier. Heads and guts were ripped out and flying, fish parts airborne; ...all falling into the resort's immaculate swimming water.

"What's going on?" I asked Bugs.

"Cleaning fish," he responded.

I was silent but couldn't help but wonder what the heck he was doing. Some of the fish scraps became floaters and quickly roamed the surface to make their way to the white sand beach. Other scraps moved suspended in mid-water to drift along the shore, just under the water. The sinkers, heavier bony parts, found their way to the bottom and moved more slowly on the polished sand floor.

Great, we're going to get kicked out of here for chumming the waters and littering the beach, I worried. What was Bugs thinking? He could have put the scraps in the trash to dump at sea. Now we have blood and fish guts floating all over the place. The poor tourists, they don't have a clue. They've become the feeding station for all the tiger sharks in the area. Someone is going to get hurt, I just know it, and we're going to get kicked out, I can just feel it. Fish scraps and blood were everywhere.

Bugs continued on and prepared the ulua sashimi style, and then stowed it on ice. I was informed that dinner would be postponed, as Budd and Bugs made plans for shore leave. The next thing I knew, both were over the back of the swim step, ignoring the fish remnants, swimming for shore. Once onshore, they dried off in the sun then waltzed into the resort like they were paying guests.

The two ragtag sailors walked up past the golf course, through the resort, and into the hotel building atop Black Rock. Wearing only flip flops, wet swim trunks, and the dry shirts they carried over their heads when they swam to shore, they strolled through the lobby like they belonged there. It's a wonder they weren't asked to leave. Bugs went to the phone to report our progress to his wife, while Budd went out back to admire the view.

After Bugs finished with the phone, they both walked the grounds, taking in the sweet smells of plumeria, pikaki, and the other local flowers. It was a welcomed change to the smell of each other and stinky fish, but when they passed the restaurant the smell of hamburgers nearly sent them over the edge. There was no telling what they would do for a burger. If they had any money on them it would have been a done deal, hamburger dinners for two. But without money, other than the quarters they had for the phone, their splendid afternoon at the resort did not last long.

Some time later I decided to swim to shore and look for them. As I swam, the shadows of our discarded carcass floating on the bottom lurked in a blurred view from above. I wondered how smart it was to swim to shore alone. The tigers have had ample time to smell the appetizers we set for dinner. I nervously looked around for large dark shadows in the water. Thank God there were none.

I was on the beach as relaxed as a tourist. I walked the shoreline but ignored and avoided the fish parts washed up on the sand. I sunned myself like a vacationer to wait for my wayward crew. I had thoughts about joining them but decided not to leave sight of the boat. I also knew I wouldn't make a good impression, unshaven and looking like a castaway. No, I was not fit for a hotel appearance.

While I sat on the sand, a freckled seven year old boy walked up the beach with his mother a short ways back in tow. When he got closer to me, he yelled, "Mama, look! Look!" He pointed to the bulging white eyeball in the ulua head washed ashore, courtesy of Bugs. It laid there with scant portions of hanging flesh presented on pure white sand like a culinary delicacy placed on Waterford China.

His Mom caught up to see the dead fish and reacted in disgust, "Get away, don't touch it!" He didn't listen. A typical boy, he bent over to touch its eye with his right index finger. But before he made contact, she zoomed in and grabbed his hand to shake him away from the scene. I sat there and pretended to ignore it all, lest I might be connected to this gruesome remnant in some way. Bugs' discarded scraps. I shook my head.

A little after sunset the boys returned and the three of us swam back to the boat. I was much more comfortable swimming now, knowing that there was only a one in three chance that I would be a predator's choice. We swam to the boat without incident.

As darkness closed in on us, we enjoyed the change from day to night floating in a most splendid setting. Looking ashore, we could see the tourists in their high-dollar rooms and on their oceanfront lanais. It was obvious that many happy vacationers were preparing for dinner out in the resort.

I could only imagine the fancy fare that would be their evening's meal. Any of the several upscale restaurants would be well stocked with maitre d', wine sommelier, tuxedoed waiters, and busboys all in service to every whim of their guests. I had visions of juicy steaks smothered with garlic butter mushrooms, all presented by well-educated fine dining servants. I imagined that it would be a night for many of the guests to remember.

Ah, but we three captains floated offshore in the heart of the old whalers' territory. I wondered how the sailors dined on the old sailing ships. I could envision them at anchor. Dinner would be served in shifts, eaten below in the bowels of their beaten wood ship. Crusty characters would slurp down moldy shepherds' pie made with beef, carrots, and potatoes gone to rot in the ship stores. Tack bread speckled with mold from weeks at sea chewed like leather. This was the food of real men at sea. Perhaps our evening's grog had loosened my imagination a bit.

We were on the *Mafatu* in modern times. "*Mafatu*," a.k.a. "The Floating Gourmet Restaurant," provided us with somewhat more of a banquet than those whalers. Dinner was served in stages. Bugs served the sashimi with wasabi soy sauce on the chopping board. Budd fed us wet green lettuce from the bottom of the cooler tossed in a plastic container with ranch dressing for a salad. Then I presented the crew with sticky rice cooked in an aluminum camping kettle and a heated concoction of chili-stew in a pot. We dove into the grub as gentlemen vultures, moving in here and there for this and that. We ate heartily and dined like career admirals in the Royal Navy.

Early the next morning we pulled anchor from our beach bungalow for a good start at stretching our day. *Mafatu* headed out to sea to explore the south coast of Maui then fuel-up at the famous Lahaina Harbor.

Years ago Lahaina served as the whaling capital of the Pacific. The port is strategically located at the top of an inner-ocean triangle of Maui Nui and the humpback whale nursery. I felt it an honor for *Mafatu* and crew to pilot into a harbor so rich in marine history.

Today the Lahaina Harbor is a popular tourist destination. The charm of the old whaler's culture, the laid-back atmosphere, and the natural protection of the Mauna Kahalawai slopes makes this seaport a wonderful place to visit. For boaters, the entrance to the harbor is somewhat challenging, as shallow reefs crowd both sides of the narrow entrance. Then, just when you are close to the wharf, fuel dock and floating museum, the harbor opens up to your immediate starboard side. A captain must turn fast to hard starboard or lose his vessel to the rocks.

We navigated through the sharp right jog of the harbor entrance with all the boasting of whalers headed for shore leave. Bugs wore a fresh shirt and sat at watch on the port side combing looking like the ship's sergeant at arms. Budd was also on deck, serving as lookout on the bow. He struck the pose of an officer of the Royal Navy who had come from afar to see the natives of Polynesia. We took a complete tour of the harbor before realizing that it was full, not an empty slip in sight.

Without our usual morning breakfast of coffee and cereal, we were starving. I had to find a slip and get some breakfast. *Mafatu* and her crew would not be denied a stop at the infamous Lahaina Harbor, so we temporarily tied up at the fuel dock. Bugs and Budd went into the village for the harbor master's permission and to search for an overnight slip. At the same time, they would get the gas card from the Lahaina Yacht Club so we could refuel. But most of all, they needed to find breakfast. I stood guard on the boat because all of our gear was in plain view, easily taken by wharf rats.

The crew's reconnaissance proved only partially successful. While Budd did get the fuel authorizations, the harbor master had nowhere to put us. His best advice was to anchor outside the harbor past the surf line and dingy it into the village. Most importantly, the crew did return with a miracle of miracles: McDonald's breakfast meals with large coffees. What a treat.

When our fuel tanks were topped off, Budd and I went back to see his sailing buddies at the Yacht Club. Bugs was left to guard the boat. By the time we got to the club, Budd's friends had gone on about their business, so we played tourists on Front Street for awhile. We gawked at all the souvenir shops and friendly tourists. It was a good change of pace, but we were weekend ocean warriors, not shopping mall metro-men. Soon we were weary of cruising the shops.

Budd and I headed back to the harbor. The whaling ship museum, "The Carthaginian," floated right next to the fuel pier where *Mafatu* lay tied up. As Budd and I neared, we noticed a disturbance and a sea of bubbles floating in the water that entangled the whaler and the surrounding areas. Visitors onshore and on the deck of the museum were looking intently into the water toward the bubbles. It looked like someone had dumped boxes of laundry detergent in the confined space. We soon discovered its cause.

When *Mafatu* came into view, we saw Bugs on the back deck with the fuel dock's fresh water hose in one hand and his other hand waving in the air to balance his body in a strange, primitive dance routine. Stepping in and out of two five gallon plastic buckets with his feet, Bugs was boogieing to some unknown rhythm as he washed his clothes on deck. It looked like he was squashing grapes and making cheap wine with his feet. It was his dirty clothes in the buckets that he was kneading. He was laundering his personal wash with free water and dish cleaning soap, but he overloaded the soap!

He danced on his feet from bucket to bucket in wash and rinse cycles. The bubbles ran out of the buckets, on deck, out of the boat, and into the harbor. I panicked. I feared we would be cited for the pollution of the historic harbor. I picked up my pace and confronted Bugs.

"What the heck are you doing?"

"Cleaning clothes," he responded calmly.

"Look at all the soap in the harbor." I pointed.

Budd kicked in, "The harbor master's going to be pissed."

Bugs was silent, knowing that the soap suds had created a stir. He could see the tourists on the museum giving us the looks.

"Okay, finish up, rinse off, we're shoving off," I commanded.

Budd stowed the gear and crammed his wet clothes below deck, then he cast us off. With that, we bolted out of the harbor like thieves in the night. As soon as practical, I opened the throttle up to get as far away from the scene of the crime as possible. I didn't need a Coast Guard fine.

Our excursion to Lahaina was over. We had been in Maui for fewer than 24 hours and were stirring up trouble. First, we stumbled onto a fish preserve, loaded with fishing poles and spearguns in a fully-rigged fishing warship. Then, we went to Kaanapali, the Waikiki Beach of Maui, to anchor 50 yards off the pearly sands of a resort to lay fish heads and guts all over the beach to attract sharks for unsuspecting tourists. Finally, we come to the old-time whaling capital to pollute the harbor with soap suds within an hour of arrival.

I knew it would be too hot for *Mafatu* in Maui for awhile, so we skipped out to Lanai as fast as *Mafatu* could take us.

CHAPTER ELEVEN

MAFATU'S GRAND ADVENTURE II: LANAI & MAUI

Mafatu blasted out of Lahaina Harbor and high-tailed it toward the north coast of Lanai in seas of 1 to 2 feet. We sliced though the small surface chop without hesitation or tribulation.

Trolling wasn't in our plans today since both Bugs and I were anxious to spear some fish, but to take advantage of all the angles we set two trolling lines way off the back of the boat running at a high speed ...just in case something was fast enough to catch our lures. It didn't take much time to travel the Auau Channel between Maui and Lanai since it was a mere eight nautical miles in distance. Less than a half an hour later we were down the Lanai Coast past Kanounou to Shipwreck Beach.

Bugs and I investigated potential dive sites along the coast but passed on every one of them since we were windward of the island and the shoreline was full of reefs and shoals. In addition, every time we saw promising mountainous coastal terrain it was too far back from the shoreline. It was unlikely that the terrain would continue underwater with any real significance.

Near the northwestern tip of the island a huge rusting freighter lay stranded in the surf. Of course, it was called Shipwreck Beach. With the wind blowing hard onshore and the treacherous shoals undersurface, it was natural that this would be a graveyard for the unwary ship captain or our aggressive dive crew.

269

We continued on and turned the corner of the island to head away from the wind to the protected northwest shore. It was as smooth as a glassy lake. Silky, rich waters of blue lapped gently against a lava coastline; it just screamed of the potential for premier diving. Between Kaena Point and Keanapapa Point a small lava formation pierced into the sea forming a mini-peninsula with a visible underwater reef of good size. Such an underwater contour should encourage closer inspections by larger fish from the deep. We got into position in 60 feet of water and put the hook down about 40 feet back into the reef. This would allow us enough anchor line to be close to the drop off but still above the reef for an easy dive entry.

Bugs was excited, his eyes bright and eager. He dragged his gear to his side of the boat and started to suit up. I was enthusiastic to explore this new territory as well. While we attended to our own diving interests, Budd set a bottom fishing-rig to keep him occupied while he listened to his radio headset tuned in to a distant Honolulu station. Music on a boat was a relaxant that some fisherman enjoyed but it really wasn't for me. I must say that Budd was a good man to be considerate of my distaste for music at sea. He used the headsets for communal peace and quiet.

As we suited up, Bugs' weight belt caught my curiosity. A homemade relic, it often caught my interest. In all my years of diving, I had never seen anyone that used such an unusual belt. It starts with black nylon webbing and a stainless buckle, but the whole thing is encased in a flattened canvas fire hose. Slits run through the hose where the webbing protrudes and the weighs are hung.

If asked, Bugs will tell you that he made it himself and used it in the commercial diving business. He likes it because it's more comfortable, doesn't slip, and is wider and easier to handle. If you ask me, he's been trying to set a new fashion standard for belts, but none of us bought into it, not just yet. All of the divers continue to use the standard web belts.

We were ready to dive and fell over the side. The water clarity was exquisite. Before our eyes, the underwater bluff worked itself out into the sea, creating a huge lava face as it fell into a deep valley. This dropped into greater depths beyond our field of view.

It was all I could ask for in a dive: no currents, clear warm water, terrific ocean topography, lots of corals, and plenty of fish life.

Bugs and I dropped down along the face of the bluff and went our own way to look for lobsters, squid, and the larger trophy fish that might ascend from the deep. Both of us passed on shooting the smaller parrot fish, hoping to be prepared for a larger score of giant ulua or omilu. After close to 45 minutes of bottom time, we surfaced empty-handed but thrilled to have been diving. As it turned out, this was a perfect sightseeing dive in beautiful new territory.

Back onboard, we stowed our gear and prepared for a second dive farther down the coast. We relaxed and scrounged up some lunch. After a little rest and lazy sunbathing for a safe surface interval, we pulled anchor and moved on to the Five Needles area. Our ninja divers had talked about this spot, telling us that it was a well-known dive icon that we just had to dive. Needles is a series of lava fingers that jut from the coastline to form a dramatic tableau along the cliffs. The lava formations are slender and tall, like a patch of needles.

We motored in close to a main geologic structure and threw our hook next to a lava pinnacle inside toward shore. It was about 50 feet deep. Ahead of *Mafatu* lay the shore, to the right the lava structure, and to the left and behind us deeper water. We floated at anchor in a protected area with wonderful underwater ground to explore. This was a good spot for Budd, too; the proximity to the bluff became an invitation for him to explore the protruding cliff at the water-line with mask and snorkel.

Bugs and I suited up and attached our catch bags to the weight belts and stowed our fish stringers in our vests. We fell backward off the rails and then swam toward the bluff to a 40 foot depth. The territory was gorgeous. Multiple layers of ancient magma worked itself down from the base of the pinnacle into the deep. With a complete underwater view, we could see how nature formed the mound. There were corals and marine life throughout, with many tropicals and small reef fish swimming freely, undisturbed by our presence. We dropped down to the 70 foot range where similar terrain continued deeper.

There seemed to be no real advantage to the greater depths since the fish were of similar size, shape, and quantity. I casually moved back up a little to stretch my air. After all, we were here to explore, so we might as well take advantage of it. I looked for lobsters in crevices, fish hiding in holes, and other creatures that would make for a good dinner. Bugs and I separated. We dove together but always with plenty of space between us for some elbow room. How could you enjoy a dive with someone in your face all the time? When diving with a buddy, he has to be there for you, but he has to keep himself almost out of sight. As we were fond of saying about buddies, "If you need 'em, you gotta go get 'em!"

I was investigating a small recess in a ledge when a bull parrot came into view. He wasn't paying me any attention, just grazing on a small coral. He would make a good target, so I slid into range with very little movement. Then he noticed me. I paused and looked down at the corals in a humbling stop. He expressed some curiosity at my presence but didn't get excited. I kept calm, relaxed, and slowed my breathing down. There would be no excessive noise or trail of bubbles coming from my regulator.

He turned back away to continue eating. I flicked my fins to slide forward, aimed the long-gun with the fore and aft sights blocking out the fish's head and squeezed the trigger gently. "Slam!" An ideal shot. Red blood, fish scales, and dark volcanic sand blew everywhere as he thrashed about for his life. I moved in to dispatch him to my higher purpose and to quickly ease his pain.

I strung him on my stainless steel fish holder and continued on with the dive, looking for the next kill. Unfortunately there would be no others. Soon I was down to 400 pounds of air and reluctantly made my way back to the boat for a safety stop. Budd helped me with the dive gear as I went on to tell him about the dive. Bugs surfaced a few moments later. He wasn't even in the boat yet when he bubbled over with excitement.

"Did you see me cover your ass?" Bugs boasted.

"Cover me? No."

"Yeah, I covered your butt!" He continued with pride as he crawled over the rail into the boat.

"What are you talking about?" I ask.

"You don't know?"

"Know what?" I started to get a little impatient.

"The shark was going for your ass!" Bugs said emphatically,

as he removed his gear looking more animated by the moment.

"Bull crap, there was no shark!" I replied.

"Oh, yeah! 6 foot grey reef. He saw you fighting with the parrot and came in for your fanny!"

"Nah! You're pulling my leg. Bullshit!" I told him.

"I kid you not! You were working the parrot. Blood's everywhere. I was a ways behind you. Then, I saw this thing come up past me on toward you. It freaked me out! He went straight for you."

Budd chimed in, not knowing whether to believe him or not. "Really mate? Lying is punishable with twelve lashes at the mast!"

"Honest! He was going to take a piece of your butt. I put my 38 on the three-prong and moved in quickly behind you. He moved cautiously back and forth checking you out before I chased him away."

"I didn't see a thing."

"I was ready to blast 'em with the power head. I stepped in between you both. He backed off. Here, look at my three-prong." Bugs pointed to the 38 that was screwed to the tip.

"Why didn't you tell me on the bottom?" I asked.

"I was going to, but before I could get to you, you swam off looking for more fish. I wasn't going to waste my air chasing you down, I had fish to shoot. I saved your ass!" He threw his fish stringer in the boat with two good-sized parrots, one wekee, and one omilu. What a nice catch. Bugs was always a top shooter in the group.

I wasn't the least bit aware of how close I was to a "butt-biting" but felt thankful for an attentive dive buddy. We stowed our gear and didn't think about it again. The day wore on at sea and before long it was time to decide on an evening berth.

Mafatu motored on to Manele Bay some ten nautical miles away where we prearranged for a slip at the boat harbor. We passed Kaumalapau Barge Harbor and soon blew past Palaoa Point to round the southeastern tip of the island. *Mafatu* navigated on to Manele Bay, a drowsy, small boat-launch harbor. Manele boasts a scenic coastline with two bays separated by a natural geologic outcropping. White Manele Bay is a wonderful white sand beach and bay to the south of the imposing coastal bluff and the offshore Puupehe Rock. Thus the name: White Manele. To the north of the lava landmark is the dark lava coastline and bay called Black Manele. It's all rock, lava outcroppings, and close-in jagged shoals. The state maintains a harbor designed with a breakwater to shelter a small band of boats from the open ocean by tucking itself back into the shoreline bluff.

Mafatu headed into this unknown harbor with caution. Everything in the area was carved out of lava, not great material for boats in the event of navigational error. Passing the lighthouse on the breakwater, we turned hard port and moved toward the tiny crescent of boat slips at the end of the channel. This was it, 24 boat slips and a ferry wharf.

I spied a few open slips that we might use for the night. We chose one on the shore side, farthest from the boat launch, and tied *Mafatu* into the slip. With the turn of a key, the motor ceased. Silence. Our ears were numbed by the persistent sound of a diesel engine. After a long day in the open ocean, it was heavenly... peace and quiet, a motionless boat, a solid dock, dry land, and an endless supply of fresh water at the end of a hose. Life was wonderful.

We reconnoitered a bit, with Billie Budd cleaning the boat while Bugs attended to the fishing and diving gear. Both men were exceptional at caring for equipment. Budd is a stickler for rinsing and re-rinsing everything on a boat. Keenly aware of the damage that salt could do, he was fastidious about his freshwater rinses. He was such a nitpicker that when we washed his boat down after fishing, he would wash it again later that evening in secret. Bugs was just as meticulous with the gear. We were all taught at a young age that both boat and gear must be maintained to strict standards, as our lives and our haul of fish depend on their performance at sea.

While the boys cleaned up, I went ashore to find the harbor master so I could give notice of our arrival and make sure our slip was approved. It turned out she already knew we had arrived and was waiting for my visit. Everything was approved, so I gave her the state's modest fee for a two-night stay and went back to the boat to help with the chores.

Mafatu and all her gear were washed, cleaned, and stowed. Dinner preparations commenced. Budd prepared the salad and libations, Bugs battered fish for frying, and I cooked a pot of rice. We would have plenty to feast on tonight.

Docked at the next slip over was an older, 26-foot Radon deep V fishing boat with no one aboard. Strewn with coolers and other items stowed on deck like a parked pickup truck at a tail gate party, it looked messy, but somehow it was in perfect order for this country atmosphere.

A short while later an aged silver pickup truck made its way down the dirt road to our dock and landing. Three hunters with high-powered rifles got out and walked to the Radon. Now it all made sense–they were hunters that had come over from Maui for the mouflon hunting season. They nodded a hello of acknowledgement but went about their own chores. It was curious: a boat full of sheep killers armed to the teeth, berthed next to a bunch of spear-toting fish killers.

Bugs planned on fresh fish for dinner fried with a light Japanese batter. In the middle of breading the fish he struck up a conversation with one of the hunters having a beer on deck. A ways though the conversation, they agreed to a swap. Mouflon steaks came over to our boat and fish fillets went over to their boat. After being around fish for a few days, a fresh thinly-sliced mouflon steak would be a welcomed extravagance. Drinks were shared and stories told from ship to ship. As usual, Billie Budd was first rate with the cocktails. What a gourmet dinner. The steaks were phenomenal, more than any of us could have imagined.

Dawn came early at Manele, but the *Mafatu* crew would have none of it. After mid-morning coffee and breakfast, we launched out of the harbor and motored back to the southern tip of Lanai in hope of more terrific diving.

As we drove past the coastline of Palaoa Point and Kaunolu Bay I was amazed by the thought that King Kamehameha I kept a summer home here and fished the perfect waters we would dive today. King Kam was the famous chief who united the Islands into the Kingdom of Hawaii in 1810 and gave rise to the rule of the Kamehameha line. Kaunolu Bay served as a fishing village located in a natural lava rock inlet at the ocean's edge where the eastern and southern tips of the island met.

Years ago the king's royal compound sat on the bluff at Kaunolu village near Halulu Heiau (a hallowed place of worship.) I could just imagine the King's double hulled canoes and royal fleet anchored in this protected paradise. Fishing was so impressive here because the hilly terrain protected the ocean from wind and swell and then dropped off deep into oblivion very close to the island. With the colliding currents coming from both sides of the island, it encouraged big-game fish to gather. There were only a handful of spots around the islands that measured up to this superior fishing.

Mafatu skimmed across the water as I scouted the coastline looking for the perfect shallow-water dive spot to nurse the crew back to life. There it was ahead, just past the King's harbor, next to the cliffs and rock slide. I moved the boat in close for Bugs to drop a shallow anchor. The water was clear, and the undersea terrain held the promise of fish. It might be a good spot for parrot fish, kumu and other shallow-water game.

Bugs snorkeled, not wanting to go through the trouble of strapping on heavy gear and blowing a tank of air in shallow water. I dove with a tank eager to accept whatever the ocean would provide. If nothing else, it would be a relaxing and enjoyable sightseeing trip. This area intrigued me with its small lava structures rising from the ocean bottom and large black boulders that littered the sea floor.

Budd captained the boat and would use this time to bottom fish and read more of the classics. Bugs and I were suited up and in the water heading for the cliff line. We always enjoyed shallow dives for reef fish as it brought back memories of our childhood spearfishing. Before long we separated. I was having the time of my life chasing fish through the shallow rock bottom while Bugs was closer in to shore doing the same fish chase.

Past each boulder and at each lava formation, reef fish congregated in the most inquisitive and tame behavior. It was if they had no fear of me. They pranced about unaware that they were in the presence of the Fish Reaper himself. Thankfully for these little creatures I was only concerned with large edible fish, not these small fry.

Probing the underwater crevice of a bluff that towered up to the surface, my head and shoulders moved in and out of the void with deliberate purpose. I looked for signs of lobsters or any telltale hints that there was something good to eat in this lava formation. Sometimes the lobsters hiding way back in a crack will remove themselves from sight but dangle the end of their antennae out just far enough from their hole to keep abreast of what's going on in their domain. They're hidden but still receiving communications from the nest. Every once in a while I might lure a spiny out if its curiosity got the better of it. Then, once in the open, a swift hand pinning against the rock would buy some time to get a secure handhold to pry the creature from its lair.

I was thinking about lobsters and tasting the delicate white meat in rich lemon-butter sauce when I felt an unusual presence from above. I rolled out sideways and turned to look up. There above me were two pairs of white legs with fins. What the heck is going on? I questioned.

At first I only got a glance of the legs as the overhead ledge impeded my view, but I improved my vantage point and the legs exposed two whole bodies. As near as I could assume, one was a young boy of twelve or thirteen, the other an older man in his forties. It must be a father and son snorkeling together. Where the hell did they come from? They're in the middle of nowhere. There were no sounds of a boat pulling up. It was clear they were tourists, not locals. They floated above pleased to watch me work the bottom.

Soon a whole boatload of snorkelers swarmed the pinnacle. Evidently a tourist snorkel boat out of Maui must be using this spot as a day-trip destination. I slowly got over the disappointment of thinking that Bugs, Budd, and I were here in the wilderness alone. I rationalized their presence to make peace with the intrusion: this is a historic area, the water's calm, the fish plentiful, and it's a great place to showcase the wonders of Hawaiian marine life. I played the script over and over in my mind and came to accept our fate. These visitors might also explain why the fish were so tame, as tourists love to feed the fish. My mind gradually moved to a nobler path. I felt a sense of happiness that so many would see and feel the beauty of our oceans.

This new excitement put me in a giddy mood for play. It's an awesome sight to watch a scuba diver underwater from a floating view above. I always enjoyed the experience of watching my dive buddies below as I decompressed near the surface. It was like watching a movie that you are a part of but detached from. You're watching the other character in the same movie, but he's not really watching you. It's a panoramic view of his past, present, and future, all rolled up into one vision from above. It must be something like the angels watching us from the heavens.

I wondered what I could do to enrich the experience for these visitors. That's it–I'll put on a show. There was no game to shoot here, especially now that fish camp arrived. I decided to put on a play. They wouldn't know it's a charade, but I would do my best to give them something to watch besides the pretty fish. I started to work the area for game, consciously searching the nooks and crannies for something to shoot. I performed like a skilled fish stalker searching for fish and extended my spear here and there preparing to shoot whenever some poor tropical of any size showed up in the distance. I didn't think they'd wonder why I was picking on such small fish. They wouldn't know any better, and besides, they'd be too busy watching the action to question it.

The undersea stage portrayal of the lone hunter gave me a thrill. I imagined I saw myself from their vantage point above. I became conscious of my form and style in the skillful hunt I tried to render. Quite naturally my body slimmed and my gut sucked in to provide a leaner hunter physique. I looked intently into cracks and crevasses, staging an authentic hunting scene. Bubbles rose to bathe the growing group of snorkelers who had trailed my every move. I crept along the bottom as smooth as a moray eel on a silent but lethal mission. There was no script, only my ingenuity of showmanship and good form.

I got to a small boulder and hunched over it looking at a poor undersized parrot within shooting distance. It was too small to shoot, but there I was, the big hunter with the perfect shot. I couldn't take it in good conscience. I also couldn't shoot and miss; it would be an embarrassment. There must be some other stage trick I could use to unwind the drama of my own silliness.

Ah, yes. It came to me. While in the perfect position on the rock, I moved my head back and forth, squinting my eyes in a show of difficulties with my vision. I acted like it was a serious problem that needed immediate attention. Then I set in action the resolution of the conflict. I put my gun on the side of the boulder and proceeded to clean my imagined fogged-up mask.

First, I carefully removed and swooshed it around. Then, with a few strands of seaweed which were close at hand, my fingers polished the lens inside and out. I swooshed it around again and put it back on my face full of water. I tilted my head back, filled the mask with air, and the water receded. The result: perfect clarity. I looked forward again and surprise, the parrot was gone. The curtain was drawn and this silly stage show concluded. With the audience amused and the actor running out of fresh lines or a decent plot, I rushed away to look for other fish away from the prying eyes of the paparazzi audience.

I swam off to find Bugs. He was easy to locate snorkeling the shallows closer to shore. I told him about the tourists. Then we headed back to the boat together; it was obvious that we wouldn't catch any fish with this army of snorkelers.

As it turned out, the wilderness we dreamed of wasn't really a wilderness at all; it was now a popular dive destination. *Mafatu* pulled anchor and headed back to Manele Bay. As we neared King Kam's fishing area, there were three large charter boats anchored with hoards of snorkeling tourists.

We left the dive boats behind and decided to do a second dive on one of Hughsan's spots close to the harbor, an underwater mountain a quarter of mile off the coastline. This dive would be deep; the very top of the domed sea-mound was over a 100 feet from the surface. It would be a fitting last dive of the day.

Once we were on the site, Bugs and I prepared for the dive while Budd circled for a final position sighting landmarks onshore and studying the depth finder. He knew we were very close to finding the spot when all of the onshore indicators lined up. Then he followed the line of marks out to sea until the depth finder showed a hill at 100 feet from the surface. This dive would be a little deeper than I would prefer, but this being a special trip, I slackened my self-imposed depth limits just this one time.

Ready for round two, we checked and rechecked our masks, fins, weight belts, air, and guns. Bugs and I splashed in off the side descending as fast as our fins would take us before the currents had a chance to blow us away from the plateau.

The water clarity was poor, brown and thick with microscopic marine life. We couldn't see the mound from above or anything else in this thick soup. I hoped Budd dropped us on the spot and we would land on something before we were pulled out to sea. Being swept out to sea would surely ruin our dive. The cloudy water was only a hint of the poor visibility that we would find. Bugs and I stayed close knowing that it would be easy to lose each other.

With a bit of luck we landed on the rounded dome. It was more like we unknowingly fell onto it rather than successfully navigated to the site since it came up at us on our way down without warning. With so much marine debris filtering out the sunlight from above, this place was difficult to figure out, much less enjoy. It was an uncomfortable dive swimming in a dark broth that hindered my viewing experience of this unique underwater formation.

The currents were moderately strong, sweeping parallel to the coast. I landed on the forward edge of the structure and took refuge from the driving current that threatened to sweep me off this precarious perch. Nestling myself into a small indentation behind a larger rock mound, I worked to get my thoughts organized on how to execute this dive. My breathing labored heavily from hoofing it down against the current, so I paused to calm myself and breathed slowly to relax my body and conserve air. I told myself with each breath, "Relax... slow down... breathe easy." After several verbal suggestions I became calm and began my search of the area. Bugs went on his own mission and was out of sight but I was not worried as I knew he would be close by.

I ventured forth and peeked over the top of the structure to see if there was a visible bottom. Nothing but the cloudy black depths met my eyes. It was an eerie feeling looking at an endless abyss. Then, there in the distance, below and away from the mound were the hazy outlines of two large ulua swimming in tandem. The predator fish skirted the lava pinnacle and kept a safe distance.

They played with me, taunting my eagerness to get a shot. They swam in circles, twisting and turning like butterflies, challenging my patience with no visible concerns or cares. What crafty fish! They knew they were safely out of range. I swam down to greet them, hoping to squeeze a shot off before they vanished. The small one was closest; I would take him if I could get close enough. He was a beautiful ulua, big, beefy, black, sporting a blunt head and a bulldog jaw line.

I got close, so close to having a good shot. He started to turn away; I fired my gun in the desperate hope for a solid hit. "Bam!"

The rubbers of the long-gun sent the stainless steel shaft onward with a bolt of speed. It went straight on and then dropped like lead from its intended target missing by a mere 6 inches. Damn it! It was too long a shot. I quickly pulled up from my deep descent to return to the pinnacle for a reload. I was tempted but decided not to chase him down for another shot. It was too deep for my bones.

Out of the current and back in the protection of my nest, I reloaded the three-band long-gun and waited for a target. It was only a matter of time before I noticed a few large parrot fish nibbling on corals to the right of my position. These stately blue males paraded in the open as they dined on their favorite meal. There were a few small reddish-brown females father in the distance, but I ignored them. The males were my favorite target since they were bigger, stronger, and meatier. Parrots are a little tougher chew than most fish, but prepared by steam with Chinese sauces, they provide a culinary treat. A tough fish becomes unusually tender when steamed and showcased in a delicate Asian sauce.

I slipped out of hiding and proceeded to move discreetly to the blue males. The current would not let up, so I hugged the rock bottom and slithered hand-over-hand slowly forward to the parrots. A casual cat-and-mouse exchange ensued between us. When my movements were slow and relaxed as I skimmed over the rocks, the feeding parrots took very little notice of me and went about their routine, but when I tried to quicken my advance past a crawl, they'd take a keener interest and keep an attentive eye on me. During my more pressing advances, they would float back and feed on corals farther away. The more I advanced, the more spooked they became.

I didn't want to scare them off, so I took to psychological gamesmanship. When I advanced too fast and saw the parrots getting jittery, I'd stop and lower my head to the rocks to pretend to feed as they did. There was a layer of algae growth on the rocks that offered the perfect food for grazing. I went through the motions mimicking their behavior in perfect character of a large, algae-eating vegetarian. At every sly opportunity, I peeked out the corner of my mask to see what they were doing. This game could have gone on for hours, but my dwindling air dictated that

I end this and take a shot as soon as it presented itself.

Pretending to nibble on a lovely green moss salad, I got even closer to the fish, but I was still barely in shooting range. Then a large blue moved in closer to a rock for a bite of fresh corals. He was nervous, but the tantalizing morsels were just too tempting. This unusual wet-suited veggie eater was a bit too close for his comfort. His eyes tracked my every move, fixated on the slight movements of my every muscle. I tried not to make eye contact, but I couldn't help being drawn to his cautious beady eyes.

We stared at each other for a moment, and I wondered if he knew of my intentions. With a look of sincere compassion in my eyes, I tried to communicate that I would take him for food. I believe this was God's way of nature: I would be respectful of his sacrifice. It would only bring honor to his long life to allow him one last brave fight. While I did not say these words in a sort of conversation, I did sincerely feel these emotions hoping it would be conveyed to the spirit of the fish. Nature just is–it's neither cruel nor kind.

I made my move. Lying on the bottom, I leaned to my left side and took in more air to get the buoyancy I needed to lift my body off the rocks without causing a stir. Carefully my gun was moved into position. My right hand slid down the shaft and felt its way to the trigger grip as I extended the long-gun forward in slow smooth motion. Then I moved ahead with a slight movement from my fins. The gun sights blocked each other on the head of the parrot. I squeezed the trigger, "Slam" the shaft flew forward to smack the target head-on. The parrot went ballistic and moved in a flurry of panic and sought the bottom for refuge. Blood was everywhere. I rushed in to secure my catch with the three-prong. The gift of the parrot's life was complete; he would be dinner.

Time passed so quickly. Bugs caught up with me at the top of the mound toward the end of our dive. He had his own success, bagging a nice-sized squid, a spiny lobster, and a big parrot. In spite of the poor visibility and limited bottom time, Bugs and I had a very productive dive even though it was a creepy experience. We worked our way up to the surface and ended a quarter mile down current to signal Budd with our dive whistle. Budd immediately sped over to pick us up.

Bugs and I tidied up and stowed the gear. Once we were relaxed, the conversation moved on to our plans for the evening and the remainder of our trip. We talked about spending another night in Manele and diving more of the Lanai Coast. Budd threw out the idea of leaving Lanai and heading back to Molokai for another night at Kalaupapa before heading home. Bugs thought about heading back to Lahaina Harbor for an evening's entertainment. Then we could dive the north coast of Maui before heading home.

I did see the merits of heading back to the north coast of Molokai or Maui, and a final visit to Lahaina Harbor was also very enticing. Then there was a personal issue that weighed heavy on my mind. Sandy and I were scheduled for our first Lamaze class in a few days. I didn't want to miss that, soon to be a new father and all. How would it look if she had to go alone? I could just imagine what the other hormonal women in class would think when they asked her where her husband was. "Oh, he's fishing with his friends." I reasoned that I'd be the scourge of fatherhood. If at all possible, I would try to avoid that scenario.

After some deliberation we agreed that we'd head to Lahaina for the night. Then, the next day we'd travel to Molokai either via the north or south route, depending on the seas. For our time constraints, diving the north coast of Maui would be too far out of the way. After a night in Lahaina we'd be in a good position to have a great shot at Molokai the next day. With this Lahaina plan we could even have a nice dinner and night out on the town, like old-time whalers on leave. We took off straight for Maui.

Mafatu slid across the flat water of the Auau Channel with the greatest of ease. No wave or chop inhibited our progress. I was concerned about the reception we'd have after the harbor soap incident, so when we arrived *Mafatu* sheepishly motored in hoping that no one would remember us. We searched through the harbor for an empty slip. None. We were forced to take an anchorage offshore, just past the surf line in clear view of Front Street, the Sunset strip of Lahaina.

Once we were safely anchored, the crew expressed their determination to go ashore for an evening's entertainment. Budd and Bugs blew up the life raft and put it in the water. There was a common feeling among us that we had been in the ocean too long, so we all agreed that we should enjoy dinner and the night life of this harbor town.

I was a little uncomfortable about leaving *Mafatu* unattended as anchors slip, lines fray on corals, boats float away, and thieves steal things. To ease my fears, I dove on the anchor and made it steadfast by wrapping the anchor chain around a few rocks. As a precaution against piracy, we also locked the expensive gear in the cabin. The cabin was near burglar proof. *Mafatu* had special stainless steel security bars designed and installed for theft prevention. With these measures, I felt I could be comfortable leaving *Mafatu* unattended for a brief evening ashore.

Bugs, Budd and I took turns washing on the swim step with the freshwater deck hose in full view of the tourists roaming Front Street. We were far enough offshore that only high-powered binoculars would reveal our bodily details. All of us felt that such a remote possibility could be safely ignored. Washed and bathed in aftershave, we donned our best t-shirts and shorts for dinner.

Three large men boarded the tiny two-man dingy in a tangle of legs, arms, butts, and torsos. The poor little raft was overloaded. It was one thing to be overloaded when everyone was wet diving, but when dressed for dinner, filled beyond capacity could mean getting soaked on the way to shore. Dinner in a fancy restaurant would not be enjoyable drenched.

Any bodily movement brought the waterline farther up the rails of the tiny craft, so we all strived to keep still and calm. This was more difficult than we would imagine, as we were in a mood of merriment. Rowing through the surf line would be our greatest challenge to staying dry. One wave, one slight move, and all of us might be in the drink. From a tourist's sidewalk view on shore, we stood out like the three stooges.

Fortunately for us, the surf was not very active; there were only occasional swells bouncing up on the reef. If the surf had been larger, a dry landing would have been impossible. It was mass confusion in the dingy with each captain telling the others how and when to row so as not to splash each other. With loosened tongues we bossed each other around and teased mercilessly. We survived the first few hundred yards and reluctantly learned how to work together to keep the dingy dry.

As we crossed the surf line, every small wave threatened our continued floatation. There were times of great tension followed by howls of laughter punctuated by sharp hysterical jabbering.

The constant movement in the boat and short rowing strokes eventually splashed water on us and our dinner clothes.

A group of tourists gathered on the street, wondering if we were in trouble or just stupid. We tried to ignore them, but a crowd amassed to see the spectacle. Thank God the waves were kind to us.

We neared shore arguing and laughing. The crowd grew larger on the seawall to watch this unusual fiasco and how it would end. Three grown men were coming in through the surf on a rubber raft like seal team commandoes. Finally the show was over; we landed on the sand beach at the foot of the highway with no dignity at all.

There were a few claps and some cheers from the crowd when we beached on the sand upright and uninjured. Not a word was spoken, but each of us knew instinctively not to embarrass ourselves in front of the onlookers. We ignored the crowd, even as there was clapping and muted cheers for our success. Budd stowed the raft under the wall of the street, and we rushed to dinner like we knew nothing of those clowns in a rubber dingy. In a few minutes we blended in with the people on the street and became anonymous.

It was a group decision: we dined at Keone's Restaurant. Each of us examined the menu carefully and ordered entrees that struck our individual tastes. Budd had the mahi and Bugs and I had juicy t-bone steaks. It was fabulous; here we were in the luxury of air conditioning, a dinner table with chairs, fancy place mats, a full set of silverware, starched cloth napkins, and a pretty woman serving us. We felt like three kings. How different a dining experience this was from eating on *Mafatu* where you grabbed your grub, sat on the engine box, and ate off hand-me-down camping equipment.

Our elegant dinners were consumed with the greatest passion. It was wonderful, so tasty and full of flavor. After dinner we roamed the streets and took in the nightlife. Civilization was marvelous but it came to an end all too soon.

We were tired after a long day at sea, so once we had our fill of the night life, we went back to the beach to retrieve the dingy. We were relieved to find it wasn't stolen. Otherwise, it would have been a long swim over shallow rocks and sharp corals back to the boat. Our comic beach scene was repeated again, but this time we slipped into the darkness without a crowd gawking at our every move.

We couldn't see much of the water or waves beyond the raft in this darkness. Our course was set to the far off anchor light of *Mafatu* as we hoped that no tsunami would come our way. Any noise of oncoming water became a cause for concern. The usually welcomed sound of a gentle wave breaking became a chill of danger and dread of swamping; we didn't want to swim all the way out to the boat at this time of night.

Any odd movement of our dingy up or down could signal peril. It was an uneasy transit. "Sometimes God protects those who are too foolish to protect themselves," my father would say. This must have been the case with us.

We finally reached the boat nearly soaked, but safe. Bugs, Budd, and I dried off, slipped into fresh clothes, and settled down to our bunks for the night. Unhappily, not one of us had a good night's sleep. The surf and swell kept us rocking uncomfortably all night long. Moderate but unpredictable chop from every direction never allowed us to get used to its pattern. The swells were coming from every which way without a rhythm, so our bodies couldn't relax. The chop kept us rolling around in our bunks and slapping against the side of our berths. It was a very different situation when the direction of the waves was consistent and your body became one with the rhythm of the waves.

Sunrise came none too soon. We took our time about it, eventually rising to the glorious view of Lahaina town at early morning. It was splendid watching the city come alive from offshore. We enjoyed a cup of coffee and had a quick breakfast. Then Budd tidied up the boat, Bugs pulled anchor, and I studied the nautical charts one last time. We would travel back to Molokai and see what the day might bring for another day of fishing and diving.

In short order we sped away from the surf line and crabbed at an angle up the coast past Kaanapali. This dead reckoning would put us in the best angle heading northwest to Cape Halawa and on to Kalaupapa, then later to the northwest end of Ilio Point. If this course became unworkable, it was also a respectable take-off heading for the far southwest end of Laau Point. It would all depend on the ocean conditions and whether the north passage would be passable. In any case, channel conditions would dictate how we'd transit to Molokai.

If we took the northerly route, we would be windward in rougher waters. There were very few spots to take shelter along the cliffy north coast, but if the water was good, Kalaupapa would be the perfect destination for a few dives and our last overnighter. Then we could do a fast Kaiwi channel crossing the next morning. So what if I showed up at the Lamaze class just off the boat? With lots of aftershave, no one would be the wiser.

If we went south, we'd be leeward of Molokai in calmer water. Kamalo Harbor was close but did not offer much protection from the sea. Located midway along the coast, Kaunakakai Harbor was the main supply line to the island. It would be perfect for long-term shelter. Then there was the barge harbor at the very west end of the island, Haleolono Harbor. In any case, there were better options along the south shore if things got too rough at sea.

When we got to Honolua Bay I fell off from Maui and into the Pailolo Channel. All weather conditions seemed normal with an average of 2 to 3 foot swells. Then a few miles out into the channel we hit the wind line blowing down the channel slot between the islands. In the course of seven minutes the wind and seas built to uncomfortable proportions. This change in the ocean came at us with no warning; we were blindsided. We traveled straight into a funnel of squalls that quickly became the most dangerous seas I would experience in Hawaii.

We should have known better. Not one of us experienced boatmen thought to listen to the marine weather station before departure. This was an especially foolish mistake on my part as captain. Here we were at the very start of our channel crossing, and the ocean was already damned mean. In no time the seas grew from 6 to 14 feet. In only a matter of ten minutes we were in very dangerous conditions for an overloaded 25-foot boat.

Swells battered *Mafatu* from the northeast, hitting our starboard aft. Fierce breaking wave-tops buffeted us as they pushed *Mafatu* down the channel toward the south of Molokai. There was no way to fight these seas heading north; a northerly leg would only be suicide. I turned the helm south and would make the best of our course, come what may. *Mafatu* blew down the Kalohi Channel at a very swift speed without much throttle.

I kept to the helm since I was most familiar with how my boat handled herself at sea. My major concerns were broaching sideways or pearl diving forward while going down these giant waves. If such a tragedy arose, we'd flip over, the boat would sink, and we'd have no way of calling for help.

It was fortunate that I had worked *Mafatu* aggressively in the past. In smaller seas I often surfed the boat home from Molokai, swell to swell. It saved gas and sped up the crossing. I was also known to ride the waves with *Mafatu* coming home in the Hawaii Kai Channel entrance.

I kept reminding myself to keep calm, as only a cool head would take us through this crisis. I reassured myself with the knowledge that I had surfed all my life; this was just surfing with a larger board on bigger waves. It wasn't really working. Today, in this ocean, it was hard to believe my positive thoughts. I was dreadfully concerned for our safety. Never had the *Mafatu* been in an ocean so rough. Many of these waves topped 14 feet or more. They were monsters.

When we left Maui in the morning, the boys set an abbreviated spread of high- speed trolling gear. Who would have imagined that this crossing would turn into a test of survival rather than the perfect opportunity to fish? As our situation worsened, we fed out more line to let the lures run long. It was probably my wishful thinking, but I hoped dragging all that line might help run the boat more stable in this wicked sea. Bugs and Budd attended to the fishing gear and did all they could to keep the trolling lines from fouling as they hung on for dear life.

Any angler in his right mind would have thought them crazy. I would not question their craziness since their added weight on the back deck helped to put the boats aft lower in the water. This would hold us down into the sea and tilt our bow up. Wave after wave, we slipped and skidded down these mountainous swells. *Mafatu* was smoking along at an unusually fast speed with her throttle barely in gear.

We could hardly hear each other through the driving wind, so we took to shouting. The howling gusts whistled through the poles and fishing lines. The boat rose and fell between waves like a fishing bobber being pushed uncontrollably by a hurricane of wind. We hung on to any part of the boat we could reach with both hands. Stinging wind-driven spray blew everywhere. Two bilge pumps were put to work even though *Mafatu* had scuppers in her self-bailing deck. Too much water was seeping into the bilges. We rode up one monster wave after another; up and down we went at steep angles without choice or recourse.

We moved in and out of blue valleys onto crests of mad white ocean waves as *Mafatu* was slammed and slapped without mercy. Out of the turmoil of this churning ocean brew, several waves collided and combined into the perfect wave that leaped high above our boat. We were riding up its massive crest when it blew its top off and a heavy wall of white water cascaded into our boat from above. I froze. Budd and Bugs were soaked, speechless, nearly knocked to their knees. All of us were stunned. Would *Mafatu* stay afloat? The decks were covered in white water. I thought of Sandy's experience on the sinking boat.

In a split second, I prayed that this one wave be a rogue and that there would be no others to finish us off. It would be so easy to sink *Mafatu* at this most vulnerable moment. Somehow we continued our forward momentum near-buried and riding low in the water. Then slowly up another wave we went, but *Mafatu* was way too heavy for any speed filled with all that sea water. As the bow rose, the water rushed back to the transom and started to gush out through the scuppers. The weight of the water on the aft deck could have, but did not sink us; we had just enough forward momentum to plane out and angle up the next wave. That might save us.

Miraculously, most of the saltwater stayed on deck and did not flood the motor box. The two super-duty bilge pumps went into high gear to drain what water had seeped in through the motor hatch vents. After a few more waves all the water was purged from our decks. *Mafatu* had made it through; we were safe.

I felt more confident than ever that the *Mafatu* was prepared to take on whatever this sea would throw at us. At that very moment, I was the proudest and most confident young man of Niu Stream. This SeaSport boat had proved worthy of its christened name, *Mafatu*, the "stout heart."

We continued on in these conditions, ever watchful of this threatening ocean. Then, at the height of these rough seas,

"Bam!" The fish line screamed out of the starboard Penn reel. "Fish on!" Bugs yelled.

"Why now? We're trying to survive here," I complained to myself. "These guys are both nuts!"

Budd and Bugs were now oblivious to our danger and went into fish catching mode. In a delicate balancing act amidst the driving wind and spray, they worked the lines on deck like long-legged crabs. Orders were barked back and forth between them in a push and pull of the fish, boat, and sea. It was a truly marvelous sight, an inspiration to any angler.

A few moments later, the line peeled out on the port reel. "Fish on!" The wind whipped the water and needled the crew's faces. Bugs and Budd traversed the decks to these heaving seas with not one slip, fall, or uncertainty. One man was focused on the fish and reel, the other on the fish and gaff. I was watching agile anglers choreograph a most hair-raising fish hunt. When the performance was over two yellow fin tuna were in the box. I salivated at the image of fresh sashimi.

In less than three hours after leaving Lahaina, *Mafatu* arrived at the southwest coast of Molokai near Haleolono Harbor. We decided against taking refuge here in the harbor and pressed on past the southerly tip of Laau Point to a northerly heading for anchorage just offshore at the Molokai Hotel. We anchored up in the lee of a small hill next to the golf course beach frontage. We would use this time for a short rest before we finalized our plans for the rest of our day. We turned in to the weather channel for news of the ocean seas that we just survived.

It was unbelievable. The VHF blared out the report. "National Weather Service report ...marine conditions for the Kaiwi Channel ...winds of 25 to 35 knots from the north, northeast ...ocean swells of 18 to 20 feet. Caution is advised." We were stunned. What a dire forecast. The Kaiwi Channel was blowing 18 to 20 feet seas. We were in trouble. Our moods turned serious.

We were safe for now here in the lee of Molokai. *Mafatu* was sheltered close to shore in about 9 feet of water. This would be a good anchorage if we couldn't cross the channel. It would protect us from wind and wave, and I was comfortable here in waters I was familiar with. We had lunch and discussed our options and risks.

Should we attempt the channel crossing to Oahu today or wait for better weather? The conversation was serious. Bugs needed to get back, as he was in the midst of a home purchase in Texas; I had to get back for the Lamaze class; and Budd, the true sailor, he could have stayed another week or two.

Against my sound judgment, we prepared for the worst and decided to take our chances to attempt the crossing. Bugs and I didn't want to be stuck on Molokai for another week if the seas turned even worse. Since we had perfect weather all this time, I surmised this weather system must be just moving into the Islands. We should try to make it back before it got any worse or it stalled here for a prolonged period.

Budd, Bugs, and I strapped everything down, put all the weight in the lowest parts of the boat and prepared the life jackets and overboard supplies... just in case. We left immediately while there was plenty of daylight. There was no laughter or casual conversation as we pulled anchor and headed out into the Kaiwi Channel.

Mafatu made her way briskly into the channel with each man to his own unspoken prayers. We neared the wind line a few miles offshore and prepared for the worst. As expected, the seas grew and the size of the waves increased. In no time we were battling forceful 8 to 10 foot swells. The waves came at us from an aft starboard angle with a greater period between peaks. That allowed us to take a slightly smoother ride through peak and trough. I guessed the larger Kaiwi Channel didn't funnel the winds and waves as tightly as we had just experienced in the Kalohi Channel. We didn't run fishing lines on this crossing; we were prepared for an emergency.

I guided *Mafatu* carefully up and down the heaving swells as she carved the blue mountains with a smooth style and practiced grace. I knew the waves of this channel. I felt the watery ground we floated on and anticipated what was to come from this waterway. With the longer swell period, *Mafatu* was more at ease and took these enormous swells in a confident but cautious stride.

My eyes moved over the ocean, scanning for conditions that might prove dangerous. I studied the waves far ahead for any exceptions to their primary direction. Any swell condition that would cause us to fall down the face of a monster was my continuous worry. Falling straight down to bury the bow in a trough would be our doom.

I wanted to surf *Mafatu* in a controlled glide down the wave's face at an angle to slide safely forward to the lower part of the wave but not straight to the bottom. Cross chop and counter waves were also a concern. They would affect the trajectory of a lightweight boat such as the *Mafatu.* A small counter wave could slow the hull or throw the boat off course down the wave into a danger point.

I also checked the waves on both sides of the boat to see what might be coming at us from the starboard and how we handled what was leaving us from the port. I took the time to look back at our wake every once in a while. This would allow me to see our trail in the water and how it tracked with our intended direction.

These swells were white monsters for *Mafatu.* Power and maneuverability were the keys to handling waves of this size. I listened intently to the sounds of *Mafatu*'s motor. A steady and strong monotonous rhythm was our desired song of security. Any hiccups or deviation of tone would peak my concern. The sound of the motor, the rpm of the engine, and boat speed were keenly intertwined. Any slight change was carefully evaluated.

But above all, the most important thing about crossing this channel safely was the feel of the boat on the waves. The sense of wind and wave and its strength against the boat, the rising and falling of the ocean, the feeling of the motor thrust against the wave as the boat moved–these were all important factors to be aware of in an ocean of this intensity. All of my senses were tuned in to the swells and the interaction between the waves and the boat.

For a worrisome thirty minutes the waves built to a consistent 10 feet, then to 12 feet. We went for twenty minutes or so without further wave elevation. We managed quite well, but still I waited for the killers to come. Where were the 18 to 20 foot swells? Be it by our prayers or good luck, there were none. After building some confidence, I ventured an observation. "Guys, I think this is it! This is all we're going to get."

Budd responded immediately, "Bonezie, went 'round the horn, we did. Conquered the seas, mate!"

He pulled me right into it again, like he always did. With my best whaler English, I belted out my response. "Aye mate, we stared them blue monsters in the face... laughed... and spit them in the eye, we did."

"Aye, that we did Captn Bones."

With that little bit of dialogue, all of our tensions were relieved. Certainly we knew we weren't out of danger, but we all felt comfortable that we'd make land safely. I took great joy in surfing *Mafatu* on every wave that offered a safe drop and slide toward our direction. It became fun. *Mafatu* flamed home in record time.

An hour and a half later we rounded the Koko Head landmark on the eastern point of Oahu. Budd, Bugs, and I motored into the marina relaxed but drained from our high seas ordeal. Tonight Mafatu would rest. We would be in the company of our families, sleep in the security of our own beds, and reflect on our voyage dreaming of our adventures to come.